Nietzsche Trauma and Overcoming

The Psychology of the Psychologist

Uri Wernik

Vernon Series in Philosophy

VERNON PRESS

www.vernonpress.com

In the Americas:
Vernon Press
1000 N West Street,
Suite 1200, Wilmington,
Delaware 19801
United States

In the rest of the world:
Vernon Press
C/Sancti Espiritu 17,
Malaga, 29006
Spain

Vernon Series in Philosophy

Library of Congress Control Number: 2017953549

ISBN: 978-1-62273-294-4

To the memory of my parents, Giza Rosenblum-Stoltzberg and Reuven Goldberg-Wernik, who hardly overcame their Holocaust traumas, and their entire families who were not given a chance to try. To the happy and peaceful life of the new generation of our family: Yonatan, Maya, Amit, Yael, Eitan, Adi, and Anne.

One should speak only when one may not remain silent; and then speak only of that which one has overcome—everything else is chatter, "literature," lack of breeding. My writings speak only of my overcomings.

(Friedrich Nietzsche, Human All Too Human, Assorted Maxims and Opinions, 1).

CONTENTS

REFERENCES

The italicized words in the following list will stand in the book for the full titles. When possible, I have used, with slight modifications, the most readily available English translations in public domain. References will include a first level division (parts, essays or sections, according to the case) followed by numerals or literal headings. This will enable the interested reader to examine the German original, or any other existing translation.

The *Birth* of Tragedy Out of the Spirit of Music, 1872.
  An Attempt at Self *Criticism*
Untimely Meditations:
  David *Strauss* the Confessor and the Writer, 1873.
  On the Uses and Disadvantages of *History* for Life, 1874.
  Schopenhauer as Educator, 1874.
  Richard *Wagner* in Bayreuth, 1876.
Human, All Too Human: A Book for Free Spirits, 1878.
  Assorted Maxims and Opinions, 1878.
  The *Wanderer* and his Shadow, 1880.
Daybreak (also translated as Dawn): Thoughts on the Prejudices of Morality, 1881.
The *Gay* Science (also translated as The Joyful Wisdom): La Gaya Scienza, 1882.
Thus Spoke *Zarathustra*: A Book for All and None, 1883-1885.
Beyond Good and Evil: Prelude to a Philosophy of the Future, 1886.
On the *Genealogy* of Morality: A Polemic, 1887.
The *Case* of Wagner: A Musicians' Problem, 1888.
Twilight of the Idols, or How One Philosophizes with a Hammer (completed 1888), 1889:
  Maxims and Arrows
  The Problem of *Socrates*
  Reason in Philosophy
  How the 'True World' Finally Became a *Fable*
  Morality as Anti-Nature
  The Four Great *Errors*
  The 'Improvers' of *Mankind*
  What the *Germans* Lack
  Skirmishes of an Untimely Man
  What I Owe to the *Ancients*
The *Antichrist*: Curse on Christianity (completed 1888), 1895.

Ecce Homo: How One Becomes What One Is (completed 1888), 1905:
 Why I am so *Wise*
 Why I am so *Clever*
 Why I Write Such Good *Books*
 Why I am a *Destiny*
 An Attempt at *Self-Criticism*
Nietzsche *Contra* Wagner: Documents of a Psychologist (completed 1888), 1895.
Dithyrambs of *Dionysus* (completed 1888), 1892.

Posthumous publications:
The *Greek* State (written 1871).
On *Truth* and Lies in a Nonmoral Sense (written 1873).
Philosophy in the Tragic Age of the Greeks (unfinished, written 1873).
On the *Future* of Our Educational Institutions (five lectures, delivered 1872).
We *Philologists* (written 1874).
The *Will* to Power (an edited selection from Nietzsche's 1883-1888 notebooks), 1901.

FOREWORD

Some say my traumatic experiences began in Vietnam as a US Marine. They really began when I started studying other combat veterans; listening to war stories and experiencing their anguish, confusion, and anger. This is when I shifted from being a researcher of the traumatized to being a practitioner as well as a scholar for the traumatized. I was the only psychologist my research participants had ever known. What I learned in those early days reminded me of this book.

To a psychologist or anyone engaged in understanding and especially helping people, Friedrich Wilhelm Nietzsche was one of the many philosophers studied in humanities or philosophy courses. Unfortunately, for students interested in helping others, Nietzsche would not be among their relied upon small book collection.

Uri Wernik makes a strong case for all of us to reconsider the utility of Nietzsche. Nietzsche was a professor of philology (the study of language) and a scholar of the classics by the age of twenty-four. He had to resign his position for health reasons. Most of his important work was only written later.

Wernik, a second-generation child of Holocaust parents, made in his previous book *Nietzschean psychology and psychotherapy,* the convincing case that Nietzsche was actually a psychologist addressing the fundamental issues of humanity, who had much to teach us about human behavior and coping. In this new book, Wernik asserts that Nietzsche was greatly influenced by the trauma he experienced in life. Here, the reader is helped to appreciate the deeper understanding of the phenomenology of trauma and abuse in general. After all, it was Nietzsche who wrote "Out of life's school of war: What does not destroy me, makes me stronger" (*Twilight,* Maxims, 8) that led to other axioms shared by ministers' sermons, Marine Corps drill instructors' assurances, and advocates of "post-traumatic growth."

The book's core is helping us understand trauma by learning how Nietzsche endured and overcame his life traumas. Nietzsche's "multifaceted tortures" concept, notes Wernik, is compatible with Post-traumatic Stress Disorder (PTSD) as a frame of reference, not as a diagnosis. The book cites and applies the lessons suggested by Nietzsche and even teaches how we can be the poets of our life. The book shows how life is the real test of the worth of philosophy and psychology.

The book shows that Nietzsche's adulthood trauma-like symptoms were due to his childhood experiences of physical and emotional suffering, specifically childhood sexual abuse. But much of the book helps us understand how he overcame these traumatic stressors and was eventually able to provide such profound insights into human experience and thriving despite setbacks.

The book notes that the conceptualization of trauma, according to Nietzsche, is not a fixed entity such as an entry in the DSM V but rather a spectrum, a constellation of characteristics; not pathological, but expected reactions and strategies of adaptation.

You do not need to be a Nietzsche scholar or a psychologist to enjoy and apply the lessons revealed in this book. Psychology is discussed extensively as a field and provides extraordinary evidence of the contributions Nietzsche has made, including the psychology of being a psychologist (see *Will*, II, 426).

The author notes in the third chapter, for example, that trauma, according to the Online Etymology Dictionary, was first recognized as a physical wound (its Greek origin means wound). The concept of trauma being an emotional shock emerged in the mid-1800s when explaining the syndrome experienced by some survivors of train accidents and other traumatic events. Thus, the area of psychological trauma was born.

The book is filled with wise and practical observations about trauma and healing revealed in the writings of Nietzsche. Pay close attention to the rhythm of this book; its lyrical essays and insights on topics and concepts familiar to trauma researchers and practitioners alike. As I look back at the start of my career, I wish I had this book as a template for not only understanding Nietzsche and his contributions to trauma psychology but also understanding the life-long influences of trauma for both good and harm and forgetting.

Charles R. Figley, PhD

Tulane University, Kurzweg Distinguished Chair and Professorship in Disaster Mental Health, New Orleans

ACKNOWLEDGMENTS

After my graduate studies, I did not pursue the academic route, for fear of the "publish or perish" burden. I learned to enjoy my clinical work and started to write anyway. Where did I find the passion for solitary independent study? I was given a certain temperament. I was fortunate to have unconventional inspiring teachers, and lucky to have conducive conditions, namely a happy family life.

I remember fondly and with gratitude Kalman Shulman, an apostate former Rabbi, Abraham Fisher-Ophir, a scholar of Sanskrit, Eva Ullman, who instilled in me the love of English, David Flusser, who kindled my interest in Early Christianity, and O. Hobart Mowrer, who taught me the meaning of integrity. Friedrich Nietzsche, who I continued reading intermittently from my youth, was my great teacher of skepticism. I hope that I have repaid him well "One repays a teacher badly if one always remains nothing but a pupil" (*Thus Spoke Zarathustra*).

Amia Lieblich, is my model for qualitative research in psychology, My brother Paul Groffsky, is always my first keen reader. Thank you, Christos Iliopoulos, the author of *Nietzsche & Anarchism*, for your helpful suggestions. Thank you, Rafi Youngman, a friend, and colleague, for bringing to my attention the literature on post-traumatic growth. Many thanks go to my enabling and supportive team at Vernon Press, my editor Caterina Sanchez, Argiris Legatos and Javier Rodriguez, who turned my words into a book.

Many of Nietzsche's works were written in Italy, and it is there that I had my most productive days in writing this book. I thank our friends Roberta Volante, Roberta Danieli, and Andrea Maniezzo in Padova, Simonetta Della Seta and Massimo Torrefranca in Rome, Clara and Dario Basso in Bassano del Grappa, for their hospitality and encouragement. My beloved life-partner Elanah-Irene stood by me and gave me good advice, as she has done with all my books. Our children Haran and Dana, Edan and Neta, Sahar and Dan, all persevered without complaints through my lectures on Nietzsche, and in talking with them many issues became clearer to me.

Rome, May 2017

INTRODUCTION

Must I begin by elaborating on the importance and significance of Friedrich Nietzsche's work? You, the reader, even if you did not realize that he considered himself and in fact was a psychologist, must have known why you chose this book. It is almost impossible to characterize Nietzsche with one label, as any of the following will be correct: philosopher, philologist, psychologist, doctor of the soul, poet, musician and teacher (*Beyond*, IV, 63), and all of them combined would be closer to the truth. Everything he wrote was in a distinct style, blending polemics, short aphorisms, and poems. Critics, versed in the methodology of social sciences, could argue that Nietzsche's psychological work is not based on controlled studies and an investigation of a sample of subjects (nowadays, usually undergraduate psychology students, participating in experiments for credit).

Let us not forget the other eminent psychologists, who relied on their observations and life experiences to reflect and theorize about human beings, among them Sigmund Freud, Carl R. Rogers, Abraham Maslow, Eric H. Erikson, Carl G. Jung and Alfred Adler.[1] I hope to convince you that it is worthwhile to pay attention to the observations and experiences of an especially talented person. One with a developed sense of what is pertinent and humanly universal, and with an ability to generalize to others his own experiences and struggles to find meaning in life (*Human*, Preface, 7). He described himself as an observer "A man who constantly experiences, sees, hears, suspects, hopes, and dreams extraordinary things; who is struck by his very own thoughts as if from outside, as if from above and below, as if they are experiences and lightning strikes tailor-made for him" (*Beyond*, IX, 292).

In another book, I explored Nietzsche's original psychology and psychotherapy, which philosophers usually understand in circumscribed ways, and psychologists hardly know.[2] Here, I am going to extract Nietzsche the person, out of his writings, and thus, display what he called "the psychology of the psychologist" (*Will*, II, 426). Then, in a "circular transaction," I will take advantage of what was learned about him, to examine and understand the text again. My first hypothesis is that Nietzsche experienced the consequences of traumatic events in his life and that he most probably suffered from abuse as a child. The second hypothesis is that we can understand his psychology and central themes in his philosophy as his ways of coping and self-healing, which he wanted us to learn and adopt. The third hypothesis is that Nietzsche's ordeal can be understood pertinently in terms of the psychological literature and studies of Post-Traumatic Stress Disorder (PTSD) and Childhood Sexual Abuse (CSA). The knowledge gained in these fields will help us understand a significant part of Nietzsche's writings in a new light. Once we realize that he wrote about his tribulations and ways of contending with them, we will gain a deeper understanding of the phenomenology of trauma and abuse in general. We will also find in Nietzsche inspiring directions for dealing with such situations, in our own lives, and the lives of those we care about. His aphorism "Out of life's school of war: What does not destroy me, makes me stronger" (*Twilight*, Maxims, 8), is often quoted in texts on Post-Traumatic Growth (PTG), but we will learn that he had much more to say on this issue.

♦

Why bother with him as a person? Are not his books sufficient and self-evident? Nietzsche's writings have been and continue to be the subject of many scholarly books, and most commentators had something to say about Nietzsche the person, and the relation between his life and his ideas. *Amazon.com* listed 630 books under "Nietzsche and biography" (May 2017). Even if the examination of the person is justified, are there not enough biographies,[3] Philosophical-biographies[4] and psychobiographies[5] about him already? My answer, similar to other authors' who wrote one more book on an extensively treated topic, is that my perspective, focusing on his traumas and overcoming is, at least, different and new. Nietzsche came to our help and supplied us with answers to these questions, invited us to solve his life riddles and instructed us on writing meaningful psychobiographies as well. For him, the test of a philosophy and a psychology is in their application to living, which is "The only method of criticizing a philosophy that is possible and proves anything at all, which is a manner of criticism untaught at universities, where only 'criticism of words by other words' is practiced." Because the proof a philosophy lies in life, he found reading Diogenes Laertius' *Lives of the Eminent Philosophers* to be more useful than reading academic publications. Thus, the best test of a theory is the life of the philosopher "since everything depends on the character of the individual who shows the way" (*Untimely*, Schopenhauer, 8). Hence, by studying him, we examine his philosophy.

We can safely disregard the author in reading most philosophy and psychology books, as the ideas or information speak for themselves, and we find them either agreeable or useful, or not. Knowing that citizens in Konigsberg, Kant's hometown, used to set their clocks the moment they saw him coming out to take his daily stroll, is not going to add or distract from our understanding of his abstract and systematic work. However, in some outstanding cases, a book makes us wonder about the life of its author. Such writers live in their books' pages, and what they wrote is connected with what they experienced themselves. Nietzsche wrote with the blood of his heart (*Zarathustra*, I, Reading and writing) and he felt that he gave birth to his books, his children. In his classic essay *Why Read the Classics,* Italo Calvino explained that such books "exert a peculiar influence, both when they refuse to be eradicated from the mind and when they conceal themselves in the folds of memory, camouflaging themselves as the collective or individual unconscious." This kind of a book "has never finished saying what it has to say," and the reader continues to be in a dialogue with it, feeling a particular kind of rapport, naturally wanting to get to know the author better[6]. Margaret Sanger, expressed the feeling of many readers, in writing about Nietzsche that "It is impossible to apply his philosophy or to study or know him before first getting an insight into the tremendous personality which so strongly reveals itself through every line of his work in every aphorism of his mind."[7]

We wish to understand, and are fascinated by the lives of prominent persons, those who shape culture and history, who are exemplars of the highest achievements or most awful calamities; be they generals, politicians, artists or scientists. Perhaps, we want to understand our human potentials and characteristics, as if touching them will transform or teach us lessons about life. We pay attention to the way they dealt with setbacks, disappointments, and frustrations encountered on their way. We are interested not only in their thoughts and actions but also in the way they died, as is exemplified in the figure of Socrates. Geniuses are a riddle to those of us, not as talented as them. Exceptional ideas, forcefully stated, invite attention to the person behind them. Life shrouded in mystery calls for elucidation, and indeed Nietzsche's last ten years of life in a state of unexplained mental paralysis became a topic of investigation and speculation by scholars, physicians, and psychiatrists in particular. Being a single man without life-partners, his love-life is another area of exploration and search for clues, aiming to uncover his secret, culminating in claims that he had affairs with this or that person, or that he had this or that sexual orientation. Nietzsche, like Heraclitus, at whose proximity he felt "warmer and better than anywhere else" (*Ecce,* Birth of tragedy, 3), can be called "the dark one," as so much of his life remains under cover. I am a psychologist, and not surprisingly I see Nietzsche as a psychologist, who in writing about "the psychology of the psychologist" (*Will,* II, 426), tried to understand his own life. Like him, I feel that "I have a nose" (*Ecce,* Wise, 1) for psychological issues, and see them where others have not suspected they exist. He described himself as "a born psychologist and lover of a "big hunt," one who explores the intricacies of the soul (*Beyond,* III, 45), and this hunter is now the subject of our hunt.

♦

The biographer's forte is that she knows many things her protagonist did not report (but cannot protest, deny or reaffirm). Psychologists and therapists, on the other hand, relate only to what their subjects say directly. They do not visit their subjects' hometown, kindergarten or high school; do not interview their families, friends, and colleagues; and do not take into consideration what persons with their agenda wrote about them, as was the case of his sister, Elisabeth Förster-Nietzsche. Unlike a biographer who wishes to discover new facts, a psychologist-therapist can only offer new interpretations, suggest hypotheses and try to examine them from as many perspectives as possible. I will thus relate only to what Nietzsche himself had to say, wrote, and wanted us to know, as found in his publications and letters to friends. I am going to take into consideration his diaries, edited after his death, in what is known as *The Will to Power*, assuming that he intended to make a book or books out of them. It is certainly possible to combine the two roles: psychologists can write biographies; biographers can use psychological theories and speculations.

In addition to connecting with the literature on trauma and abuse, this book is tied in with the discipline of psychobiography, and I will, therefore, begin my exploration with the issue of the author-text connection, the relation between the person and her writings and the possibility of retracing, extracting the person from the writings. Nietzsche himself, we will see, had what to say about these questions as well. I will then go on to review, criticize and reject the prevalent psychological attempts to analyze and portray him, and follow it with an examination of Nietzsche's autobiographical writings and the extensive use of riddles in them. A careful reading will show us that this psychologist's "multifaceted tortures" are compatible with what is known today as Post-Traumatic Stress Disorder (PTSD).

A reservation is in order here. Everything that I will claim about Nietzsche's Post-Traumatic Stress Disorder in adulthood, his pain and suffering, poisonous upbringing and childhood sexual abuse, is based on circumstantial evidence, and for this reason is open to more than one understanding. Apparently, one could choose different texts and offer different interpretations. To make my case, I have combined pieces of information from diverse sources, which eventually support each other. My first line of argumentation is based on gleaning, juxtaposing and interpreting, passages from his writings, which were overlooked until now, or not understood as referring to Nietzsche, the person, and as indications of trauma and abuse. How ironic it is, that we did not have to be detectives, looking for clues in faraway places, which Nietzsche did not discuss, or did not want us to explore. The answers only lay in front of us, in what he wrote. As the prophet said, we are persons who "have eyes but do not see; who have ears but do not hear" (*Jeremiah*, 5, 21). You, my dear reader, are going to find many quotes from Nietzsche's writings in this book. I felt that it would almost be a crime to reduce them into my ordinary language. I hope that you wish that there had been more of them.

My second line of reasoning is based on a reanalysis of the figures of Dionysus and Jesus that hold a central place in Nietzsche's writings and which, I will argue, he saw as representing him. Nietzsche considered his idea of the Eternal Recurrence to be especially sublime, and with tremendous implications for life. What looks like an unexplained over-evaluation is understood in a new way, once his secret, the one he called "midnight's voice," is deciphered. These readings will supply us with indirect evidence for the presence of a traumatic theme in his life. The third line of argumentation will consist of the striking parallels found, between Nietzsche's reports of mental anguish and difficulties in life, and the findings of the psychological studies of survivors of Post-Traumatic Stress Disorder and the consequences of adverse childhood experiences and sexual abuse. At this point, we will be able to characterize Nietzsche, as the survivor par excellence, which will bring us to the last part of the book, where we will deal with overcoming.

I will present Nietzsche's original conceptualization of pain and suffering, and three modes of coping and overcoming trauma, which can be drawn from his writings: the ways of the sage, warrior, and creator. These conceptualizations pass the Nietzschean test of relevance to life, as in studying them, we gain thinking and acting tools for coping with hurt and distress to the best of our ability. Similarly, we will find that his search for meaning and self-healing following his traumas, formed the foundation of his central ideas, the triad of the Will to Power, the Eternal Return and the Superman. All of them will be shown as different ways of overcoming. The new light shed on these much-discussed themes, from a psychological-biographical perspective offers an additional vindication of our position.

♦

Nietzsche, who said about himself "I am no man, I am dynamite" (*Ecce*, Why I am a destiny, 1), rarely fails to move his readers, who respond either with admiration of his unconventional thinking and way with words or with almost hostile opposition to his ideas. These responses are often accompanied by a heightened sense of irony, which is also used in his writings as a literary device.[8] Ironies were abundant in his own life as well, which revealed marked contrasts between what he intended or what could be expected from his writings and what actually took place. The three Moirae (Fates), who come uninvited, must have worked overtime in his case. I will conclude my introduction, with a rundown of some such ironies:

The Barefoot Shoemaker: Nietzsche is one of the great teachers of life. He is the teacher of the Superman (I will use, not to be a hair-splitter, the most common Thomas Common's translation of *Übermensch* into English, having it stand equally for men and women) and the Will to Power. He is also the disciple of Dionysus, the laughing dancer, the champion of earthly desires and being an "animal with a good conscience" (*Gay,* II, 77). In his own life, as we will see, he was a hermit, locked in his cell of pain, isolation, and deprivation. He demonstrated insight into human behavior that did not involve him. He gave valuable advice on managing life and self-advancement, but as far as he was concerned, we will see that he emerges from his writings, to say the least, as unassertive, inflexible, inhibited and without a highly developed pragmatic emotional intelligence. And yet, I wonder how many therapists can disagree with Zarathustra's statement "Many a man cannot loosen his own chains, and yet he is a savior to his friend" *(Zarathustra,* I, The friend).

Beware of pity: Zarathustra said "Alas, where in the world have there been greater follies than with the compassionate? Woe to all lovers who cannot surmount pity!" *(Zarathustra,* II, The compassionate). Moreover, he argued that creators must be hard, and that great love and pity are incompatible, and pity is obtrusive and offensive *(Zarathustra,* IV, The Ugliest man). Still, it is usually reported that on January 3, 1889, on the Piazza Alberto in Turin, he saw an exhausted and ill-treated carriage horse. In what could be the last gesture of a still sane person or the first signs of mental breakdown, the same person, who decried pity and empathy in such high terms, flung his arms around the horse's neck, wept and then lost consciousness. He never wrote again and sank into a state of daze and withdrawal.

Anacleto Verrecchia, who investigated Nietzsche's "catastrophe in Turin," concluded that the above description, often mentioned and taken to be factual, in what consists of a double irony, is probably a myth only. He found out that the story was first reported unsigned, in a tabloid, eleven years after Nietzsche's death. The more graphic details of the story appeared in another newspaper item forty years afterward, seeping from there into more serious publications.[9] We have here another variation on *facta ficta* (*Daybreak,* IV, 307), and a justification of the low esteem Nietzsche held for journalism "Sick are they always; they vomit their bile and call it a newspaper" *(Zarathustra,* I, The New Idol).

On how to die: after Nietzsche's breakdown in Turin, he was kept in psychiatric clinics in Basel and then Jena. Later he was placed in his mother's care in Naumburg, the town where he grew up. After her death, his sister Elisabeth Förster-Nietzsche took care of him. Much of the time, he was bed-ridden and incommunicative. Again ironically, in the years before his mental collapse, Nietzsche detested his sister, yet she took upon herself to run his archive and edit, or more accurately censor and distort his works. He died in his sister's villa on August 25, 1900, apparently of pneumonia in combination with a stroke. With another wry twist, the person who attacked Christianity vehemently had a Christian funeral and was buried near his father in his hometown church's graveyard. The circumstances of his death are much removed from what Nietzsche had to say about timely death. When Nietzsche wrote, on two separate occasions, about Socrates and Jesus, he saw their deaths as a mirror of the truthfulness of their life-tasks.

Nietzsche who taught the doctrine of voluntary death "Die at the right time," did not know that he was describing the exact opposite of his own, indeed, not voluntary death. Dying well, meant dying not too late, nor too early, turning death into a celebration of a full life. A death willed after one had a goal and an heir to continue one's cause; avoiding unnecessary prolongation of life "Sour apples are there, no doubt, whose lot is to wait until the last day of Autumn: and at the same time they become ripe, yellow, and shriveled" *(Zarathustra,* I, Voluntary Death).

On falling between the cracks: Nietzsche studied and was later a professor of philology. He never had formal training in philosophy, and when he wrote about himself as a philosopher, it meant simply "a lover of wisdom," usually qualified with adjectives such as real, tragic, pessimistic or experimental. He examined philosophy from the point of view of psychology and argued that quite often, the errors of the greatest philosophers in constructing false ethics were based on wrong explanations of human behaviors and feelings (*Human*, I, 37). Nietzsche took upon himself to expose the philosophers' errors "I have asked myself whether, taking a large view, philosophy has not been merely an interpretation of the body and a misunderstanding of the body" (*Gay*, Preface for the 2nd Edition, 2).

Nietzsche describes himself as a psychologist from birth "a born and inevitable psychologist and analyst of the soul" (*Beyond*, IX, 277) with an "innate refined sense concerning psychological questions in general" (*Gay*, Prologue, 3). This role-identity continued throughout his life, culminating in his becoming "an old psychologist and pied piper" (*Twilight*, Preface). A good reader, Nietzsche believed, will certainly discover the fact that "my works bespeak a psychologist who has not his peer" (*Ecce*, Books, 5).

None of the philosophers before him were real psychologists like him; on the contrary, they were "superior swindler," and "Idealists," which made him conclude that "Before me there was no psychology" (*Ecce*, Destiny, 6). In those instances where he wore the hat of a philosopher, he was not a "philosophy laborer," and he singled out his idea of the philosopher "by miles from the idea which can admit even a Kant, not to speak of the academic ruminators and other professors of philosophy" (*Ecce*, Untimely, 3). However, this is not how he is perceived now, as a simple *Google* search (May 2017) reveals: twice as many results were found for the combination "Nietzsche + philosophy" as compared with "Nietzsche + psychology." An *Amazon* search for books with the same combinations found a ratio of three to one. Most of the discussions of Nietzsche as a psychologist are from the perspective of depth psychology, seeing him as a precursor of other admired psychoanalytical authorities. For this reason, supposed similarities between them are highlighted, while to my mind, the differences are much more interesting. Mainline psychology, in contradistinction, treats him as if he never existed. Thus, recent clinical psychology books, discuss multiple-selves and acceptance therapy, without even once mentioning Nietzsche's idea of multiplicities and *Amor fati.* The bottom line is that those he rejected, adopted him; while the ones he wanted to be part of, stayed clear of him.

On scholars: Nietzsche was a critic of the academic establishment and no fan of scholars. This part of his work is unsurprisingly usually disregarded in academia. A philosopher, a lover of wisdom, is not only a great thinker but also a real human being with an "immediate perception of things." Scholars, however, lose touch with reality, letting concepts, opinions, history and other books and articles step between them and things (*Untimely,* Strauss, 7). Their books are oppressive, with the typical specialists' shortcomings: zeal, seriousness, fury and "overestimation of the nook in which he sits and spins." Their books "also mirror a soul that has become crooked; every craft makes crooked" (*Gay,* V, 366).

In his discourse on scholars, Zarathustra-Nietzsche stated "I have left the house of scholars and slammed the door behind me." He had enough of being a spectator and preferred the open air over dusty rooms. He lost his patience with the cunning little sayings and little truths; with "weaving the stockings of the spirit." Scholars, he felt, are sly poisonous spiders who "know how to play with loaded dice" *(Zarathustra,* II, Scholars). He reserved his sharpest remarks for the scholars studying the philosopher who was his educator: "A corpse is a pleasant thought for a worm, and a worm is a dreadful thought for every living creature. Worms fancy their kingdom of heaven in a fat cadaver; professors of philosophy seek theirs in rummaging among Schopenhauer's entrails, and as long as rats exist, there will exist a heaven for rats" (*Untimely,* Strauss, 6).

Allow me to check Google twice more and be done with it. I found 413,000 results for "Nietzsche + academic articles" and 1,900 for "Nietzsche + Ph.D. Dissertations." My guess is that there must be more than a hundred references per article or book. How ironic it is that the severest critic of scholars became their very favorite body, not to say corpse, of study. I must admit that with this book, I might be joining the crowd.

Chapter 1

NIETZSCHE *AD HOMINEM*

We are trained not to link the validity of an idea with characteristics of the person expressing it. Ideas, we are taught, should be impersonal and examined on their merit. However, in Nietzsche's case, in particular, it is almost impossible to separate the person from his books. Nietzsche will not let us disregard him, as he talks about himself openly but also implicitly when we least suspected it. At this point, someone could ask, did not Nietzsche write "I am one thing, my writings are another" (*Ecce*, Books, 1)? And this would also be the opportunity to be reminded that he taught that there are no facts, but only interpretations of facts (*Will*, III, 481). I will use this one sentence to show the many ways of understanding a Nietzschean text. Some readers will take the statement that he and his writings are not identical at face value, and will even be content to transcribe it into I=A, My books=B, and A≠B. Non-literal readers will not be surprised to learn that a person is not a book, and will ponder other possible interpretations, some of which are based on Nietzsche's other reflections, understanding this statement as if he is saying:

- There is more to me, hidden from view, than what I reveal "Every philosophy also hides a philosophy; every opinion is also a hiding place, every word is also a mask" (*Beyond*, IX, 289). Also "The flame is not as bright to itself as it is to those it illuminates: so too the sage" (*Human*, IX, 570).
- I change, and my views can change; I have a future in front of me, while my books are frozen in time. Such an interpretation does not preclude the opposite one. Namely, the fate of books and persons is different—humans are final, they die; books keep on living, are understood in newer ways, and keep impacting their readers.
- What I teach and what actually happens in my life, are not identical. My writings are not only about what I am but also about what I wish to be. The answer to his disciples' question "But why does Zarathustra speak to his pupils differently - than to himself?" *(Zarathustra,* II, Redemption), is that he is a teacher who uses his life story to make a point, and for that reason, his writings include mostly material that he found to be instructive for his students-readers.

- The experienced life, being vast and time-bound, unchangeable and unrepeatable, cannot be reduced to words:

> Alas! What are you, after all, my written and painted thoughts! Not long ago you were so variegated, young and malicious, so full of thorns and secret spices, that you made me sneeze and laugh—and now? You have already doffed your novelty, and some of you, I fear, are ready to become truths, so immortal do they look, so pathetically honest, so tedious! (*Beyond*, IX, 296).

We will see time and again in this book, that connecting two particular sentences or passages, as I did above, written by Nietzsche in different times and places, whose connection was not realized until now, can support a hypothesis offered about the first and clarify the second, which remained obscure until the two were introduced to each other. I will also put side by side, quotes by Nietzsche and by researchers of trauma, letting my readers draw their conclusions.

The Author-Text Connection

Nietzsche had defined views on the author-text connection, and reviewing them will prepare the way for studying his life. He started with the general observation that one cannot not write about herself, and therefore, everything we say, says something about us. Instead of debating Kant's categorical imperative, he just raised the question "what does such a claim tell us about the man who makes it?" (*Beyond*, IX, 187). The personal factor will always remain in the background, and even when one gained much knowledge, even if one is as objective as possible "ultimately he reaps nothing but his own biography" (*Human*, IX, 513). Not only is it unavoidable, but it might as well be a condition for artistic excellence. Nietzsche who at one time admired Wagner's "great, good and perfect" musical masterpieces, explained that unlike other musicians, he suffered deeply and put himself into his music (*Contra*, 1).

He readily admitted that all significant psychological expressions in *Thus Spoke Zarathustra* and his other books, whether they were written about Zarathustra or Wagner, were also about him and described his own traits and nature (*Ecce*, Birth, 4). Zarathustra's task of "saying Yes to the point of justifying, of redeeming even all of the past," was his task (*Ecce*, Thus, 8). With philosophers, he concluded, there is nothing that is impersonal, while with scientists the situation might be somewhat different: "Gradually it has become clear to me what every great philosophy so far has been: namely, the personal confession of its author and a kind of involuntary and unconscious memoir; also that the moral (or immoral) intentions in every philosophy constituted the real germ of life from which the whole plant had grown" (*Beyond*, I, 6).

Other thinkers shared this insight: Will Durant, subtitled his *The Story of Philosophy* "the Lives and Opinions of the Greater Philosophers," indicating that their lives and ideas were connected.[10] Durant found William James, who stated that "The history of philosophy is to a great extent that of a certain clash of human temperaments," to be a major spokesman for the idea. James distinguished between tender-minded temperaments—which prefer definite dogmas and truths, and being believers, have no problem to talk about free will, idealism and optimism, and skeptical, tough-minded temperaments—irreligious, empiricists, materialistic and pessimistic. This dichotomy is not absolute, as contradictions and combinations of toughness and tender-mindedness in different domains are possible.[11] Professional philosophers influenced and biased by their own natures, more than by objective data, try to hide this fact, not accepted conventionally as legitimate, in favor of impersonal reasons. Similarly, people accept or reject philosophies according to their temperaments, interests, and needs, and not in light of some "objective truth."[12] What matters to people, is not whether a philosophy is logical, but rather the implications of putting it to use in their own life. In other words "Pretend what we may, the whole man within us is at work when we form our philosophical opinions."[13] James concluded that "We know that arguments are dictated by our needs; and that our needs cannot be dictated to by arguments."[14] Thus, an intellectual discussion is inherently insincere, as we all deny that we trust representations of the world that suit our temperament, and reject as mistaken representations that stem from different temperaments.[15]

Johann Gottlieb Fichte, like James, added the reader to the equation of text and author, explaining that, "What sort of philosophy one chooses depends, therefore, on what sort of man one is; for a philosophical system is not a dead piece of furniture that we accept or reject as we wish; it is rather a thing animated by the soul of the person who holds it."[16] Commenting on the process of writing *Death in Venice*, Thomas Mann remarked: "The truth is that every piece of work is a realization, fragmentary but complete in itself, of our individuality."[17] Thus, this perspective of seeing an intellectual creation and its appreciation as a reflection of one's biography is valid for you, the reader, and for me, the author. Our decision to study Nietzsche, as well as our way of understanding him, and our acceptance or rejection of the ideas of other scholars and commentators, stem from our autobiographies and is influenced by our temperaments.

Travel Books and Masks

Can the examination of Nietzsche the person serve as a formula to decipher his writings? It is certain that we must take the person into account, but this is no simple task at all. Nietzsche, this time in the role of a hermit, did not believe that philosophers express their real and conclusive thoughts in their books, and moreover, they write books intending to hide what they really think. The hermit went on and wondered whether in the case of the author-philosopher "behind every cave there does not still lie, and must lie, an even deeper cavern [...] an abyss behind every reason, under every 'foundation'" (*Beyond*, IX, 289). Using a different image, Nietzsche did not wish to remove his mask but rather asked for "One more mask! A second mask!" (*Beyond*, IX, 278). And yet, it was Oscar Wilde who said "Man is least himself when he talks in his own person. Give him a mask, and he will tell you the truth."[18]

The ability to generalize one's own experiences to others is a characteristic of free spirits, who figure out that their struggle to find meaning in life must also take place in others (*Human*, Preface, 7). Nietzsche felt that his experiences "the history of an illness and convalescence," were not intended to remain his alone. His "travel books" were meant to be sent out on a journey and be an experiment for others (*Human*, Assorted, 6). He knew that only listing his pains and suffering would make him a "melancholy author," and to be a serious one, he had to tell us "what he suffered and why he now reposes in joy" (*Human*, Wanderer, 128).

In some cases, however, Nietzsche advised us to separate the person from the work, and treat him only as "the precondition for his work, its maternal womb, the soil or, in some cases, the dung and manure, on and out of which it grows." Concentrating on the person might only detract from the enjoyment of the work, and besides, "Homer would not have written a poem about Achilles or a Goethe a poem about Faust if Homer had been an Achilles or if Goethe had been a Faust." An accomplished artist is always separated from actual life, or in other words, the creation and the creator are not identical (*Genealogy*, III, 4).

Furthermore, the possibility of intentional disinformation must be taken into consideration. Writing about Alfieri (Count Vittorio Alfieri, 1749 –1803, an Italian dramatist and poet), Nietzsche was practically confessing indirectly, that not only did he make a poet of himself, but that he also did transform, with much effort, his life story into a noble meaningful narration. Such rewriting is a painful process which necessitated being a despot toward oneself in creating one's language and style —"he finally found a rigid form of sublimity into which he forced his life and his memory." Thus, it is better not to give much credit to a self-written history, be it Plato, Rousseau or Dante (*Gay*, II,

91). Nietzsche commented that "all matters are not only two-sided but three or four-sided" (*Human*, VII, 417) and this typical Nietzscheanism, holds true with the issue at hand. A text could be some or all of the following: an autobiography and confession, a self-serving alibi and confabulation, and finally a means for a personal bonding with a teacher of life, who opens a window to his experiences to instruct and transform his students. At times, it feels as if Nietzsche hoped that his readers would become his disciples and study him, thus allowing his suffering not to be vain.

Nietzsche agreed with Schopenhauer, his teacher and educator that all great philosophy is saying "this is the picture of all life, and learn from it the meaning of your own life." The student-reader-disciple enters a dialogue with the text and through the text with the author which in her ideas and personal life holds "the hieroglyphics of universal life. The students-disciples compare their life with the life of the teacher, who must give a good example. Thus, the ancient Greek philosophers taught "Through their bearing," by the way they dressed and ate, by their morals, and not by words, articulated or written (*Untimely*, Schopenhauer, 3), and this is also what Nietzsche, in the role of a teacher, set to do. The first part of the following quote served as this book's motto, and I will also quote it toward the book's end:

> One should speak only when one may not remain silent, and then speak only of that which one has overcome—everything else is chatter, 'literature,' lack of breeding. My writings speak only of my overcomings: 'I' am in them, together with everything that was hostile to me, *ego ipsissimus* [my very own self], indeed, even if a yet prouder expression be permitted, *ego ipsissimum* [my innermost self] (*Human*, Assorted, 1).

Nietzsche's Quest

Psychobiography became at the beginning of the 21st century a respectable sub-specialty of personality theory, examined and discussed in comprehensive reviews and handbooks.[19] It studies and helps us understand historical, literary, artistic and political figures.[20] The present book is thus, a psychobiography of Nietzsche, but it is also *psychologicis* and a descendant of the quest for the historical Jesus, which the pioneers of psychobiography disregarded. Let me explain these terms and their relevance to my work.

The quest for the historical Jesus (as a living human being) began in Germany with H. S. Reimarus (1694-1768), who wished to extrapolate the real person from the *New Testament*, using objective historical study, giving up dogma and avoiding ecclesiastical control. The quest continued with David Friedrich Strauss' *The Life of Jesus Critically Examined* (1835) and Ernest Renan's *Life of*

Jesus (1863) and culminated with Albert Schweitzer's *Quest of the Historical Jesus* (1909). Since then, many books on the same topic appeared in what is known as the second, third and even fourth quests. Nietzsche was a critic of this quest and offered his own view of the historical Jesus. He did not use the term psychobiography, and his little-known distinction between psychology, *psychologica* and *psychologicis*[21] is relevant to our discussion. The last two words are simply the Latin equivalents of psychology, as found in titles of older textbooks. Psychology is the naturalistic science that studies, as objectively as possible, human behaviors and motivations. *Psychologica,* in contradistinction, is a particularly biased perspective with its own value-laded world-view, interests, desired ends and assumptions about people. While *psychologicis,* is the largely speculative analysis of individuals and human conditions, in light of psychological theories of the two former kinds. Nietzsche felt that the German depth psychology of personalities, in comparison with the French one "lacked subtlety and divination in *psychologicis*" (*Will,* I, 107). These, I pray, will be found in my work.

Davis Strauss' *The Life of Jesus Critically Examined* had a strong influence on Nietzsche and contributed to his giving up the Christian belief and leaving his theological studies.[22] It was only later, when Strauss published his *The Old and New Faith,* that Nietzsche wrote a vicious polemic, *David Strauss: the Confessor and the Writer,* criticizing him as a paragon of cultural philistinism. He did not lose the opportunity to ridicule his once admired first book, for misunderstanding Jesus' asceticism and self-denial; for a simplistic view of the Resurrection; and for the portrayal of Jesus "as an enthusiast who nowadays would scarcely have escaped the madhouse" (*Untimely,* Strauss, VII). The last sentence is an apt description of the later scholarly treatment of Nietzsche himself.

Nietzsche criticized the interpretation of historical figures, not in their own terms, but in terms of later biased commentators (*Antichrist,* 29) and he saw such attempts as "proof of a contemptible psychological frivolity." He criticized the interpretation offered by Renan "that buffoon in *psychologicis,*" who tried to "read the history of a 'soul' out of the Gospels," and in his reading completely misrepresented Jesus, the person. The more significant target of Nietzsche's criticism, however, was the Church, which by using "acrobatic feats in *psychologicis*" (*Contra,* Preface), conceived and portrayed the figure of Christ, its *raison d'être,* in a distorted manner to fit its needs and support the morality it promoted. The church turned belief and faith in salvation through Christ, the antithesis of his Gospel, into the core of Christianity, disregarding Jesus' way of life and state of being. Jesus, like all people, did not live by faith, but by his instincts. He, therefore, concluded that the *psychologicis* of Jesus, which disregarded the reality of his life, his actual "conditioning fundamentals" (also translatable as nature or being-determinative) was radically wrong (*Antichrist*, 39).

Nietzsche treated the "the fundamentals of life" on two additional occasions. To return to them, we must identify, challenge and discard the influences of education, society and culture, which include the fantasies of "God, soul, virtue, sin, Beyond, truth, eternal life..." (*Ecce*, Clever, 10). The fundamentals are the natural biological functions "Whatever originates in the stomach, the intestines, the beating of the heart, the nerves, the bile, the seed," which cannot be judged in moral terms (*Daybreak*, I, 86). Thus, the Church's biased, misleading interpretation of Jesus is "in fact as an almost criminal fraud in *psychologicis*" (*Ecce*, Destiny, 7). Nietzsche, who, we will see, felt a strong affinity with Jesus, wanted to set the record straight and described Jesus as he felt he was. Not less important, if the Church's *psychologicis* of the figure of Jesus is disqualified, the rug is pulled out from under the feet of its morality, and ultimately, so he hoped, bring it closer to its demise (*Antichrist*, 39).

In virtue of his review of the different approaches to the understanding of the historical Jesus, and in light of his own notions, Nietzsche, the subject of our study, became a critic and commentator on *psychologicis*, the project of depicting a person based on a written text. Moreover, he suggested how to evaluate such an endeavor. He was clear about the proper way to extract the psychology of a person (Jesus) from a text (the Gospels), resulting in neither merely factual information nor impersonal ready-made labels such as hero and genius, offered by Renan. This holds true for psychiatric diagnostic categories, later used to explain Nietzsche as well. Instead, he called for a lively psychological understanding of what makes up a person in a given role, and how it came to be; in other words, make the particular person emerge, touch us, and impact our lives.

On Psychological Types

In addition to identifying the actual "conditioning fundamentals," Nietzsche suggests that coming to investigate a person's life and work, we must, most importantly, ascertain the type of the individual:

> What concerns me is the psychological type of the Redeemer. This type might be depicted in the Gospels, in however mutilated a form and however much overladen with extraneous characters [...] It is not a question of mere truthful evidence as to what he did, what he said and how he actually died; the question is, whether his type is still conceivable, whether it has been handed down to us (*Antichrist*, 29).

It is arguable that the following Nietzschean core concepts and many others, actually constitute a gallery of types: masters, slaves, priests, last man, the Superman, free and bound souls, strong and weak types, parasites, nobility, poets, philosophers, artists, commanders, practical persons and good Europeans. There are much more types "Reality shows us an enchanting wealth of types, the opulence of a lavish play and change of form" (*Twilight*, V, 6). Nietzsche believed that the wish to change persons according to some preconceived design is naive and hypocritical. The question for him is not how to change one's type, but rather how to act optimally in accord with it, in the words of the subtitle of *Ecce Homo* "How One Becomes What One Is." The word "type" is mentioned forty-eight times in *The Antichrist*, and it seems that it is equivalent to a "state of being." The different types interact with each other and "gravitate differently physiologically; each has its own hygiene, its own field of work, its own sense of perfection and mastery" (*Antichrist*, 57). Before we can consider Nietzsche's life fundamentals or formative experiences, we must examine the existing approaches to understanding him as a person and their implications for the understanding of his work. I hold that these attempts simply obliterated the person, clouded our view and did not enlighten us about Nietzsche's type.

Chapter 2

STEREOTYPES AND SPECULATIONS

Nietzsche, we saw, criticized the imaginary causes invented by the Church (God, soul, ego, spirit, free and un-free will) that disregard real life contingencies and natural-physiological causes, in favor of "the sign-language of religio-ethical balderdash" (*Antichrist,* 15). Modern psychobiographies are not immune to inventing similar imaginary causes, derived from theory and not from life. Nietzsche supposedly threw his arms around a suffering horse in Turin, Italy, before he descended to mental paralysis. Writing about a situation that probably never happened,[23] Eva M. Cybulska determined that this "was for Nietzsche a synthesis and culmination of so many of his own repressed thoughts and feelings. Dreams, experiences and ideas merged into a symbol." She added that according to Freud, a horse could symbolize the father, and the wish for his protective love, a theme also found in Schubert and Dostoevsky.[24]

Being intrigued by Nietzsche's life, and offering new ways to understand him, is commendable. Presenting a hypothesis as a fact, without supporting evidence, and without raising alternative explanations, is a different matter. Nietzsche concluded that "All the attempts that I know of to read the history of a 'soul' in the Gospels seem to me to reveal only a lamentable psychological levity" (*Antichrist,* 29). The attempts, reviewed in this chapter, to read Nietzsche from his writings, I am afraid, did not do much better.

The Ills of Diagnosis

Psychiatric diagnosis, I argued[25] in line with Thomas Szasz,[26] is a major component of the new *psychologica,* serving the state and the pharmaceutical industry.[27] A psychiatric diagnosis, as found in the DSM (Diagnostic and Statistical Manual), and especially of dead persons, is a guessing game, consisting of fitting a list of symptoms with a list of diseases, a kind of "cookie cutter," that catches only what is formally defined as pathological and disregards what is unique and different in the individual. It is an anti-therapeutic act, which instead of finding human commonalities, between the observer and the observed, declares the two inherently different, one healthier and better than the other. If I decide that you suffer from delusions, I am practically asserting that I am normal and you are not; I am almost invalidating whatever you say.

One of the first to use his authority as an alienist (as psychiatrists were called, in the nineteenth century) was Max Nordau, who with an apparent antipathy to Nietzsche's critique of his times' society and culture, declared him insane. He explained, that while ordinary readers must get used to Nietzsche's style, it was evident for him, that the writings were not different from those written by patients he had sent to the asylum. He did not mince his words, determining that a careful reader will hear in everything Nietzsche wrote a raving madman "So far as any meaning at all can be extracted from the endless stream of phrases, it shows as its fundamental elements a series of constantly reiterated delirious ideas, having their source in illusions of sense and diseased organic processes."[28]Additional medical and psychiatric assessments appeared after Nietzsche's death. The first article in English, unlike Nordau's, was devoid of hate and annihilation of the person and had some degree of empathy and irony. The author commented that Nietzsche, who wanted people to banish pity, was turned into a man who depended on the pity of others, and rather than diagnosing him, described a gradual slow process of disintegration, beginning at youth, loss of restraints and passing from sanity to insanity. His madness is evident in the writings, which are worth nothing as a contribution to psychology "He never proves anything, never indeed tries to prove anything, but contents himself with arrogant and absurd assertions."[29]

Paul Möbius was asked by Nietzsche's mother and sister to examine his case to deny the rumors that he died of syphilis. However, he announced in his *Nietzsche's Pathology* that he did suffer from syphilis of the brain (also known as GPI, general paresis of the insane), and he warned Nietzsche's readers, that in his writings "If you find pearls, don't think that they all are genuine. Be suspicious, because this man has a sickness of the brain."[30] Years later, in a more sympathetic approach, Eva Cybulska claimed that Nietzsche had psychiatric problems and suffered from delusions. His cardinal ideas, the death of God, the Superman and the Eternal Recurrence, were explained as a coping mechanism, a conceptualization which did not detract from the value of the work.[31] In another article she offered a more detailed diagnosis, arguing that Nietzsche's clinical picture was one of "bipolar affective disorder, consisting of brief manic episodes with some psychotic features."[32]Another psychiatrist, Richard Schain, suggests that Nietzsche would have been diagnosed today as suffering from manic-depressive psychosis (bipolar disorder) and that after a few years without improvement he would have been re-diagnosed as sick with chronic schizophrenia.[33]

Malek Khazaee, examining "the case of Nietzsche's madness," tried to find "how many of Nietzsche's books, if any, were written under the spell of madness." However, madness was seen by him, not as a psychiatric diagnosis, but rather as a description of uncommon ways of thinking, in Nietzsche's words, "it was madness that prepared the path to the new idea, that broke off the spell of a venerated usage and superstition. Do you understand why it had to be madness that did this?" Besides, madness might be an essential element in creativity "wherever there is madness there is also a grain of genius and wisdom, something 'divine,' as one whispered to oneself" (*Daybreak*, I, 14).[34]

Reviewing the different diagnoses of Nietzsche's final illness and reason for his death, one can indeed conclude only that he died; the reason for it remains an open question. Most of the modern scholars dealing with the issue saw it as their duty to vindicate Nietzsche from the hearsay that he suffered from syphilis. They use similar arguments, mainly pointing to the unusually extended period of time from the alleged exposure to the bacteria to the appearance of symptoms. They vary on the alternative diagnosis suggested. Only one scholar, going against the stream, brought arguments why syphilis cannot be ruled out.[35] The alternative to the diagnosis of syphilis is usually a neurological-organic disease: meningioma,[36] Frontotemporal dementia,[37] slow-growing medial sphenoid meningioma,[38] and CADASIL (cerebral autosomal dominant arteriopathy with subcortical infarcts and leukoencephalopathy) with dementia.[39] Brian Domino, contended that believing that readers need to know about the mental condition of authors, requires accepting as valid the following false assumptions: that the insane are always insane; that the readers cannot discriminate between the ideas of geniuses and lunatics; that the ideas of the insane are always harmful; and that knowing that the author is insane will help them appraise the work. He concluded, "Why, then, would an interpreter of Nietzsche's works care whether he suffered a progressive and rapid loss of mental acuity?"[40]

The absurdity of posthumous diagnosis is shown by Lucien Karhausen, who pointed out that at least 140 different illnesses have been proposed by various scholars as the cause of Mozart's death "Mozart's death has become a free for all, a grabbing of hypotheses." he was also diagnosed with twenty-seven different mental illnesses, invented by "data torturing" and by disregarding the differences between common manifestations and their more extreme pathological forms. In this way, sadness and moodiness were turned into depression; justified anxiety and worries into neurotic anxiety; and a sense of humor into immature personality or manic behavior. The list of pathologies included pathological gambling, attention deficit hyperactive disorder, obsessive compulsive disorder and dependent and passive-aggressive personality disorders.[41]

Karhausen suggested that such an abundant harvest of speculations, more than saying anything about Mozart's physical and mental health, illustrates our need to feel superior to creative geniuses, which we accomplish by portraying them as neurotic, psychotic or deviant, thus cutting them down to size and pulling them down from their pedestals. By degrading an outstanding creator, we mitigate our envy and can bear better our mediocrity.[42] Still, we must not forget the role of pure, healthy curiosity in such diagnostic exercises, and that understating something in different terms is the definition of a creative act.

The Father Complex

Maxine Harris interviewed persons who lost a parent early in life and, among others, mentioned Nietzsche as an example. A child who lost a parent will always remember the catastrophic death, changed into images of violent death, disasters, and destruction. Ideas of death and dying and a pessimistic outlook can continue for the rest of their life. Some children change from being spiritual and religious into ones who are unable to love, and even hate a God who let their parent die, and made them uncared for orphans. Observing a slowly dying parent, changes their conception, seeing weakness and helplessness, where strength and security existed before. Harris made the often forgotten point that the effects of the loss are mitigated or aggravated by the emotional state and functioning of the remaining parent.[43]Her conclusions are convincing, although it is arguable that some children become more pious, especially when they believe in some form of life after death; some children with living parents can grow up to be pessimistic nevertheless, and anxious people often think about death as well.

Nietzsche's loss of his father is treated from a dynamic or psychoanalytical perspective as a key factor in his life and work. Freud's Wednesday Circle had chosen Nietzsche as their subject for discussion for their meetings in April and October 1908. They discussed different aspects of his personality among them his sadism, repressed homosexuality and his father complex.[44] Interestingly, the following theoreticians feel comfortable writing about the effects of loss of a father, as if they were unconnected with the nature of the surviving mother and the resulting new family constellation. In an article trying to "unriddle" the vision of the Eternal Return, Eva Cybulska connects the idea with Nietzsche's early loss of his father. A loss that left him with a sense of deadness and abandonment, and with grief mixed with unconscious rage and resentment; feelings which were also projected onto God. His relationship with Wagner is explained as an attempt to recreate the past, the experience of sitting on his father's lap, his love and music fused into one. His break with Wagner and the love he felt towards his wife Cosima Wagner, were likewise explained as the result of the impossibility of solving the rivalry with his own father, having Wagner and his wife as substitute players in his Oedipal drama. The "ambiguous kernel of the eternal return of the same" is explained on the same grounds "With some dreadful inevitability, the whole cycle of love, abandonment, resentment, and rage had to repeat itself; the 'return of the dead' was complete. Wishing to go back to the lost paradise became bound up with the fear of losing it again; moreover, the paradise had to be lost."[45] In another article, this author connected the idea of the *Übermensch* with the same early loss of the father, which deprived him of "meaningful mirroring" and a chance to learn how to deal with realistic disappointments. Nietzsche, she argued, developed an inclination for idealization "his proverbial Achilles' heel and the source of repeated disillusionments and sorrow." The ideal of the *Übermensch* was a means to deal with his vulnerability "a mask of hardness that was designed, if unconsciously, to ward off any future assaults on his fragile self."[46]

Kyle Arnold and George Atwood argued that Nietzsche's emotional life, philosophical work and eventually his madness, stemmed all from the death of his beloved father at the age of four years. A trauma that confronted him too early with the finitude of life, the certainty of death and loss. The trauma shattered his emotional world, leaving behind chaos and fragmentation, the ground of the later breakdown. Already as a boy, he made "restorative efforts" in trying to overcome his grief and devastation by identification with his lost father, adopting a pastor's manners; as if bringing him alive again, by being him. Such efforts to overcome the nothingness of traumatic loss continued throughout his life, with many written indications that Nietzsche felt and was aware of the similarity of disposition and fate with his father "I am merely my father once more" (*Ecce*, Wise, 1). These authors, like Eva Cybulska, suggest that the very attempt to restore and perpetuate his father resulted in a tragic and recurrent return to his own psychological annihilation and finally to a breakdown. Here, they feel, lies the essence of his doctrine of the eternal return of the same.[47]

Such explanations are tempting at first sight, as they readily confirm preconceived theoretical notions and seem to offer one elegant solution to many queries. On second thought, doubts appear and questions, not considered by these authors, are raised: how can the lost-father hypothesis be disproven? Are all fatherless children doomed to madness? Do all fatherless children "discover" ideas similar to the Eternal Recurrence or the Superman? Does identifying with an absent father always lead to creativity or destructiveness? Is identification with a dead father, different from identification with a living one, and what happens when the father, dead or alive is abusive? Are there any alternative explanations for Nietzsche madness, if he was mad at all? Is the missing father the only motivation for the themes of Eternal Return or the Superman? Finally, what in Nietzsche's life and work, cannot be explained by the loss of his father? Another important question that Nietzsche would have raised is how does this theory contribute to life, and what are we supposed to learn from it? Such questions, of course, can and should be raised about my hypotheses as well.

Reading Nietzsche's various references to his father and father figures raises uncertainties as to whether the picture of the loving father is not an idealized one. The 13 years old boy wrote in *Out of my Life* "On August 2nd the mortal cover of my beloved father was entrusted to the womb of the earth [...] Then the coffin lowered down into the ground, and the dull words resounded, and he, our beloved father, has gone away from all of us mourners. The earth has lost a believing soul; the heaven received a watching soul." The elegiac style, I find, is ornate and somewhat stereotypic, as if he used a familiar formula for such occasions, perhaps repeating what was expected of him and what he heard in many funerals and eulogies at church. A dream he recorded at that time, contradicts the spirit of these words "... suddenly a grave opens and my father, dressed in his shroud, climbs out of it. He rushes into the church and after a short while he returns with a little child in his arms. The grave opens, he enters, and the cover sinks down again on the opening. Immediately the thunderous sound of the organ stops, and I wake up."[48] Arnold and Atwood, accept the avowal of love as authentic and the portrayal in the dream of a threatening, dangerous and even murderous father, as something in need of psychodynamic explanation, namely, as an expression of unconscious anger at the father's desertion. At the beginning of this essay, Nietzsche expressed reservations about his recollection "Although I am still not an adult and have hardly left the years of childhood and boyhood behind me, there is much that has disappeared from my memory, and the few things which I can remember are probably only due to tradition." I propose that the dream might reveal a truth obscured in reality and that the son's love is not self-evident. In any case, five years later, in another essay and for another audience,[49] love was not declared, and the father's death was mentioned in a matter of fact manner.

Outing Nietzsche

Was Nietzsche a homosexual? Such a question begs additional questions: what does it say about the person asking it, what is meant by the word "homosexual," and why does it matter? The questioner must have an essentialist binary view, that people are either heterosexual or homosexual, and that the two are inherently different entities. Alfred Kinsey suggested in his seminal study that people range on a scale of six grades, from exclusive homosexuality to exclusive heterosexuality. He also found that a significant number of heterosexuals had homosexual experiences in their childhood and adolescence.[50] Besides, homosexuality is historically and culturally dependent: in ancient Greece, it was different from what it is today; in Teheran, Iran it is not the same as in San Francisco, California. In addition, sexual fantasies, urges, actual behavior, self-perception and social roles, do not necessarily overlap, and one or some of them can exist, without the others.

Nietzsche studied in a boys' boarding-school, and hardly had any exposure to girls. In such situations (like in a *Yeshiva*, a school of the ultra-orthodox Jewish community) the young males' close bonds and feelings of love towards mates are expected, accepted and not at all derided. Nietzsche was a devotee of classical Greek culture, in which friendship between men was treasured, and the beauty of boys celebrated. In the domain of same-sex relations, separate and independent forms and shades can exist in different combinations: homophilia (loving and having close emotional bonds with members of one's own gender), homoeroticism (being able to see persons of one's own gender as handsome and sexually attractive), homosexuality (having actual sexual relations), and being gay (defining one's self as gay, adopting cultural characteristics and belonging to a gay community).[51] Perhaps, at the beginning of the 21st century, when adjectives such as genderqueer, genderfluid, agender, pansexual, and trigender, are increasingly flaunted in forums on the web, all the previous distinctions are becoming obsolete.

On top of the ambiguity, and unfortunately still common negative connotations, Freud's discussion of Nietzsche's "repressed homosexuality" just increased the murkiness. It is a problematic notion, as only manifest homosexuals can prove that they are not repressed ones.[52] Among Nietzsche's biographers, Curtis Cate and J.R. Hollingdale did not find Nietzsche's sexuality important enough to put under their microscope.[53] Walter Kaufman discussed it in one footnote only. He pointed out that construing Nietzsche's love to Wagner as homosexual in nature (as did the psychoanalyst Wilhelm Stekel, one Freud's earliest followers and co-founder of the Psychoanalytic Society), is based on a tenuous knowledge of Nietzsche, misunderstands his intellectual celebration of male friendship; disregards Nietzsche's love feelings toward Cosima, the heterosexual imagery in *Thus Spoke Zarathustra* and his poems, and his later demand for women, in the asylum.[54]

Joachim Köhler treated the question in depth and did not leave any stone unturned, aiming to prove that Nietzsche was a homosexual and that it was the most significant feature of his life. He argued that it is the ground of his most significant contributions: his attack on Christianity, which is hostile to sexuality, prohibits homosexuality and deems it a sin; and the ideal of the Superman (and Superwoman), who live passionately and determine their own value system.[55] His argumentation becomes overkill, finding secret homosexuality behind innocent childhood poetry for example, without considering any alternative interpretations. Nietzsche used an image of a lizard in the sun, to describe the pleasure of lying on a beach in Italy, and Köhler had to comment that "Sardes, author of a third-century Greek anthology of pederastic literature, calls the penis of his young lover a lizard."[56] Freud supposedly said that sometimes a cigar is only a cigar, and this holds true for lizards too, as can be learned from Randy K. Milholland's witty remark "You make me understand how wonderful it is for little lizards when they find that one special rock that's perfect for sunning themselves on. You make me lizard-happy."

Rüdiger Safranski acknowledged Nietzsche's homoeroticism, as one element in his "quest for intimacy." Nietzsche, he said, titled the fourth book of *The Gay Science* "Sanctus Januarius," a saint and martyr depicted in churches' pictures and statues as a man with androgynous characteristics, feminine beauty, associated with bleeding. Nietzsche explained to a friend that this part of the book reveals much about him. Some interpreters, Köhler included, find here evidence of homoerotic tendency, a conclusion which especially after my visit to Naples, I find unconvincing. Saint Januarius (In Italian Gennaro) is the patron saint and the former bishop of Naples in the 4th century, who was martyred by beheading. Some remains of his skull and a reliquary containing some of his solidified blood, are kept and venerated in Naples' cathedral, in which three times a year, in an extraordinary rite, the blood liquefies miraculously. However, Saint Januarius, similarly to Saint Anthony of Padua for example, is depicted in some paintings as a rugged man, or as a more delicate spiritual person in others. I assume that the different artists chose, according to their own interpretations, to transmit a message of either strength or piousness. Incidentally, the miracle of a liquefying blood occurs with a few other saints, such as Saint Pantaleon in Ravello. I, therefore, suggest a different interpretation, namely that Nietzsche experienced in Naples a return to health and liveliness as if his blood started to flow again, and he, the nonbeliever, somewhat tongue in cheek, gave thanks to the city's patron saint.

Safranski mentioned in this context the suggestion by H. J. Schmidt that it was the poet Ernest Ortlepp, a drunkard, vagabond and a recognized abuser of boys, known to Nietzsche and his school friends, who probably seduced or raped the young Nietzsche. Leaving him traumatized, exhilarated and with an altered sexual orientation. Although indirect evidence can be found in Nietzsche's writings for Schmidt's hypotheses, Safranski chose not to go into it, and he cautioned against "reducing the immense range of life that inspired Nietzsche's thought to the secret history of his sexuality and making it the privileged focal point of truth." This equation of sexuality with the truth of individuals, he suggested, is our area's "most prominent fiction regarding the nature of truth."[57]

Assuming that Nietzsche was a homosexual, as Köhler claimed and Safranski did not rule out, or according to my reading that he had a complicated, if not disorganized sexual identity, we must put such assertions to the Nietzschean test as we did before regarding the hypothesis of the 'father complex." Do we understand any better Nietzsche's critique of culture and religion or his doctrine of the Superman in this light? Does it enrich our own life, helping us be more passionate or creative? Do we have now a better conception of Nietzsche's type? Although the claim cannot be rejected, the answer to these questions remains negative.

Chapter 3

AUTOBIOGRAPHY AND RIDDLES

Nietzsche, in effect, wrote two autobiographies (not to count his juvenile autobiographical essays). One is Apollonian and the other Dionysian. One is analytic and systematic; the other, poetic and prophetic. One is direct, where Nietzsche discusses himself and reviews his writings; the other is indirect where Nietzsche uses a mythological-religious figure as a mouthpiece. One is conceptual and evaluative, the other associative with many images and sensations. I am referring to *Ecce Homo* and *Thus Spoke Zarathustra*. The two books are not merely autobiographies, as Nietzsche used his own life experiences to make a point. In the former it is to teach "how one becomes what one is." It is much harder to pinpoint a single goal in the latter. Perhaps "how to overcome what one is" could come close enough.

Nietzsche, it seems, wrote each part of *Thus Spoke Zarathustra* in ten days. The tone of his messages is urgent and emotionally involved. Words are flowing from his soul or unconscious to ours. Zarathustra is a teacher and prophet, and prophets have revelations and use their own life as a metaphor. In the case of the prophet Hosea, the Bible recounts that God had told him "Go, take yourself a wife of harlotry and children of harlotry; for the land has committed great harlotry by departing from the Lord" (*Hosea*, 1, 2). Interestingly, Nietzsche felt that he had to forewarn his readers "No 'prophet' speaks here, no horrible hybrids of sickness and the Will to Power, called by men founders of religions" (*Ecce*, Preface, 3).

Nietzsche's two autobiographies share a substantial use of riddles. He poses riddles and Zarathustra is described as riddles solver "a hard nut-cracker" *(Zarathustra,* III, The ugliest man), whose life taught him how to solve riddles of the heart *(Zarathustra,* II, Self-overcoming). Zarathustra says "Calm is the bottom of my sea: who would guess that it hides droll monsters! Unmoved is my depth: but it sparkles with swimming riddles and laughter" *(Zarathustra,* II, The sublime men). He, "the father of the book," calls himself "the ruminator and riddle-lover" (*Ecce,* Self-Criticism) and sees himself as a natural born "guesser of riddles" (*Gay,* V, 343). In his books Nietzsche mentioned numerous times the famed riddle of the sphinx, solved by Oedipus "what walks on four legs in the morning, two in the afternoon, and three in the evening?" (Human beings, as they age).

Zarathustra solved the riddles posed by the magician *(Zarathustra,* IV, 5), the ugliest man *(Zarathustra,* IV, 7), the voluntary beggar *(Zarathustra,* IV, 8) and the daughters of the wilderness *(Zarathustra,* IV, 16). Posing and solving riddles is a hallmark of human beings "And how could I stand being a man if a man were not also the composer, riddle-reader, and redeemer of chance?" *(Zarathustra,* II, Redemption). In a moment of grace, the world seems like "Not riddle enough to scare human love from it, not solution enough to put to sleep human wisdom" *(Zarathustra,* III, The three evil things, 1). Zarathustra teaches how "to compose and collect into unity what is fragment in man, and riddle and fearful chance; – As composer, riddle-reader, and redeemer of chance, did I teach them to create the future, and all that *had been* – to redeem by creating" *(Zarathustra,* III, old and new tables, 3).

In her *The Poetics of Riddle in W.S. Merwin's Poetry,* Norma Procopiow explained that "Through the centuries, the riddle has varied in significance from childish rhymes to ribald innuendo." She pointed out that Aristotle described it as *aenigma,* a figure of speech in which ordinary meaning is overtly changed or turned[58] and quoted Northrop Frye's description of riddle as "a fusion of sensation and reflection, the use of an object or sense experience to stimulate a mental activity in connection with it [...] The idea of the riddle is descriptive containment; the subject is not described but circumscribed, a circle of words drawn from it."[59] Her analysis of Merwin's use of riddles as a literary device applies to Nietzsche, whose riddles also "generally comprises a question or statement couched in deliberately puzzling terms." The two of them used metaphors, whose rhetorical purpose was "to turn on verbal artifacts that continue to absorb us, even after we have answered them."[60] Merwin himself added that riddles, like poetry, seek "a finality of utterance," wishing to remain "irreducible and unchangeable."[61]

I hope to show that Nietzsche's life and writings are interrelated: each of them will help us understand the other one better. Nietzsche himself was playing hide-and-seek with us, a game of inviting and dissuading us from getting close to him. And then, finally, when it seems that he let us get closer, he did not say things directly but talked in riddles. The second part of *Human All too Human* is titled *The Wanderer and his Shadow,* and Norma Procopiow aptly pointed out that "There is perhaps no metaphor more universally fraught with the dialectical potential for riddle than the shadow. As an obscurity, the shadow attests to space and light. As nothingness, it reflects substance."[62] Riddles, when told in kindergarten or a pub, are meant to instruct or amuse; otherwise, they hide, not a funny, smart retort but a secret. Carl Jung sensed that Nietzsche lived with a secret and in his *Memories, Dreams, Reflections* wrote that upon reading Nietzsche, he was held back by a secret fear not to be like him: living with a secret, isolated from his environment, with inner experiences and insights of which he wrote, but no one seemed to understand.[63]

Painful Riddles

The riddles which Nietzsche or Zarathustra (which also stands for Nietzsche) solved are mostly philosophical; the riddles he posed to his listeners and readers are biographical, alluding to painful undisclosed life events. It seems that he was torn between a need to reveal information about himself and concurrently a need to keep it hidden. The first chapter of *Ecce Homo* already begins with a riddle:

> The happiness of my existence, its unique character perhaps, lies in its fatefulness: expressing it in the form of a riddle, as my own father I am already dead, as my own mother I still live and grow old. This double origin, taken as it were from the highest and lowest rungs of the ladder of life, at once a decadence and a beginning, if anything, explains that neutrality, that freedom from partisanship with regard to the general problem of life, which perhaps distinguishes me (*Ecce*, Wise, 1).

The problem is that the solutions to Nietzsche's riddles do not appear in his books' appendices, as they do in textbooks of mathematics. Nevertheless, let us try and tackle this riddle, limiting ourselves to three trials. Nietzsche is talking about the double origins of his life. One of them represents the highest rung of life and the other the lowest, and it is another riddle whether the rungs relate to his parents or to something else. I will limit myself to the first part of the quote, and I will return to the second part at a later opportunity.

Different possible solutions come to mind: the first is based on realizing that Nietzsche mentioned in the same section his own physical decline which started at the age of thirty-six, precisely the age when his father died. Thus, objectively, like his mother, he is alive; while subjectively, as far as quality of life is concerned, he feels like the living dead and is more like his deceased father. This reasoning is supported by "perhaps it is only a prejudice to suppose that I am living at all" (*Ecce*, Preface, 1).

The second possibility would see his parents as symbols of the male and female principles. For Nietzsche, the genders are and should be essentially different. The male is strong and active, produces change and makes things safer and better. The female is weak, dissatisfied and sensitive, one who makes life more beautiful and profound. She is romantic, seeks "happiness," willing to be deceived and intoxicated (*Gay*, I, 24). In a word, "This is how I would have man and woman: the one fit for war, the other fit for bearing children..."

(Zarathustra, III, Old and new law-tables, 23). Nietzsche is thus disclosing that his warrior male part is defunct, while his female part, the one pregnant with ideas and the one that gives birth to books is intact.

A third possibility would be that Nietzsche is discussing two problem areas or two psychological difficulties that brought havoc to his life, but also rebirth. He came to terms with his "father" theme, which is now a dead issue. His "mother" theme, however, continues to bother him, and it will not go away as long as she and he are alive. A segment that was intentionally omitted by his sister Elisabeth Förster-Nietzsche, from the 1905 edition of *Ecce Homo,* and reintroduced in later versions reads:

> The treatment I have received from my mother and my sister, up to the present moment, fills me with inexpressible horror: there is an absolutely hellish machine at work here, operating with infallible certainty at the precise moment when I am most vulnerable – at my highest moments [...] for then one needs all one's strength to counter such a poisonous viper [...] But I confess that the deepest objection to the 'Eternal Recurrence', my real idea from the abyss, is always my mother and my sister (*Ecce,* Wise, 3).

Thus Spoke Zarathustra is full of riddles. Midnight is frequently mentioned, and it hides a secret. Zarathustra asked, "What says deep midnight's voice indeed?" *(Zarathustra,* III, The second dance song, 2). And he asked again "O man! Take heed! What says deep midnight's voice indeed?" *(Zarathustra,* IV, The drunken song, 12). The question was repeated once more "Hear you not how it mysteriously, frightfully, and cordially speaks to you, the old deep, deep midnight?" *(Zarathustra,* IV, The drunken song, 3). Midnight talks and hints at something menacing, but we find it difficult to understand "Now does it speak, now is it heard, now does it steal into over wakeful, nocturnal souls: ah! Ah! How the midnight sighs! How it laughs in its dream!" *(Zarathustra,* IV, The drunken song, 3). Although he posed the riddle, he is unable to reveal its solution "Ah! Ah! The dog howls, the moon shins. Rather will I die, rather will I die, than say to you what my midnight-heart now thinks" *(Zarathustra,* IV, The drunken song, 4). For a moment it seems that the secret is going to be revealed "Ye higher men, it is getting on to midnight: then will I say something into your ears"— something mysterious and frightful, spoken by the "midnight clock-bell," something experienced by "more than one man," something that cannot be heard by day, but something that eventually remained unsaid *(Zarathustra,* IV, Drunken song, 7). The sighs in the above quotes intimate that midnight's deep voice has something excruciating to say. The dictionary (*thefreedictionary.com*) reminds us that in addition to being 12 o'clock at night, midnight also means intense darkness and gloom, also called "the witching hour," when supernatural events are thought to occur, and witches are supposed to appear.

The fourth part of *Thus Spoke Zarathustra* is populated with many colorful figures which give the commentators room for a "who is who" guessing game. I will concentrate on some grave riddles appearing in the chapters *The vision and the riddle*, *The adder's bite*, and *The ugliest man*—the solving of which will help us understand the secret of Nietzsche. The key to solving the riddles is that Nietzsche's psychological observations seemingly about others, stem from and are actually about himself. He explained, "Every psychological passage that is significant is concerned only with me—you need not hesitate to substitute my name or that of 'Zarathustra' wherever the text gives the name of Wagner" (*Ecce*, Birth, 4). He also pointed out "These were Schopenhauer and Wagner, or, in a word, Nietzsche..." (*Ecce*, Untimely, 1). Nietzsche suggested that "Plato made use of Socrates in the same way, that is to say, as a means of expressing his own ideas" (*Ecce*, Untimely, 3). I would like to improvise now and add "Zarathustra, Dionysus, and Jesus, or, in a word, Nietzsche..."

Suffering and Trauma

It is impossible to understand Nietzsche or the "psychology of the psychologist" (*Will*, II, 426), without taking into account the centrality of pain and suffering in his life. Suffering is suffering, is suffering. It is beyond words, and no one can comprehend another person's pain. Four kinds of suffering fell to Nietzsche's lot, or to be more exact, his massive suffering can be divided into four related domains, which I will examine later. Firstly, he suffered mental anguish and was ridden with terrible flashbacks and suicidal thoughts. Secondly, he suffered from sickliness which included debilitating bodily pains, weakness, digestive problems, headaches, and eyestrain. Thirdly, he experienced extreme tearing mood swings, alternating between melancholia and euphoria. Fourthly, his interaction with fellow human beings was troubled. He was shy, introverted, easily hurt and unassertive. Although he had a few friends, most of the time he suffered from loneliness and lack of love and was ridden with feelings of contempt and disgust towards others.

In the last chapter, we rejected the attempts to diagnose Nietzsche and see him as suffering from this or that psychopathology, warranting labeling him with a psychiatric tag. Nietzsche criticized the mentalistic concepts of ego, soul, and self. He saw all of them as "blunders of psychology," instances of turning fictions into concrete objects.[64] He went on using these very concepts, realizing that otherwise, communications with his readers would not be possible. Following him, for the sake of clarity, I will use the term Post-Traumatic Stress Disorder (PTSD), not as a diagnosis, but as a frame of reference to describe the psychological aftermath of trauma. Not as a fixed, standardized entity, but rather as a range and constellation of individual characteristics, taking to heart Alfred Korzybski's dictum "the map is not the territory."[65] The consequences of trauma are not pathological; the person suffering from them is not abnormal. The person is unfortunate, and the reactions are normal reactions to an abnormal condition.[66] I suggest that Nietzsche suffered from a severe psychological trauma whose consequences continued to trouble him for the rest of his life. Before I let Nietzsche talk, that is to say, confirm my claim, I will elaborate on the map, to make what is in the territory more noticeable.

The Online Etymology Dictionary explains that since the 1690s the term "trauma" was used in medical Latin for "physical wound." The word derived from Greek trauma "a wound, a hurt; a defeat." Only since 1894 was, it used to indicate "psychic wound, an unpleasant experience which causes abnormal stress" (*Etymonline.com*). Human beings, however, have always suffered from harrowing experiences, when attacked by wild beasts, assailed by fierce enemies, crushed by nature's disasters, hurt in accidents, raped and sexually abused. After violent, life-threatening events like these, it would be surprising to see persons continue with their life as if nothing has happened. Even after the physical trauma is healed, the devastating psychological effects can continue for years.

Descriptions of trauma can be found already in ancient Greece and Rome, in the medieval ages, and in the16th century Renaissance.[67] The terms Post-Traumatic Stress Disorder was introduced only in 1980. Before it, similar phenomena were conceived, among others, as nostalgia, homesickness, soldier's heart, neurasthenia, shell shock and combat fatigue.[68] As the manifestations are the result of an interaction between individuals and their environments, which do not stay permanent, the nature of the experience itself is not identical in different periods and situations. PTSD is not a universal fixed entity, and thus soldiers in antiquity, in WWI, or in Vietnam, experienced wars differently, and when traumatized, responded differently too.[69] The fifth edition of the DSM considers experiencing, as well as witnessing a threat to survival, serious injury or sexual violation, as triggers to PTSD, and it describes four typical clusters of indicators (I avoid using the word "symptom") for the condition:

1. Re-experiencing: trauma victims are prone to re-experience the initial trauma, in the form of short flashbacks, or with prolonged psychological distress, whenever spontaneous memories of the traumatic event are aroused, and when related contents appear in recurrent nightmares and dreams. 2. Avoidance: people who experienced trauma try to avoid external reminders of the event, and, therefore, refrain from talking about it and tend to suppress distressing memories, thoughts, and feelings. 3. Negative cognitions and

moods: trauma survivors often suffer from a persistent and distorted sense of self-blame and faulting. They feel distant from others, numb, forgetful and less interested in activities. 4. Hyperarousal: after the occurrence of trauma, people are liable to remain on alert—tense, vigilant, restless, suffering from sleep disorders, difficulties in attention and concentration; with frightening thoughts, and occasional shaking and sweating. Having a lower threshold of frustration and problems in restraint and deliberation, persons who experienced severe trauma can easily become moody and irritated, aggressive and involved in self-destructive behaviors.

In addition to the delineation of the above four clusters, the DSM recognizes two subtypes of PTSD, the first in children younger than six years, the second, with prominent dissociative symptoms, namely feeling detached from one's own mind or body, or experiencing the world as unreal, dreamlike or distorted.[70] Furthermore, attempts at self-medication make these persons prone to alcoholism and addictions. These, together with the other disturbances, resulting in a higher prevalence of relationship breakdowns, phobias, anxiety disorders, severe depressions, headaches, stomach problems, dizziness, chest pain, body aches and pains, weaker immune system and difficulties at work.[71]

Why, until now, have other scholars not raised the hypothesis that Nietzsche suffered the consequences of trauma? Perhaps, because Nietzsche's philosophically-minded readers did not find in the following statements any abstract ideas to be analyzed, and therefore they were just overlooked. As these passages were dispersed in many of Nietzsche's books, their combined weight was ignored. Also, Nietzsche talked in general, as if commenting on some psychological phenomenon, without saying specifically that it was about him. Besides, it is often difficult to see at first glance, an animal blended into its habitat, and only if its presence is suspected, and the landscape is scrutinized, can it suddenly be discovered. I will now let Nietzsche talk, and the reader will find it an easy task to insert each of his sentences into one of the four categories of PTSD indicators.

The Trauma of War

The fifth edition of the DSM, we learned, considers not only experiencing a direct threat to survival and severe injury but also witnessing them as triggers to PTSD. Nietzsche's letters, describing the experiences of a twenty-six years old man, serving in the Swiss voluntary ambulance corps, during the Franco-Prussian war (19 July 1870 – 10 May 1871), with ghastly details and evidence of their detrimental impact, suggest an alternative hypothesis to account for the source of his trauma. In a letter to his mother (August 28, 1870) he wrote: "I am sending you a souvenir of the terribly devastated battlefield, strewn with countless sad remains and smelling strongly of corpses." Two weeks later

(September 11, 1870) he updated her "I went as far as the outskirts of Metz and conducted a transport of wounded from there to Karlsruhe. And as the result of this, the terrible state of all the wounded in my hands, the constant bandaging of their septic wounds, and sleeping in a cattle truck in which six severely wounded men lay on straw, I contracted the germ of dysentery."

In his next letter (September 21, 1870) addressed to Ritschel, his professor, he recounted the same events, adding that "The strain of the whole undertaking was considerable, and I am still struggling against the recollection of all I saw during those weeks, as well as against an incessant wail of which I cannot rid my mind's ear." Nietzsche added that he arrived at his hometown, wishing to recuperate and recover from the stress and fatigue, through peaceful work, however, despite his best intentions "one's own paltry personality with all its wretchedness and weakness comes and trips one up. Once more, alas!" We have here evidence of intrusive memories followed by an experience of an emotional meltdown.

The last letter from the front was sent to his friend von Gersdorff (October 20, 1870). In it, he told about repeatedly dressing the wounds of two soldiers who have contracted hospital gangrene, and later had charge of six other wounded soldiers for three days and nights, without any rest, in smelly closed-up trucks, two soldiers suffering from dysentery, and the other two from diphtheria. After he had delivered the invalids to a hospital, he fell sick himself "Besides, the atmosphere of my experiences had spread like a gloomy mist all about me, and for some time I never ceased to hear the plaintive cries of the wounded."[72]

In his books, Nietzsche did not refer to these experiences. The atrocious memories continued for "some time" only, and therefore it seems that the label Acute Stress Response would better fit the situation. In the letter to Ritschel, Nietzsche implied that he felt similar emotional difficulties before his war experiences. His symptoms of pain and moodiness were apparent already when he was a high-school student, and his personality's characteristics were probably set in earlier stages of his life. The studies of Adverse Childhood Experiences, which I will review later, show that they increase the susceptibility to trauma in adulthood. The conclusion called for is that the later war trauma was added to the past childhood trauma, to make it more devastating.

The Multifaceted Torture of the Psychologist

Nietzsche's severe suffering might well be the explanation for his condemnation of pity. He did not want to pity himself, and he did not want others, we included, to pity him, as pity implies recognition of impairment and investment in solace rather than in coping. In the following quote, Nietzsche is observing as a psychologist other "exceptional examples." But this precisely is what he is himself—an exceptional and a "lofty person." Hence, as a psychologist, he is writing about the process of studying the only subject he knew well—himself, and this knowledge is then projected onto others. Any other reading does not make sense, as it would portray Nietzsche's statements as wild hunches (who and how many "lofty persons" did he examine after all?), and groundless generalizations (are all "lofty persons" indeed identical?). Besides, it is not reasonable that discussing other human being's "corruption and destruction," will pose a danger of "suffocation from pity," while this would be expected in remembering one's own:

> The multifaceted torture of the psychologist who has uncovered this destructiveness, who once discovers and then almost always rediscovers throughout all history this entire inner 'hopelessness' of the loftier people, this eternal 'too late!' in every sense, can perhaps one day come to the point where he turns with bitterness against his own lot and attempts self-destruction—where he 'corrupts' himself (*Beyond*, IX, 269).

The continuation of this paragraph asserts that such "lofty persons" are in a constant need of healing and require "some sort of refuge and forgetting." They experience fear of their memories, are sensuous, childish, impulsive, careless in trust and mistrust. And the description gradually becomes appalling "With souls in which some fracture or other normally has to be concealed; often taking revenge in their works for an inner slur, often seeking with their flights upward to forget some all-too-true memory [...] often struggling against a long disgust, with a recurring ghost of unbelief..." (*Beyond*, IX, 269).

Is it possible to read these lines, without feeling that Nietzsche was pouring his heart out in them? I reiterate—he talked about his complexities, his "inner hopelessness," his self-destructiveness, his suicidal ideas and his "eternal too late" (failing and understanding what he should have done only after the fact). He alludes to a severe trauma "some internal fracture," leaving him hurt, abiding with intrusive memories, internal defilement and a sense of disgust, with problems of trust in people, being in need of healing. Whatever transpired was disastrous, a murderous ritual, a historical turning point "the crowd worshiped a god—and the 'god' was only a poor sacrificial animal!"

In the introduction to the second volume of his *Human, All Too Human*, dedicated to free spirits, he wrote openly about his "innermost solitude and self-restraint over long intervening years," and about himself, a psychologist "who has a lot of painful things *beneath* him, *behind* him, yet subsequently identifies and as it were *jabs firmly* at them with the point of a needle." Thus, he concluded, it should not be surprising, if this psychologist had blood on his fingers, and not only on them (*Human*, Assorted, Preface 2ed, 1). In addition to this admission, there are other testimonies, interspersed in his writings, suggesting that a severe childhood trauma must have taken place in his life:

> My friends, it was hard for us when we were young: we suffered youth itself like a serious sickness. That is due to the time into which we have been thrown—a time of extensive inner decay and disintegration, a time that with all its weaknesses, and even with its best strength, opposes the spirit of youth [...] Everything on our way is slippery and dangerous, and the ice that still supports us has become thin: all of us feel the warm, uncanny breath of the thawing wind; where we still walk, soon no one will be able to walk, (*Will*, I, 57).

Nietzsche apparently talked here about some dreadful experience. Had it been losing his father, it would have been, quite easy and simple to express it. It is not clear yet how he was made a "sacrificial animal," what caused the fracture in his soul and the "extensive inner decay and disintegration." Neither is it given "What is the gnat that will not let him sleep," the memory he tries so desperately to suppress and finally, what was it that changed so drastically his attitudes towards life and ability to love:

> We all know the curious way in which unpleasant memories suddenly throng on us, and how we do our best by loud talk and violent gestures to put them out of our minds; but the gestures and the talk of our ordinary life make one think we are all in this condition, frightened of any memory or any inward gaze. What is it that is always troubling us? What is the gnat that will not let us sleep? There are spirits all about us, each moment of life has something to say to us, but we will not listen to the spirit-voices. When we are quiet and alone, we fear that something will be whispered in our ears, and so we hate the quiet and dull our senses in society" (*Untimely*, Schopenhauer, 5).

Nietzsche highlighted the time dimension of trauma, in which the past intrudes upon the present, coming back as a ghost haunting and disturbing "A leaf is continuously released from the roll of time, falls out, flutters away—and suddenly flutters back again into the man's lap" (*Untimely*, History, 1). Humans are historical creatures who live with memories of the past, which can become "an invisible and dark weight," an intruding and painful burden. The "it was" can become traumatic; turning existence into "a past tense that is never over and done with," that only death can terminate (*Untimely*, History, 1). Nietzsche described, as can be expected with survivors of PTSD, the re-experiencing of traumatic memories and the struggle to avoid them, his feelings of hopefulness, and also his anger outbursts. Hyper-alert trauma victims are often prone to having a lower threshold of aggression and exhibiting outbursts of uncontrolled violent behavior "Occasionally nowadays it happens that a mild, moderate, reserved man suddenly becomes violent, smashes plates, throws over the table, screams, stomps around, slanders the entire world." Nietzsche was unable to explain what happened to him "perhaps the harpies have flown over my table" and furious with himself, he mentioned in this context again some suffocating memory (*Beyond*, IX, 282).

In another place, he described how, as a result of failing to overcome the pain of trauma, the victim is liable to respond with malice of his tongue or withdrawal into the Nothing "into mute, rigid, deaf resignation, self-forgetting, self-extinction." He does not necessarily become "dusky, a barn owl," and can still somehow, in his way, love life, however, "It is the love for a woman who raises doubts in us" (*Contra*, Epilogue, 1). His response to human intimacy is entering a state of alarm "we cannot persuade our nose to give up its prejudice against the proximity of a human being" (*Gay*, V, 379). Already in his first book, discussing the intermixture of pain and joy in general, he wrote a sentence that can be easily understood as referring to his own life experience "At the very climax of joy there sounds a cry of horror or a yearning lamentation for an irretrievable loss" (*Birth*, IV, 40). In the next chapter, I suggest a biographical reading of this book. Was he lamenting the loss of innocence and trust?

In an aphorism titled, *Advice as riddle*, Nietzsche challenged us to understand the following recommendation "If the band is not to break, bite it first—secure to make!" (*Beyond*, IV, 140). Now, in the context of trauma and loss of trust, the solution suggests itself: one, who was hurt before in a close relationship, must check carefully, using provocation, before bonding again, to make sure the offense will not be repeated. This advice is not only a riddle, but a quandary too, as reasonable persons might leave when they are bitten, and gluttons for punishment will stay. In the aftermath of trauma, trust is lost; memories and pain resurface; and oversensitivity to injury increases. Nietzsche described the very moment of the breakdown of the defense of repression "My past burst its tomb, many pains buried alive woke up; fully slept had they merely, concealed in corpse-clothes" (*Zarathustra*, III, Involuntary bliss).

Following his traumatic experiences, Zarathustra-Nietzsche is left sore and vulnerable, lacking in resiliency "But you profound man, you suffer too profoundly even from small wounds..." (*Zarathustra*, I, The flies of the marketplace). Lower simpler souls withstand injury and loss better than noble ones whose life is more complicated, who are easily hurt, in whom trauma can turn into a direct threat to their lives "With a lizard a finger which has been lost grows back: not so with a man" (*Beyond*, IX, 276). Some people can fall and never get hurt, but this is not his case "for us life is more dangerous: we are made of glass; woe unto us if we merely bump ourselves! And all is lost if we fall!" (*Gay*, III, 154). For Nietzsche, this time in the garb of a hermit, the slightest insult could be detrimental, and the hurt extreme and he admonishes "guard yourselves against offending the hermit! But if you have done so, well then, kill him as well!" (*Zarathustra,* I, The adder's bite). We will see, in the next chapter, that when Nietzsche wrote about Jesus and Dionysus, he was also writing about trauma and himself.

Chapter 4

NIETZSCHE, DIONYSUS AND JESUS

We have considered *Ecce Homo* and *Thus Spoke Zarathustra* as autobiographies, but as Nietzsche himself said, all his books are in a sense autobiographical and all his psychological insights are also about himself. I would like to suggest that his first book, *The Birth of Tragedy*, and his one before the last, *The Antichrist*, although not usually seen as such, are autobiographical as well. I will claim in a later chapter that the *Genealogy of Morals* has autobiographical elements as well. His first book was considered by critics, and foremost among them by Nietzsche himself, to be an immature book of a young professor of philology, who had not yet found his own voice. He still wrote as a Schopenhauerian and a Wagnerian, running off in all directions—mythology, anthropology, art, music and psychology, without mentioning the last subject by name. This book introduced Dionysus, a figure-theme which went on to gain a central place in his life and writings. At the end of *Ecce Homo*, we read "Have I been understood? Dionysus against the Crucified." I am suggesting that he can also be understood as the two of them together.

Nietzsche, Dionysus, and Apollo

The Birth of Tragedy is usually read as a contribution to the understanding of culture, art, tragedy and music, in accord with its opening sentence "Much will have been gained for aesthetics once we have succeeded in apprehending [...] that art owes its continuous evolution to the *Apollonian-Dionysian* duality" (*Birth*, 1). In the reading offered here, the Greek tragedy under discussion also refers to Nietzsche facing his own fate; and the Dionysian-Apollonian forces represent two major elements in his soul.

In this interpretation, the changes in the conception of Dionysus in Nietzsche's different books are not merely conceptual shifts of theory in light of new findings, but an indication of the author's evolving phases of coping with his suffering. He started by opposing the Dionysian and the Apollonian and moved to opposing the Dionysian with the romantic and the Socratic. Finally, when the Dionysian and the Apollonian reached cooperation and integration, the two were set up against the Christian ethic "Dionysus versus the 'Crucified': there you have the antithesis" (*Will*, IV, 1052). A few years after publication, Nietzsche summed up the main point of his book in an addendum:

> Indeed, what is Dionysian? — This book offers an answer to that question — a 'knowledgeable person' speaks there, the initiate and disciple of his god. Perhaps I would now speak with more care and less eloquently about such a difficult psychological question as the origin of tragedy among the Greeks. A basic issue is [...] whether their constantly stronger desire for beauty, for festivals, entertainments, and new cults really arose out of some lack, out of deprivation, out of melancholy, out of pain? (*Birth*, Criticism, 2).

Nietzsche, I suggest, used Dionysus, as he later used Schopenhauer, Wagner, Zarathustra and Jesus, as his own mirror images, or as images of some parts in his inner multiplicity. The expressions "knowledgeable person" and "initiate and disciple of this god" indicate a firsthand experience in which one gets to know the other as one knows oneself. The title of his later offering *Dithyrambs of Dionysus* entails that it was composed by Dionysus, and only written down by Nietzsche. After his mental breakdown, he stopped using masks and openly expressed what was on his mind, signing his letters as either the Crucified or Dionysus. In addition to saying that he is a disciple and initiate of his god, he also proclaimed: "I am a disciple of the philosopher Dionysus, and I would sooner be a satyr than a saint" (*Ecce*, Preface, 2). Similarly, he stated, in a more determined tone "I, the last disciple of the philosopher Dionysus—I, the teacher of the Eternal Recurrence" (*Twilight*, Ancients, 5).

Dionysus, like Jesus and like Nietzsche, is a "sacrificial animal," a victim of trauma and mistreatment and hence, the predominant themes of some lacking, deprivation, melancholy and pain (*Birth*, Criticism, 2). Nietzsche, in his first book, still felt comfortable enough using abstract terms like "primordial," "eternal," and "ground of being," to describe and repeatedly accentuate Dionysus' pain, suffering and injury, as can be seen on many occasions. Among them "we see a reflection of original pain, the sole ground of being" (*Birth*, 4) and "the original Oneness, the ground of Being, ever suffering and contradictory" (*Birth*, 4). This is also found in "the delusion of being able thereby to heal the eternal wound of existence" (*Birth*, 18). Nietzsche, I submit, was describing life in general, but also his own life, divulging that pain and suffering are its underlying condition, existing already in childhood:

> In truth, however, the hero of Greek tragedy is the suffering Dionysus of the mysteries, the god experiencing in himself the agonies of individuation, of whom wonderful myths tell that as a boy he was torn to pieces by the Titans and now is worshiped in this state as Zagreus. Thus, it is intimated that this dismemberment, the properly Dionysian suffering, is like a transformation into air, water,

> earth, and fire [...] From the smile of this Dionysus sprang the Olympian gods, from his tears sprang man (*Birth*, 10).

This theme reappeared in the Dionysian mysteries, in the ritual of *sparagmos* (In ancient Greek "tear, rend, pull to pieces"), in which the flesh of a living animal, and supposedly humans too, were torn apart, mangled, and sometimes followed by an act of *omophagia* (the eating of the raw flesh). Nietzsche and some of his readers must have had in mind Euripides's play *The Bacchae*, which concerns Dionysus and the Maenads who pulled a living bull to pieces with their hands. Not only that, later in the play, Agave led the *sparagmos*, the ritual tearing to pieces of Pentheus, her own son.[73] The play can be understood from different perspectives. I suggest that *sparagmos* is a symbol and an image of child abuse, and indeed, at least, two authors titled their books *The Slaughter of the Innocents*, a title which also alludes to the *New Testament*. The first had the subtitle *Child Abuse through the Ages and Today*,[74] and the second, *The Many Faces of Violence against Children*.[75] Children experience sexual abuse as a ritual "which is nothing more than repeatedly engaging in an act or series of acts, in a certain manner because of a sexual need." The perpetrator, in search of arousal and gratification, engages in the act in specified ways, with repeated sequences of activities and verbal behaviors.[76]

Did Nietzsche identify himself with Dionysus, or did he understand Dionysus in terms of his own life's experience? It is entirely possible that the two processes took place concurrently. Dionysus, just like Nietzsche and Zarathustra, oscillated between pain, melancholia and trauma on one end, and intoxication, joy and occasionally rage, on the other end. Zarathustra said about himself "Into every abyss do I bear the benediction of my yea to Life," and Nietzsche commented, "But this again is the very essence of Dionysus" (*Ecce*, Zarathustra, 6). If Dionysus is Zarathustra, and Zarathustra is Nietzsche, then Dionysus is Nietzsche, and the "eternal yes" will eventually turn into the Eternal Recurrence and *Amor fati*.

Nietzsche is also Apollo, who in *The Birth of Tragedy* represents art and heroism. I do not have to say much about Nietzsche's self-image as an artist and his artistic talents as a poet, essayist and composer. The Apollonian artistic creation and fighting spirit were his aids in coping with his Dionysian emotional turbulence, at times reaching monstrous proportions. To combat the "somber contemplation of actuality, the intense susceptibility to suffering," it was necessary to defeat Titans and kill monsters, but also to entertain zestful illusions (*Birth*, 3). The merger of the two forces is mutually beneficial, the Dionysian injuries are healed and out of the "original Titanic hierarchy of terror" the Apollonian need for beauty is gradually fulfilled in the creation of an "Olympian hierarchy of joy," just as "roses are seen to break from thorny bushes" (*Birth*, 3). These two gods reconciled, can confront now another god, and Nietzsche can now commence his more mature work "The god on the cross is a curse on life, a signpost to seek redemption from life; Dionysus cut to pieces is a promise of life: it will be eternally reborn and return again from destruction" (*Will*, IV, 1052).

Two First-born Sons

The enormity of Nietzsche's suffering and pain shows up in many places in his texts, sometimes unheralded, inducing in the reader an experience of the eerie words and tune of a Requiem's *Miseria*. Without his suffering, there would not have been a Jesus. Without his own *Via Dolorosa*, his hurting and grappling with it, there would not have been a Nietzsche too.

The way Nietzsche conceived the "psychology of the Redeemer" will help us extract Nietzsche's psychology, the "psychology of the psychologist" (*Will*, II, 426). To repeat, in philosophers and, of course, in Nietzsche too, "There is nothing whatever that is impersonal" (*Beyond*, I, 6) and "Every psychological passage that is significant is concerned only with me" (*Ecce*, Birth, 4). Nietzsche often wrote about and maintained a dialogue with "lofty figures," among them Socrates, Schopenhauer, and Wagner. Nietzsche, a son, and grandson of pastors continued a dialogue with Jesus throughout his life, based on a primary and deep identification. In other words, I suggest seeing Jesus as one of Nietzsche's mirror images. Speaking about mirror images, Zarathustra, one of Nietzsche's favorite representations, can be conceived as a mirror image of Jesus, thus being a mirror image of Nietzsche's mirror image.

Jesus and Nietzsche

Nietzsche's *The Antichrist* is not at all an anti-Jesus polemic, but as the subtitle *A curse on Christianity* indicates, a critique of a particular church oriented misinterpretation of the man. Nietzsche was concerned that he too, will be misunderstood "Listen! For I am such and such a person. For Heaven's sake do not confuse me with anyone else!" (*Ecce*, Preface, 1). Nietzsche's deep identification with Jesus is reflected in the title of his autobiography *Ecce Homo* ("Behold the Man," the Latin words proclaimed by Pontius Pilate when he presented Jesus to the crowd shortly before his crucifixion). As was mentioned before, after his mental breakdown, he signed most of his notes as either "the crucified" or Dionysus. *Thus Spoke Zarathustra*, which consists of four parts, adopts the style of the Gospels, and Nietzsche wrote to his publisher in the initial description of the work "It is a 'poetic composition,' or a fifth 'gospel,' or something for which no name yet exists." The first line of the book "When Zarathustra was thirty years old" refers to "Jesus himself was about thirty years old when he began his ministry" (*Luke*, 3, 23), it has a chapter titled *The*

Mount of Olives, and the book ends with the last supper. Nietzsche himself asserted that Zarathustra stands for him. Much of what Zarathustra does and says alludes to Jesus; much of what Nietzsche says about Jesus in *The Antichrist* alludes to himself. Thus, Nietzsche is in Zarathustra, and Nietzsche is in Jesus too.

The similarities between the two are manifold: Jesus wandered in the wilderness; Nietzsche was a wanderer without a home and repose who "rarely finds his table set and his nourishment ready" (*Beyond*, IX, 282). Jesus said about himself "The foxes have holes, and the birds of the heaven have nests, but the Son of man has not where to lay his head" (*Matthew*, 8, 20), and Nietzsche described his own state of restlessness "Who are you? What have you been doing? Have a rest here: this place is hospitable to everyone—relax! And whoever you happen to be, what would you like now? What do you need to recuperate? Just name it: what I have I'll offer you!" (*Beyond*, IX, 278). In *The Antichrist*, Nietzsche described Jesus in the same terms he used to describe himself. He called Jesus a "free spirit" and portrayed him as his own law-giver. He saw him as a "strange figure" and added "Such a compound of the sublime, the morbid and the childish. In the last analysis, the type, as a type of the decadence, may have been peculiarly complex and contradictory" (*Antichrist*, 31). Likewise, he saw himself as decadent, adding that "The only thing I have always suffered from is 'multitude,' the infinite variety of my own soul" (*Ecce*, Clever, 10). This theme is beautifully expressed in a short poem (*Gay*, Prelude in rhymes, 1):

> Sharp and mild, rough and fine
>
> Strange and familiar, impure and clean,
>
> A place where fool and sage convene:
>
> All this I am and wish to mean,
>
> Dove as well as snake and swine.

Also, Jesus is described as not believing that "'truth' may be established by proofs" (*Antichrist*, 32), while Zarathustra said, "I am not one of those who may be questioned about their Why" (*Zarathustra*, II, Poets). Jesus' "glad tidings" are described as the abolishment of the concepts of sin, punishment, and rewards (*Antichrist*, 33), while Nietzsche talked about swallowing the bitterest drop of "Man's complete lack of responsibility, for his behavior and for his nature" (*Human*, II, 107). Both Nietzsche and Jesus left everything behind (occupation and family) and dedicated themselves to a cause; one to the kingdom of heaven, the other to the kingdom of earth *(Zarathustra,* IV, The ass festival, 2). The two of them, could not fit in and live a conventional and comfortable life; the two were frustrated by a lack of recognition; the two had a special place in their hearts for children and the childish state of mind. One desired to be transformed into the Son of man, the other into the Superman. One is the bearer of joyful tidings "The Spirit of the Lord is upon me, because he anointed me to preach good tidings to the poor" (*Luke*, 4, 18); the other, is the bearer of a gay science "I am a bringer of good tidings such as there has never been" (*Ecce*, destiny, 1). One loves those who are "down goers and great despisers," the other loves the meek and poor. Both are revolutionaries: Jesus criticized the religious establishment of his time and challenged their morality of written dry commandments; Nietzsche questioned morality altogether. Nietzsche, the one "who devises his own virtue" was aware of their common fate: "The good have to be Pharisees – they have no choice! The good have to crucify him who devises his own virtue! That is the truth!" *(Zarathustra,* III, Old and new law-tables, 26). They share not only a mission but also family backgrounds "O my brothers, he who is a first-born is always sacrificed. Now we are all first-born. We all bleed at secret sacrificial tables, we all burn and roast to the honor of ancient idols" *(Zarathustra,* III, Old and new law-tables, 6). Jesus and Nietzsche were both first-born and both, to say the least, did not have a happy care-free childhood.

To Be Loved and Nothing Else

Nietzsche showed a remarkable insight into the psychology of Jesus, simply, because he was also a loveless child, a martyr "a sacrificial animal." Thus, in the following lines, he is talking about his own frustrated need for love. Unlike Jesus, he did not invent hell for those who refused him love, nor invented a loving God. Nietzsche tore the morality mask off the former and killed the latter:

> It is possible that beneath the sacred story and disguise of the life of Jesus there lies hidden one of the most painful examples of the martyrdom of knowledge about love: the martyrdom of the most innocent and most desiring heart, which was never satisfied with any human love, which demanded love, to be loved and nothing else, with hardness, with madness, with fearful outbreaks against those who denied him love; the history of a poor man unsatisfied and insatiable with love, who had to invent hell in order to send there those who did not wish to love him—and who finally, having grown to understand human love, had to invent a God who is entirely love, who is capable of total love—who takes pity on human love because it is so pathetic, so unknowing! Anyone who feels this way, who

> knows about love in this way—seeks death.—But why dwell on such painful things? Assuming we don't have to. — (*Beyond*, IX, 269).

There is no reason to ask where Nietzsche got such intimate details about Jesus' early life, and why it is so painful to dwell on it, as it is almost obvious that he sees Jesus in his own image. In the following quote Nietzsche, speaking as a physiologist is explaining Jesus' problems with the expression of love through human touch. Again, no supporting facts are given, apart from Nietzsche's intuitions, apparently based on his own life experience:

> In the strict sense of the physiologist, a quite different word ought to be used here... We all know that there is a morbid sensibility of the tactile nerves which causes those suffering from it to recoil from every touch, and from every effort to grasp a solid object. Brought to its logical conclusion, such a physiological habitus becomes an instinctive hatred of all reality, a flight into the 'intangible,' into the 'incomprehensible'; a distaste for all formulae, for all conceptions of time and space, for everything established—customs, institutions, the church—; a feeling of being at home in a world in which no sort of reality survives, a merely 'inner' world, a 'true' world, an 'eternal' world... (*Antichrist*, 29).

Nietzsche accentuated this point, explaining again that Jesus' "susceptibility to pain and irritation," was so great that he could not bear to be touched and found all sensations to be too intense, resulting in an "instinctive hatred of reality" (*Antichrist*, 30). However, nowhere in the Gospels is there any indication that Jesus avoided touch. Moreover, his healing relied on touch "Holding her hand, he said to her, *Talitha Kumi*, which means—little girl, get up!" (*Mark*, 5, 41), and likewise "And wherever he went—into villages, towns or countryside—they placed the sick in the marketplaces. They begged him to let them touch even the edge of his cloak, and all who touched him were healed" (*Mark*, 6, 56). Where else can we find such an avoidance of close contact? Survivors of childhood sexual abuse show an "extreme fear of allowing others to see them as they truly are."[77] They fear being victimized again, in light of their prior trust and openness to someone in authority. Thus, most survivors of CSA feel intimacy as most frightening "To feel close to another again is to remember that this position is a dangerous one, one that might lead to being taken advantage of."[78]

Human Fathers

The neurological disorder of oversensitivity to touch, which Nietzsche posited to account for Jesus' hate of reality, seems very far-fetched. As a diagnosis of

Jesus, these quotes are not very convincing; yet as an admission of Nietzsche's problems in intimacy, these words are suggestive. In fact, Nietzsche describes himself almost in the same way. The themes of depersonalization and derealization appear in other places too. Zarathustra said, "To men, I am still the mean between a fool and a corpse" *(Zarathustra,* Zarathustra's prologue, 7) and as was mentioned before "as my own father I am already dead" (*Ecce*, Wise, 1). Nietzsche wrote in similar terms about Jesus and himself as living outside of reality, which brings up back to the dissociative phenomena in PTSD. Dissociation is the most direct defense against overwhelming traumatic experiences, consisting of symptoms of derealization (feeling as if the world is not real), and depersonalization (feeling as if one self is not real). Experiencing the world and the self from afar, enables victims of abuse, torture, and war, to escape from an unbearable and unavoidable external reality, on the one hand; and from internal distress and arousal, on the other hand. It somehow allows them to continue to live and function. In the following comment Nietzsche connected his dissociation, his being "beyond life," with a cryptic reference to his father:

> I regard it as a great privilege to have had such a father: it even seems to me that this exhausts all that I can claim in the matter of privileges—life, the great yea to life, excepted. What I owe to him above all is this, that I do not need any special intention, but merely patience, in order to enter involuntarily into a world of higher and finer things. There I am at home, there alone does my profoundest passion have free play. The fact that I almost paid for this privilege with my life, certainly does not make it a bad bargain. In order to understand even a little of my *Zarathustra*, perhaps a man must be situated much as I am myself—with one foot beyond life (*Ecce*, Wise, 3).

Mind you, he is, in fact, thanking his father for almost losing or ruining his life! We arrived at a secret again and have only hints that Nietzsche dropped such as "What was silent in the father speaks in the son, and often I found in the son the unveiled secret of the father" *(Zarathustra,* The Tarantulas). A possible benign but trivial interpretation of this sentence is that the son fulfills the father's unrealized wishes. I feel that a more forbidding understanding is called for, that the son's suffering reveals his father's wrongdoings. Additional hints can be found in a conversation, as if taken from Shakespeare's Hamlet, between two old watchmen overheard behind a garden wall, in which one says, "For a father, he cares not sufficiently for his children: human fathers do this better!" The other watchman tried to excuse the father, for being too old and incapable. Yet, this father refuses to recognize at all his responsibility

"Proving is difficult to him; he lays great stress on one's *believing* him" *(Zarathustra,* III, The apostates, 2). Moreover, Nietzsche conceived the father-son relationship as inherently problematic one "Fathers have much to do to make amends for the fact that they have sons" (*Human,* VII, 382). In chapter two, I sowed some doubts, concerning the picture of a loving father, as seen through the eyes of the 13 years old Nietzsche, and accepted as factual by some scholars. We will see that the doubts will refuse to dissipate, but no final verdict will be delivered.

Painful Things

Other commentators raised various hypotheses to account for Nietzsche's sexuality and complicated intimate relations, which are not of interest to me as such. I am not interested in what he did or did not do, and with whom; but rather in what were his "fundamentals," formative experiences; in the way he dealt with them; and how they shaped his psychology and philosophy. Our reading of his texts until now suggested, that as a child he underwent some life-threatening condition, the source of his being "unsatisfied and insatiable with love" and the reason for his "recoil from every touch."

We have already listened to Nietzsche's dispersed testimonies about living with the characteristics of PTSD. Two main themes emerge from Nietzsche's discussion of the psychology of Jesus and his rendition of Dionysus, those of lovelessness and physical abuse. The two amplify each other: lack of love in childhood, makes an abuse more devastating; abuse makes the experience of being unloved much harder to bear. The first is a possible source of his attack on Christianity, received morality and criticism of language and culture; the second of the themes of acceptance (Eternal Recurrence) and overcoming (the Superman). The former, to be discussed in the next chapter, is denoted by poison; the latter, to be considered in the chapter following it, is symbolized by a snake.

Before we go into more detail, we must answer Nietzsche's valid question "But why dwell on such painful things?" We must dwell on such painful things, because pain and suffering are essential facts of life, and Nietzsche, who saw himself as the teacher of the Superman, is actually a great teacher of the nature of suffering, who in a personal and moving way, makes us understand what impersonal, clinical studies find hard to do. We must dwell on such painful things, simply to see whether we read Nietzsche, who was convinced that he cannot be understood "we are never understood" (*Twilight,* Maxims, 15), but still kept asking, in the closing line of his autobiography *Ecce Homo* "Have I Been Understood?" We simply had to figure out what was it that made him write "One not only wants to be understood when one writes, but also - quite as certainly - not to be understood" (*Gay,* V, 381).

We must dwell on such painful things because they were the breeding ground or raw materials for Nietzsche's psychology (self-understanding) and therapy (self-overcoming). Encountering suffering is the source of his creativity. Nietzsche exemplifies growth by confrontation (*agonality*) with self, others, and circumstances "We have to give birth to our thoughts out of our pain and, like mothers, endow them with all we have of blood, heart, fire, pleasure, passion, agony, conscience, fate, and catastrophe. Life—that means for us constantly transforming all that we are into light and flame—also everything that wounds us; we simply can do no other" (*Gay*, Preface, 2).

We must dwell on such painful things for an additional reason. Nietzsche had an exceptional talent for seeing the universal in his own life and experiences, and everything he said about himself was penetrating and instructing. However, his vision of what was outside and around him, of other people, was embroiled with his own difficulties, and therefore not as clear-sighted. Knowing the source of his ideas will enable us to be more careful about generalizing his insights to our own and other people's lives.

Chapter 5

POISON AND STENCH

Michael Haneke's 2009 black and white movie *The White Ribbon* could serve as a vivid illustration of Nietzsche's upbringing. The film takes place in a German village before the First World War. People lived there in what looks like a feudal nature preserve, with a sharp division and outbursts of violence between landlords and farm laborers, and between the well-to-do and their subservient servants. The cruelty of parents and among them the local pastor and his wife are shown in different means and ways: as abuse, harsh discipline, authoritarian indoctrination and socialization. All carried out in the name of Christianity, allegedly for the benefit of their children's souls, while breaking their spirit in practice. Cruelty begot more cruelty and misery in the children. Such a microcosm makes the later developments of Fascism and Nazism, foreseen by Nietzsche, much less bewildering.

Poisonous Relationships

Nietzsche's father was a Protestant pastor and a son of a pastor. His mother came from a family of pastors and theologians as well. Helmut Walther in his article *The Young Nietzsche,* quoted from a letter written by Nietzsche's father in 1846, describing his less than two years old son: "Brother Fritz is a wild boy who, at times, can only be brought under control by his father, since the rod is not far removed from the latter; however, there exists now another, more powerful helper, that is Christ who has already won the boy's head and heart, so that he does not want to hear anything else talked about but of 'heile Kist'!"[79] His father, the one little Fritz used to see in his minister's robe, leading the Sunday worship in church, did not spare the rod at home, and we do not know if he ever stopped using it. His mother, aunts, grandmother and maid with whom he grew up after his father's death, represented Christian strictness, conventions, and traditions with few manifestations of warmth and maternal affection. Reading Nietzsche's letter to his mother, from August 1883, written when he was already 38 years old, makes us understand what he had to live through as a child who was unable as yet to protest or object:

> My dear mother: I have received everything in the way of food and the necessaries of life—unfortunately, too, your letter, which made me feel very wretched. Really, these dissertations on Christianity

> and on the opinions of this man and that as to what I should do and ought to think on the subject should no longer be directed to my address. My patience won't stand it! The atmosphere in which you live, among these "good Christians," with their one-sided and often presumptuous judgments, is as opposed as it possibly can be to my own feelings and most remote aims. I do not say anything about it, but I know that if people of this kind, even including my mother and sister, had an inkling of what I am aiming at, they would have no alternative but to become my natural enemies. This cannot be helped; the reasons for it lie in the nature of things. It spoils my love of life to live among such people, and I have to exercise considerable self-control in order not to react constantly against this sanctimonious atmosphere...[80]

Nietzsche titled the following segment, *Tragedy of childhood*, naturally adopting an impersonal, objective scientific tone. Here too, it seems that what he knew about himself helped him understand a more general problem. It is entirely plausible that "noble-minded" persons, like "lofty persons" (*Beyond*, IX, 269), stand for Nietzsche and his own childhood and tragedy:

> Not infrequently, noble-minded and ambitious men have to endure their harshest struggle in childhood, perhaps by having to assert their characters against a low-minded father, who is devoted to pretense and mendacity, or by living, like Lord Byron, in continual struggle with a childish and wrathful mother. If one has experienced such struggles, for the rest of his life, he will never get over knowing who has been in reality his greatest and most dangerous enemy (*Human*, VII, 422).

Nietzsche's *On the Genealogy of Morality* and especially its third essay *What do ascetic ideals mean* is to my mind, not only an abstract discussion of an issue but also a memoir, a description of his family's home ambiance and pedagogical practices. In one section, describing the defeatist, self-righteous outlook on life, Nietzsche has the word "poison" appear four times. Going into details of glances sighs and typical locutions, makes the reader almost visualize Nietzsche's widowed mother and unmarried aunts, economically dependent on the goodwill of his grandmother, using their weakness to tyrannize the child, trying to make him a well-behaved, disciplined, adult-like boy—"the little pastor," as he was called by his school friends.[81]

Nietzsche describes this state of affairs as "a normal pathology" and an "atmosphere of sickness" and "poisonous air" which is dangerous for healthy people. These sick people are themselves failures, stuck in their life, resentful, hopeless; believing that they are better than others, experts in "noble indignation":

> They wander around among us like personifications of reproach, like warnings to us, as if health, success, strength, pride, and a feeling of power were inherently depraved things, for which people must expiate someday, expiate bitterly. How they thirst to be hangmen! Among them, there are plenty of people disguised as judges seeking revenge. They always have the word 'Justice' in their mouths, like poisonous saliva, with their mouths always pursed, constantly ready to spit at anything which does not look discontented and goes on its way in good spirits. [...] The sick woman, in particular: no one outdoes her in refined ways to rule others, to exert pressure, to tyrannize (*Genealogy*, III, 14).

The mother-poison connection is also supported by a passage, mentioned before in trying to solve Nietzsche's riddle "as my own father I am already dead, as my own mother I still live and grow old" (*Ecce*, Wise, 1). In it, he described the horrible treatment he received from his sister and mother, who were described as *canaille* (rabble), hellish machine and a poisonous viper. (*Ecce*, Wise, 3). What is the nature of poisoning? It consists of exposing a victim, imperceptibly, to a harmful material, sometimes camouflaged as beneficial (when mixed in with food or drink), without the possibility of resisting or avoiding it, resulting in diminished strength, health, and energy, or even death. In fact, the psychologist Alice Miller used the term "poisonous pedagogy" to describe emotionally damaging child-raising practices, intended to manipulate the character of children through force, deception, and hypocrisy.[82] Nietzsche was sensitized to such poison in his childhood and could smell it anytime he felt pressure to conform, or experienced disrespect for his separateness and individuality.

The metaphor of poisoning appears in almost all of Nietzsche's writings. Another closely related simile, often used by him is a bad smell, which is not as lethal as poison but certainly repelling "Many lands have I seen, my nose hath learned to test and estimate many kinds of air" (*Zarathustra,* Daughters of the desert). Nietzsche became a poison and bad smell human detector, first in his own life and later in society and culture at large "I was the first to discover truth, by sensing falsehood as falsehood. I smelt it as such [...] my genius resides in my nostrils" (*Ecce*, Destiny, 1).

Self-poisoning and Resentment

Being a victim of poisoning by others triggers a secondary self-destructive self-poisoning. The persecution and lack of respect for one's autonomy, combined with helplessness and an inability to fight back and take revenge, lead to poisonous resentment and nihilism. Nietzsche used the French *resentiment*, rather than the German equivalent, probably to add to anger and enviousness, the nuance of rehashing of hurt feelings. This is unnecessary in English, which has the two senses in one word. He was suggesting that a child's powerlessness, the inability to resist the abuse inflicted by adults, is at least as damaging as the abuse itself. When Nietzsche was fighting resentment and nihilism in his writings, he was fighting something he knew personally very well and tried to overcome: "Choose the good solitude, the free, wanton, lightsome solitude, which also gives you the right still to remain good in any sense whatsoever! How poisonous, how crafty, how bad, does every long war make one, which cannot be waged openly by means of force!" (*Beyond*, II, 25).

Nietzsche found that "nothing consumes a man more quickly than the emotion of resentment." This is a self-damaging way of reacting, which involves an amalgam of emotions, consisting of embarrassment, vulnerability, a thirst for revenge, an inability to carry it out "the concoction of every kind of poison" in fantasy, helplessness and finally exhaustion (*Ecce*, Preface, 7). In addition to exhaustion, resentment can turn people into "refined vengeance-seekers and poison-Brewers" (*Beyond*, II, 25). The best remedy and preventive measure, not always available, in the words of the cult movie *Animal House*, is "don't get mad, get even." Nietzsche pointed out that persons, who think about revenge and executes it, might suffer from "a violent but temporary fever." However, one who lacks the strength or courage to do so, endures "a chronic suffering, a poisoning of body and soul" (*Human*, II, 60).

An Assortment of Poisons

Nietzsche saw Christianity, religion, morality and some institutions and doctrines as toxic anti-life agents. He was in this regard, Odysseus who outsmarted Circe (In Greek mythology, the sorceress who detained Odysseus on her island and turned his men into swine):

> Up to the present Christian morality has been the Circe of all thinkers they stood at her service. What man, before me, had descended into the caves from which the poisonous fumes of this ideal of this slandering of the world burst forth? What man before me had even dared to suspect that they were caves? What one of the philosophers preceding me was a real psychologist, and not its very reverse, a 'superior swindler,' an 'Idealist'? (*Ecce*, Wagner, 4).

This "real psychologist" indeed identified an assortment of poisons: "morality becomes the poisoner of life" (*Will*, II, 352), and he continued, "Christianity gave Eros poison to drink; he did not die of it, certainly, but degenerated to Vice" (*Beyond*, IV, 168) and "I understand religions as narcotics: but when they are given to such nations as the Germans, I think they are simply rank poison" (*Philologists*, 166). Religion is not the only danger, "The doctrine of equality! There is no more poisonous poison anywhere: for it seems to be preached by justice itself, whereas it really is the termination of justice" (*Twilight*, Skirmishes, 48) and "The state, I call it, where all are poison-drinkers, the good and the bad: the state, where all lose themselves, the good and the bad: the state, where the slow suicide of all—is called 'life'" (*Zarathustra*, I, The new idol). Nietzsche considered the denial of the body and its desires and pleasures as a particularly deleterious poison: "I conjure you, my brethren, remain true to the earth, and believe not those who speak unto you of super-earthly hopes! Poisoners are they, whether they know it or not. Despisers of life are they, decaying ones and poisoned ones themselves, of whom the earth is weary: so away with them!" (*Zarathustra*, Prologue, 3).

The poison of life's afflictions can be put to good use "Out of your poisons brew you balsam for yourself" (*Zarathustra*, I, Joys and passions). Yet, this is not something that everyone can do "The poison of which weaker natures perish, strengthens the strong nor do they call it poison" (*Gay*, I, 19). Some people are more susceptible to poisoning, and it seems that Nietzsche is among them, and for him, the mere exposure to others becomes a threat to be avoided. Zarathustra-Nietzsche, who suffered intensely from small wounds, heard in the marketplace "the buzzing of the poison-flies," was stung by them, and had a poison-worm crawl over his hand. Experiences which made him search for his solitude again and "flee to where a rough, strong breeze blows!" (*Zarathustra*, I, The flies in the market-place). From poisons, we will move on to the next chapter, to snakes.

Chapter 6

SNAKES AND MONSTERS

Poisoning represents a continuous negative atmosphere of upbringing, lacking in love and respect for a child's needs. Snakes, in contradistinction, represent, in the reading offered here, a direct and discrete physical abuse and harm. We are moving now from mistreatment to the realm of trauma. Snakes, adders, vipers, and serpents appear in many instances and connotations in Nietzsche's writings. When Nietzsche wrote about poison, the message was clear, and we had only to realize, or at least consider the possibility, that he was referring to his own experiences in life. A snake, however, is an image, a symbol with many shades of meanings, sometimes contradictory. I look at the vignettes in *Thus Spoke Zarathustra*, where this symbol appears, as if they were a series of dreams, of visions. Each dream reveals different aspects of the riddle, and the very repetition is an indication of the theme's weight. An image-symbol which reappears in many dreams must have a special significance. In her *Dictionary of Mythology*, Gertrude Jobes, listed alphabetically under the value "snake," the following:

> Androgyny, circle, convalescence, cunning, danger, death, deceit, destruction, divine emanation, evil, false appearance fertility, guardianship, generation, grief, health, intelligence, jealousy, lasciviousness, malice, materialism, misfortune, phallus, pleasure, power, prophecy, prudence, renewal, revenge, self- creation self-indulgence, self-sustenance, sensation, sensuality, sin, subtlety, temptation, treachery, the unfathomable, universe circle, vexations, vice, wiliness, wisdom worldliness.[83]

Klaus Vollmar saw snakes as predominantly symbols of fear. They appear unexpectedly out of the unknown; like the unconscious, they are incommunicative, secretive and frightening. A snake also stands for physical drives and sexuality, and when it appears as *Ouroboros* "A serpent, dragon or worm that eats its own tail," it represents wholeness, transformation, and rebirth (*Wiktionary.org*). A snake can symbolize healing, and in fact, two winding snakes appear in the Caduceus, the staff of Aesculapius, the god of medicine in ancient Greece.[84] In the Biblical book of Genesis, a snake is a symbol of temptation, the eternal enemy of humankind, the one who brought upon Adam and Eve the end of innocence and expulsion from the Garden of Eden. However, a snake can also be a vicious assailant, far from being a smooth talker. I will now explore some reptilian discourses and incidents in *Thus Spoke Zarathustra*, which combined will help us solve Nietzsche's gloomy riddle.

The Vision and the Riddle

The vision is a dreadful one, yet in its midst, the idea of the Eternal Recurrence (a.k.a. the eternal return of the same) is born. Zarathustra described an enigmatic and gruesome scene, which he, a lonesome person, lonely and different from others, challenged us to decipher, and I will quote it in its entirety:

> But there lay a man! And there! The dog leaping, bristling, whining—now did it see me coming—then did it howl again, then did it cry: —had I ever heard a dog cry so for help? And verily, what I saw, the like had I never seen. A young shepherd did I see, writhing, choking, quivering, with distorted countenance, and with a heavy black serpent hanging out of his mouth. Had I ever seen so much loathing and pale horror on one countenance? He had perhaps gone to sleep? Then had the serpent crawled into his throat—there had it bitten itself fast.
>
> My hand pulled at the serpent, and pulled: —in vain! I failed to pull the serpent out of his throat. Then there cried out of me: "Bite! Bite! its head off! Bite!" —so cried it out of me; my horror, my hatred, my loathing, my pity, all my good and my bad cried with one voice out of me. —Ye daring ones around me! Ye venturers and adventurers, and whoever of you have embarked with cunning sails on unexplored seas! Ye riddle-enjoyers! Solve unto me the riddle that I then beheld, interpret unto me the vision of the lonesomest one! *(Zarathustra,* III, The vision and the riddle, 2).

Reader, can you read the details of "this loathing and pale horror" without feeling shocked and nauseated? Nietzsche is Zarathustra, and Zarathustra is the shepherd, who said about himself "I am truly weary of being your shepherd, always sheepish and meek" *(Zarathustra,* III, The second dance song). Nietzsche, as was shown in the last chapter, described quite openly the deleterious effects of his Prussian-Christian upbringing. Therefore, this is not what is being discussed here. It must be something that out of shame and guilt is kept secret. An involuntary oral intromission takes place, and this scene will appear in the book again and again. Unfortunately, the hypothesis that Nietzsche had undergone sexual abuse is almost unavoidable. Zarathustra's question "Who is the shepherd into whose throat the serpent thus crawled? Who is the man into whose throat all the heaviest and blackest will thus crawl?" *(Zarathustra,* III, The vision and the riddle, 2), can now be answered.

Nietzsche's analysis of Jesus' problems with love and touch discussed before, his feelings of a shared fate of being a "sacrificial animal" and being crucified, now get a new and ominous meaning. Difficulties with touch are the first indication that a child might have been sexually abused. The chapter is abundant with references to Nietzsche's childhood and his father, who according to the report of his sister Elisabeth Förster-Nietzsche, fell to his death upon stumbling over the house's dog. She neglected to mention that he suffered from a brain disease for an extended period before this. Nietzsche was nearly five years old when he died. The whole description, including a howling dog crying for help, feels like a dream, a déjà vu, and a vivid recurrence of a familiar experience.

Other commentators until now, did not treat the different snake scenes altogether and did not find any special biographical significance in their shared characteristics. They did not conceive these snakes as phallic symbols, perhaps because clichés tend to be mistrusted, despite having a grain of truth in them. Each instance was treated separately, understood as symbolizing abstract ideas. Anthony M. Ludovici, an early commentator, argued that "In this parable, the young shepherd is obviously the man of to-day; the snake that chokes him represents the stultifying and paralyzing social values that threaten to shatter humanity, and the advice "Bite! Bite!" is but Nietzsche's exasperated cry to mankind to alter their values before it is too late."[85] In a later interpretation, Laurence Lampert understood the black snake, not as a symbol of pessimism, as suggested by Heidegger, but rather, as an expression of disdain at the possibility that the Eternal Return mandates the return of the small man. Later in his book, the ugliest man, the killer of God, is taken by him to stand for criticism of pity, and the snakes in the scene are simply disregarded.[86] However, claiming that in the different reptile scenes Nietzsche only wanted to express some criticism of modern culture or some reservations about an abstract idea raises questions. Why not say it openly and directly, rather than risk misunderstanding of such simple and straight forward meaning? Why should such claims be turned into terrible secrets? Why use the same theme repeatedly?

Snakes, we saw, is a multifaceted symbol that can stand for many things, positive as well as negative. Also, the same experience can be represented by different people, at different times by different symbols. Renee Fredrickson suggested that dreams often point to the existence of buried memories of sexual abuse "The dream world acknowledges the abuse obliquely instead of directly, through symbolic representations of the forgotten abuse [...] Snakes or other phallic symbols are often references to abuse involving someone's penis."[87] Christine Landis and Maxine Harris, retell Constance's story, diagnosed as suffering from serious mental illness, who was raped by a stranger when she was five years old. She described the onset of her nervous breakdown: "I saw snakes and felt as if they were coming after me. I was hollering and screaming and telling people to come and get the snakes off me because they were eating me up."[88] We cannot say that sexual abuse is always and necessarily represented by snake images, although it is a possibility that must be taken into consideration.

A Choking Monster

The hypothesis that Nietzsche experienced sexual abuse as a child is not based on one passage only. Snakes keep crawling again and again into Zarathustra's addresses. The above event is narrated again in another discourse with slight modifications. It is now Zarathustra, and not the shepherd, who had this experience, and the snake is called a monster. It is now Zarathustra himself, who bites the monster's head off, what he told the shepherd to do before. Here too, in this context, the idea of the Eternal Recurrence makes its appearance. What follows has the quality of a flashback, a recurring painful memory, which is so familiar with trauma victims. The triple expression of disgust, which like a mantra reappears in other instances when such a memory arises, has the quality of a conditioned visceral response of a nauseated aversion. We will see (Chapters 7 and 8) that the feeling of disgust is prevalent among victims of childhood sexual abuse:

> —And how that monster crept into my throat and choked me! But I bit off its head and spat it away from me. [...] Now, however, do I lie here, still exhausted with that biting and spitting-away, still sick with mine own salvation. [...] The great disgust at man—*It* strangled me and had crept into my throat: and what the soothsayer had presaged: "All is alike, nothing is worthwhile, knowledge strangles." [...] Ah, Disgust! Disgust! Disgust!—Thus spoke Zarathustra, and sighed and shuddered; for he remembered his sickness *(Zarathustra,* III, The convalescent, 2).

The Adder's Bite

In the third snake scene, the snake does not penetrate the mouth but stings Zarathustra's neck, which is a less gruesome, but not a less fatal occurrence. Again the attack took place in sleep, but here the snake becomes cognizant of the victim's awareness of what happens and knows that he did cause harm and offered solace:

> One day had Zarathustra fallen asleep under a fig-tree, owing to the heat, with his arms over his face. And there came an adder and bit him in the neck so that Zarathustra screamed with pain. When he had taken his arm from his face he looked at the serpent; and then did it recognize the eyes of Zarathustra, wriggled awkwardly, and tried to get away.
>
> 'Not at all,' said Zarathustra, 'as yet hast thou not received my thanks! Thou hast awakened me in time; my journey is yet long.'
>
> 'Thy journey is short,' said the adder sadly; 'my poison is fatal.' Zarathustra smiled. 'When did ever a dragon die of a serpent's poison?'—said he. 'But take thy poison back! Thou art not rich enough to present it to me.' Then fell the adder again on his neck, and licked his wound *(Zarathustra,* I, The adder's bite).

The chapter continues with the disciples asking about the moral of the story. Zarathustra explains that rather than the Christian returning good for evil, it is better to prove that the enemy did something good for you, and in the same vein when cursed, it is better to curse back a little than blessing, just as little revenge is better than no revenge at all. Zarathustra indeed responded as he taught: this time, he did not bite the snake's head off, and moreover, he thanked him, and revenge was not even considered. He also described using his imagination to pretend that he is a dragon that cannot be hurt by a snake, actually using dissociation to survive: "Traumatized children use a variety of dissociative techniques. Children report going to a 'different place,' assuming the persona of heroes or animals, a sense of 'watching a movie that I was in' or 'just floating'- classic depersonalization and derealization responses."[89] Thanking the abuser here, rings a bell, and indeed, we remember that Nietzsche claimed that he had a great privilege, a privilege that almost killed him, to have a father, to whom he owes the ability to easily enter "a world of higher and finer things" (*Ecce*, Wise, 3).

The question arises again if what he wanted to teach was ways of dealing with wrongs carried by one person against another, why use such an abominable image? The unfortunate answer again is that Nietzsche in all likelihood describes an encounter between an adult abuser and a child victim. In another place, while discussing the rare human trait of fellowship in joy, in distinction from sympathy to pain, Nietzsche interjected a hardly related sentence saying that "The snake that stings us means to hurt us and rejoices in so doing: the lowest animal can picture to itself the pain of others" (*Human*, Assorted, 62). The attributes of intention to harm and the enjoyment of the victim's suffering make it clear, that it is a human snake that is described and the situation of a sleeping victim suggests a domestic setting.

The Ugliest Man

The above impression is reinforced by a fourth snake vignette, in which Zarathustra enters a valley "which all animals avoided, even the beasts of prey, except that a species of ugly, thick, green serpent came here to die when they became old. Therefore, the shepherds called this valley: 'serpent-death.'" Zarathustra, however, became absorbed in dark recollections, for it seemed to him as if he had once before stood in this valley" (*Zarathustra,* IV, The ugliest man). The snake's color changes here from direful black to slimy green, and yet, the experience has the same quality of a flashback to an earlier time, which we met in the other snake vignettes. Some cues in the environment were somehow remindful of a past trauma, and consequently, intrusive thoughts and vivid memories resurfaced, making the survivor relive the painful events again. Zarathustra meets the ugliest man, who it turns out, is the murderer of God. The encounter has an emotional tone as if something has passed between them before; as if Zarathustra knew him before and did not want to meet him again:

> Then, however, when he opened his eyes, he saw something sitting by the wayside shaped like a man, and hardly like a man, something nondescript. And all at once there came over Zarathustra a great shame because he had gazed on such a thing. Blushing up to the very roots of his white hair, he turned aside his glance and raised his foot that he might leave this ill-starred place (*Zarathustra,* IV, The ugliest man).

Shame and guilt are almost universal reactions to sexual abuse in childhood or rape in adulthood. Shame is a deep sense of feeling "bad" as a person, in many cases encouraged by the abuser cutting off the victim from the support of other family members, forcing the victim to keep the abuse secret. Guilt is based on the belief that the abused one is responsible for what transpired. In one study of severely abused casualties, all participants showed elevated scores for shame, guilt, and dissociation.[90] Indeed, Zarathustra-Nietzsche wondered where can be found the "love that bears not only all punishment but also the guilt!" (*Zarathustra,* I, Of the Adder's Bite). He describes a twilight state of consciousness, in which one part would prefer not to recognize the figure, and another unwillingly admits it. No reason is given for Zarathustra's deep shame and blushing. The transition to dialogue suggests the resurfacing of a suppressed memory "Then, however, the dead wilderness became vocal: for from the ground a noise welled up, gurgling and rattling, as water gurgles and rattles at night through stopped-up water-pipes; and at last it turned into human voice and human speech" *(Zarathustra,* IV, The ugliest man). These words were written in 1883, and they explain a puzzling sentence that Nietzsche jotted down on a piece of paper fifteen years before, when he was twenty-four years old "What I am afraid of is not the terrible shape behind my chair, but its voice: also not the words, but the horribly unarticulated and inhuman tone of that shape. Yes, if only it spoke as human beings do."[91] We have here a fracture of traumatic memory, a bursting flashback that leaves him shaken.

The identification of this "nondescript something" with the murderer of God raises questions. First of all, why is Zarathustra so moved? Secondly, the idea of the death of God appeared already earlier in the book "Could it be possible! This old saint has not yet heard in his forest that *God is dead*!" *(Zarathustra,* Prologue, 2) and when the idea appeared for the first time in Nietzsche's writings, it was again a statement of fact "God is dead; but given the way of men, there may still be caves for thousands of years in which his shadow will be shown" (*Gay,* III, 108). The idea was later put in the mouth of a madman "God is dead, and we have killed him, you and I!" (*Gay,* III, 125). "You and I" killed God, but not an individually designated murderer. In the present discourse about the ugliest man, a matter of fact becomes a riddle, and the issue of witnessing becomes prominent: "Zarathustra! Zarathustra! Read my riddle! Say, say! What is the revenge of the witness? [...] You think yourself wise, you proud Zarathustra! Read then the riddle, you hard nutcracker,—the riddle that I am! Say then: who am I!" *(Zarathustra,* IV, The ugliest man).

Upon hearing these words, Zarathustra was overcome by pity and sank to the ground down suddenly and heavily like a log. He then got up immediately and demanded that the ugliest man let him go, adding with a stern expression, that he knows him as the murderer of God, one that cannot endure being recognized, "You took revenge on this witness!" *(Zarathustra,* IV, The ugliest man).

I would like to suggest a somewhat different solution to the riddle. Jesus is "the faithful witness" (*Revelation,* 1, 5) who also witnessed his betrayal, and is often considered by his believers, at least colloquially, as their God. Jesus himself said, "I and the Father are one" *(John,* 10, 30) and his disciple Thomas declared "My Lord and my God" *(John,* 20, 28). Therefore God here is Jesus, and the murderer portrayed here is Judas, the one who betrayed him with a kiss, leading to his crucifixion. In the traditional Passion plays, which Nietzsche must have known since childhood, the Jews were portrayed as the murderers of God, and Judas, in particular, was depicted as an ugly man, a hunched figure with a large nose and red hair who would do anything for money.

If so, this is a meeting between Zarathustra-Jesus-Nietzsche and Judas, his abuser-betrayer. Now all pieces of the puzzle, the initial avoidance, the feelings of shame and pity, the ugliness, the shock of recognition and the terror, all fall now into place and become comprehensible. Similarly, the ugliest man saying "Stay! Do not pass by! I have divined what ax it was that struck thee to the ground: hail to thee, O Zarathustra that thou are again upon thy feet!" *(Zarathustra,* IV, The ugliest man). The riddle here is directly connected with the riddle in *The vision and the riddle,* and it is also related to the fact that Zarathustra has witnessed the snake's bite *(Zarathustra,* I, The adder's bite).

The Sleepwalker Song

In this song, the themes mentioned in the previous four vignettes reappear and come together: the secret, the pain, and the ugly man. Throughout the song, there is tension between two forces. One is a past pain, encroaching on the present, represented by midnight; the other, a wish to heal and reconcile, accept and transform whatever happened, by means of the idea of the Eternal Recurrence, represented by mid-day. The midnight old clock-bell says in Zarathustra's ear "Hear you not how it mysteriously, frightfully, and cordially speaks to you, the old deep, deep midnight? O man, take heed!" *(Zarathustra,* IV, The drunken song, 3). In the following account, the intrusive nature of Zarathustra's painful memories is described. Here the snake itself is missing, but the howling dog, the spinning spider, the night, the moon, the secret that cannot be told, and the spooky atmosphere remain as they were in *The vision and the riddle* above. Zarathustra would rather die than reveal what is on his mind. Nietzsche's deep identification with Jesus and the parallel between the crucifixions and his own calamity delineated already before, are evident here too. Only fine ears can understand the hidden message:

> Woe to me! Where has time gone? Have I not sunk into deep wells? The world sleeps—Ah! Ah! The dog howls, the moon shines. Rather will I die, rather will I die, than say to you what my midnight-heart now thinks. Already have I died. It is all over. Spider, why spin you around me? Will you have blood? Ah! Ah! The dew falls, the hour comes—The hour in which I frost and freeze, which asks and asks and asks: "Who has sufficient courage for it? [...] The hour approaches: O man, you higher man, take heed! This talk is for fine ears, for your ears—what says deep midnight's voice indeed? *(Zarathustra,* IV, The sleepwalker song, 4).

In these painful words, sentences from the Gospels reverberate "The hour has come for the Son of man to be glorified" (*John*, 12, 23) and similarly "Now my soul is troubled. And what should I say—'Father, save me from this hour'? No, it is for this reason that I have come to this hour" (*John*, 12, 27) and finally "It is finished" (*John*, 19, 30). In one of his last written pieces, a postscript to *The Antichrist*, often not included in the printed book because of its violent and feral nature, Nietzsche put forward a few propositions, whose tone of a personal vendetta is now more understandable. The third one being:

> The execrable location where Christianity brooded over its basilisk eggs should be razed to the ground and, being the depraved spot on earth, it should be the horror of all posterity. Poisonous snakes should be bred on top of it (*Antichrist*, Law against Christianity, 3).

The challenge of overcoming trauma is immense. There is still the buried secret "corpses in sepulchers." There are still haunting memories "Ah, why does the worm still burrow? [...] there thrills still the heart, there burrows still the woodworm, the heartworm. Ah! Ah! The world is deep!" *(Zarathustra*, IV, The sleepwalker song, 5). Nevertheless, the chapter ends with a sense of triumph. The idea of the Eternal Recurrence has its day, impacting the lives of those who listen to it. The tension is resolved, the past and present become one, Zarathustra himself and the world and eternity become one. He is transformed:

> Just now has my world become perfect, midnight is also mid-day, Pain is also a joy, curse is also a blessing, night is also a sun [...] Said you ever Yes to one joy? O my friends, then said you Yes also to all woe. All things are enlinked, enlaced and enamored,—Wanted you ever once to come twice; said you ever: "You please me, happiness! Instant! Moment! Then wanted you all to come back again!" *(Zarathustra*, IV, The sleepwalker song, 10).

Nietzsche's transformation and message impact others as well, among them his guests, the "higher men," and first among them, the ugliest man, who I suggested represents the betrayer and alleged perpetrator of the abuse. When all those involved, accept their fate without guilt, blame, hate, and resentment, reconciliation is possible, and the distinction between abusers and victims disappears, and the ugliest man almost repeats Zarathustra's words:

> "My friends, all of you," said the ugliest man, "what think you?" For the sake of this day- I am for the first time content to have lived my entire life. And that I testify so much is still not enough for me. It is

> worthwhile living on the earth: one day, one festival with Zarathustra has taught me to love the earth. 'Was that- life?' will I say to death. 'Well! Once more!' My friends, what think you? Will you not, like me, say to death: 'Was that- life?' For the sake of Zarathustra, "well! Once more!'"— *(Zarathustra,* IV, The sleepwalker song, 1)

The motto of "once more" does not guarantee an end to pain. Its joy is not a blind happiness "It wants love, it wants hate, it is over-rich, it gives, it throws away, it begs for someone to take from it, it thanks the taker, it would rather be hated.—So rich is joy that it thirsts for woe, for hell, for hate, for shame, for the lame, for the world" *(Zarathustra,* IV, The sleepwalker song, 11).

The Type of the Psychologist

The reading offered here, suggests that the "midnight's gloomy hour" *(Zarathustra,* IV, The Magician, 1), was an hour of traumatic abuse. Now, when Nietzsche-Zarathustra's world became perfect, and midnight is also mid-day *(Zarathustra,* IV, The sleepwalker song, 10), when a resolution of the trauma has been reached, we can answer the question asked over and again "What said deep midnight's voice indeed?" *(Zarathustra,* IV, Drunken song, 12). In any case, taking Nietzsche's admonition to heart, we are not trying to find "mere truthful evidence" about a possible perpetrator, but rather asking about Nietzsche himself "whether his type is still conceivable, whether it has been handed down to us" (*Antichrist,* 32). Knowing what Nietzsche had to overcome, we can now establish Nietzsche's type, as the type of the survivor, one who overcomes his fate.

For Nietzsche surviving is the crux of life "To those human beings who are of any concern to me [...] I wish them the only thing that can prove today whether one is worth anything or not—that one endures" (*Will,* IV, 910). Nietzsche was a survivor when he could "out of poisons brew balsam for himself" *(Zarathustra,* I, Joys and passions). Nietzsche is even more of a survivor saying "Everything evil, tyrannical in man, everything in him that is akin to beasts of prey and serpents, serves the enhancement of the species 'man' as much as its opposite does" (*Beyond,* II, 44).

Nietzsche went even further in accepting, and even loving his fate, and in the spirit of *Amor fati,* he turned the snake into a symbol of renewal: "The snake that cannot shed its skin perishes. So do the spirits who are prevented from changing their opinions; they cease to be spirit" (*Daybreak,* V, 330). The serpent and the eagle became Zarathustra's friends, symbolizing earthiness combined with spirituality, shrewdness with vision *(Zarathustra,* Prologue, 1). Ultimately, the snake is transformed into a symbol of Nietzsche's great idea of the Superman. It appears in the form of a staff with a snake coiled about a sun, upon a golden haft, given to him as a present by his disciples "A symbol of the Superman, above praise and blame, a commanding will, a new good and evil, a ruling idea and a subtle soul—a golden sun, and around it the serpent of knowledge" *(Zarathustra,* I, The bestowing of virtue, 1).

Chapter 7

ABUSED CHILDREN AND ADULT SURVIVORS

During Nietzsche's lifetime, physical child abuse was mostly taken for granted. The Biblical dictum "He who spares the rod hates his son, but he who loves him is careful to discipline him" (*Proverbs*, 13, 24) was considered a sound advice, and sexual abuse was still an unspoken dark secret. Sigmund Freud suggested in his 1895 "seduction theory," that hysteria was a result of sexual abuse of children, usually committed by their fathers. In 1897 however, he changed his mind and claimed that his patients suffered from faulty fantasies of sexual violation. He continued to treat memories of physical abuse as fantasy up to 1919, as is shown in his essay *A Child is Being Beaten.* If Freud could not see the deplorable reality of abuse, how can we be surprised that others were blind to it?

The telling of the secret, already existing in the Church's institution of confession, the disclosure to an empathic listener is actually the essence of therapy, an essential condition for healing.[92] Nietzsche lived in a time and in a society which dichotomized the roles of females and males: only women could be weak and in need of protection; men were supposed to be robust and tough. Then, sexual abuse was not recognized, and adequate therapy was non-existent. Revealing his victimization, meant being perceived as womanish and defiled. Consequently, he had to keep a stiff upper lip (hidden by a bushy mustache).

Until now I have studied Nietzsche's writings, which I regarded as his encrypted testimony. Based on his testimony, I suggested before (Chapter 3) that Nietzsche, the psychologist who bared his soul to us, would have been diagnosed today as suffering from PTSD, which is also associated with surviving childhood sexual abuse. Thus, Rodriguez et al., found in a clinical sample that 86% of 117 adult survivors met the criteria for a PTSD diagnosis at some point during their lives. They also found a significant correlation between the duration and severity of the abuse and the severity and scope of the PTSD symptoms.[93] I am going now to explore studies of Adverse Childhood Experiences (ACE) and investigations of adult survivors of Childhood Sex Abuse (CSA). The striking correspondence between what we learn from this literature and Nietzsche's testimony will reinforce our conclusions. These studies will also lay the ground for understanding his pain and suffering, described in the following chapter.

Adverse Childhood Experiences

Child abuse ("the battered-child syndrome") became an openly discussed, examined and researched issue only in the 1960's.[94] Fifty years later, Vincent Felitti and Robert Anda, published a series of epidemiological studies with more than 17,000 individuals, investigating the relationship between adverse childhood experiences or trauma, and adult health, well-being, social function and life expectancy.[95]

In such a study, Nietzsche would have gotten a high score, in light of the most likely emotional, physical and sexual abuse he suffered as a child, combined with household dysfunction (his father's brain sickness and eventual death, followed by the death of a younger brother). The researchers found a high correlation between adverse childhood experiences score and poor physical and mental health, impaired functioning, high-risk behaviors including increased substance abuse and exposure to trauma in adulthood, PTSD, psychiatric problems and hospitalizations, suicide attempts, and homelessness. Most of the above can be attested to in Nietzsche's life.

Felitti and Anda documented the mental health consequences of child abuse which included disorganized attachment style (unstable and afflictive relationships), anxiety, depression and acting out symptoms; a higher prevalence of chronic illnesses with symptoms such as headaches, sinus pain, muscle pain, migraines, cough, fever and gastrointestinal problems. Children who experienced abuse or neglect are more likely to suffer in adulthood from physical ailments such as allergies, arthritis, asthma, bronchitis, high blood pressure, and ulcers.

Pain and Fibromyalgia

Fibromyalgia is a chronic pain illness characterized by widespread musculoskeletal aches, pain and stiffness, exercise difficulties, soft tissue tenderness, general fatigue, brain fog, stress, irritable bowel and sleep disturbances. Eyestrain is reported by many patients, often anteceding severe headaches. Fibromyalgia patients experience a range of symptoms of varying intensities that fluctuate over time. Several studies have found that over a half of female fibromyalgia patients reported a history of sexual abuse and it is reasonable to assume that the situation is not much different with males. Physicians started using the term "fibromyalgia" only in the 1970's, but it was known already in the 19th century as muscular rheumatism. Nietzsche was suffering from rheumatism and headaches already when he was sixteen years old. The intensity, frequency, fluctuations, and scope of Nietzsche's pains and sicknesses suggest that the diagnosis of fibromyalgia could be applied to him as well, although his case doesn't lack many other diagnoses, mostly made posthumously.

Migraines and bipolar disorder seem to be connected; 25% of men who suffered from bipolar disorder also suffered from migraines—five times higher than the expected frequency in the general population. Similar findings were reported regarding the co-morbidity of fibromyalgia and generalized anxiety disorders, manic symptoms and bipolar disorders.[96] Estimates of a history of childhood sexual abuse among a population of women diagnosed with fibromyalgia range from 50 to 67%. Walker et al. found that the relationship between fibromyalgia and a history of childhood sexual abuse increases in strength the more pervasive, invasive and traumatic the abuse.[97] Alexander et al. found that 57% of fibromyalgia patients reported a history of sexual abuse and also reported increased pain with other conditions.

Mood Disorders

There is a direct correlation between ACE scores, and the frequency of self-acknowledged periodic depression, attempted suicides, and the use of anti-depression medications. In the general population, 54% of current depression and 58% of suicide attempts in women can be attributed to adverse childhood adverse experiences. In fact, in a study that assessed a sample of 254 adults with major mood disorders retrospectively, it was found that 28% of the males and 58% of the females reported incidents of childhood sexual abuse.[98] Adults who had experienced childhood sexual abuse were twice as likely to suffer from many mental health disorders, in comparison with counterparts who were not abused.[99] Freshwater, Leach, and Aldridge found that in addition to a higher rate of depression, women who were sexually abused as children suffered from a lower self-esteem and larger discrepancy between their perceived level of functioning and the one they aspired to achieve.[100] Among men survivors, it was found that there is a ten-fold increase in suicidal ideation, related to depression, in comparison to the general population.[101]

Social Difficulties

Adult survivors of CSA display a higher prevalence of low self-esteem, maladaptive coping skills, disturbed self-identity, poor interpersonal relationships, lack of social support, and increased vulnerability to stress.[102] It is to be expected that, given this background, their intimate couple relationship will be hampered, and indeed, survivors report a lower relationship satisfaction, poorer communication skills, and lower levels of trust in relationships.[103] There is a direct link between the severity of the abuse at childhood and the problems and dissatisfaction experienced in adult intimate relationships, which in turn, becomes a mediating link between childhood sexual abuse and depression.[104]

Adult Survivors of Sexual Trauma

The traumatic experience of abuse has a significant impact on the emotional, social, cognitive and behavioral development and functioning of children. As their brains are still developing, such experiences and adaptations to them are incorporated into the organization and operation of the mature brain. Physiological hyperarousal and vigilance in anticipation of further abuse, and numbness-surrender-dissociation, at the times of abuse, are two primary adaptive responses of children. Because the developing brain internalizes and organizes incoming information based on its use, the more frequent such responses, the higher the chance that they will turn into traits and neuropsychiatric symptoms at adulthood.[105] More specifically, traumatic attachments, including episodes of hyper-arousal and dissociation, are engraved into the developing limbic and autonomic nervous systems of the immature right brain, which is responsible for stress modulation, attachments, and affect regulation. Such structural changes explain the following symptoms of PTSD and the difficulties in generating adequate strategies for coping with stress in interpersonal relations.[106]

Erwin Parson and Luerena Bannon, addressing the survivors and their caretakers, offered a sensitive description of the stress responses in victims of sexual trauma. They pointed out that CSA rarely comes to the attention of parents and teachers, and the victims suffer in silence, with their pent up emotions, and violence. Their violence is a defense against feelings of humiliation, anxiety, degradation, low self-esteem, shame, and a diminished masculine self-image. Other common responses are impulsive behavior, suspiciousness, and hostility, as well as avoidance of particular situations that can trigger memories of the abuse. Re-experiencing can also take place at night, in nightmares, which prevent restful sleep, leaving them dazed, "spaced out," as if living in a dream.

The traumatic experience distorts all the stages of the life cycle, and affects a personality alteration, with marked changes in the domains of shame, traumatic sexualization (altered patterns of desire and behavior, hypersexuality or avoidance of sex), eating disorders, self-harming habitual avoidance, and flashbacks of traumatic scenes. Survivors exhibit a sense of vulnerability, inner fragmentation, and dissociation, suppressed anger, and feelings of betrayal and helplessness. They also feel a sense of defilement, self-blame, and self-disgust. Their ambition is diminished; they suffer from concentration difficulties, amnesia and memory disturbances; pessimism about the future, powerlessness, hopelessness, problems in trust and relations. Such responses hinder effective problem-solving in living and preclude a sense of well-being and success. The intrusive nature of their ideation leads to "a lifestyle of hiding from life itself through persistent disengagement from self and world." Although diminished awareness, helps in avoiding negative feelings, it results in a developmental arrest "shutting down the self so the warmth or fire of emotions is replaced by cold numbness and emotional distancing."[107]

The Inner World of Sexually Abused Children

Erwin Parson, Dawn Brett, and Alan S. Brett described the experience of CSA in terms of transgression and their healing as a quest for the restoration of the self.[108] They based their observations and conclusions on extensive therapy work with survivors. Children who underwent sexual trauma feel that they have lost their individuality, dignity, and sense of control. The loathsome memories of the abuse intrude, reemerge and are re-enacted vividly and painfully in their thinking, feeling, and behavior, impacting their values and relationships. While victims of sexual assault are usually more resilient, victims of repeated sexual abuse and trauma, because their spirit was broken, remain more psychologically maimed.

Trauma leaves the victims with a chronic persistent state of anxiety and alertness, which impacts how they feel, act and understand themselves and the social world around them. Victims, respond in many situations with numbed emotions, turning away from particular circumstances, feelings, persons and places, which may trigger traumatic memories. Nevertheless, many try to go on with their lives, make sense of what happened, and engage in significant activities and relationships. These necessitate suppression, denial, and avoidance as means of dealing with the fears and distress that often accompany such attempts, which in turn reinforces their "dissociative vulnerabilities." The authors found that denial is much stronger in victims who knew their assailants. Following the trauma, survivors might become oversensitized to sexual cues from other people. Thus, vigilant traumatized women, scanning the environment anxiously, may perceive sexual intentions, which non-traumatized women will not see. Anticipating further assault, they avoid closeness and liveliness, remaining isolated and frozen, with fewer chances of pleasures and personal growth. Some abused children, though, develop a realistic, intuitive perception of others, their intentions, and states of mind, which enables them to protect themselves better from "adult predatory appetites." They also learn how to camouflage themselves and hide their true selves, which puts them "in a persistent state of near-adrenergic burnout," sometimes suffering from paranoid anticipations of attacks.

People tend to believe that their selves are "an inviolate and highly prized, stubbornly personal possession." The repeated sexual trauma smash this belief to pieces, causing massive mental disorganization, experienced as a transgression of the self, a violation, and infringement of the spirit, the whole self, something perceived as precious, almost holy and unique. With a broken spirit, the power to know, love and will, is diminished; the biological tendency to be with others is curtailed, and the vulnerability to further abuse is increased. The child's distress and helplessness are increased, realizing that the abuse is not recognized, nor condemned by the other family members. The traumatizing environment, often demanding secrecy, threatening abandonment and denouncement, becomes thus a place devoid of joy, warmness, and love. It becomes a place of darkness, paralysis, and buried rage, "The child suffers day by day existential malaise, and faces contradictions in mood and behavior—of appearing to be alive (or animate) yet emotionally lifeless."

The repetitive sexual molestation, the manipulative misuse of the child's body for adult sexual gratification, is experienced by the child as a transgressive manipulation, deterioration "from being spirit-infused and alive to being essence-defused and vacuous—from awesome to awful." A traumatized child cannot go on just being, but rather must grow up fast, learning to survive, avoid trusting, watch and identify possible threats, be sensitive to the moods and behaviors of threatening adults in their surroundings. Some victims who experienced severe, repeated abuse stop feeling as human at all. Reading this, I was reminded of the way Nietzsche characterized himself "I am not a man, I am dynamite" (*Ecce*, Destiny, 1).

An Idea from the Abyss

Nietzsche's idea of the Eternal Recurrence that reaches its crescendo in *The sleepwalker song* can be conceived as not particularly original: in ancient Egypt, the scarab beetle was believed to be a symbol of eternal renewal and the reemergence of life. The concept of the wheel of life is also common in Indian religions. The idea was expressed already, among others, by Heraclitus and Ecclesiastes. The idea is not so difficult to accept, especially if taken non-literally, and is without shattering implications for life if seen as an abstract idea. How can we understand Nietzsche's feelings and insistence that it is such a shocking, awful and sublime challenge?

The proposed solution to Nietzsche's riddle helps us resolve this disparity, and by this very fact, it gives additional support to the solution offered. In the "riddle chapters" analyzed in the last chapter, the idea of the Eternal Recurrence is "enlinked and enlaced" with the secret. The enormity of the concept becomes apparent, once it is realized that in his case, it is the recurrence of the traumatic secret, most probably childhood sexual abuse, which is involved. This approach is no small thing at all for him; this is for us, a profound teaching on coping with disaster. Now we can understand Nietzsche's pronouncement:

> Such things have never been written, never been felt, never been suffered: such suffering can be borne only by a God. Dionysus. [...] No one hitherto has found any clue to such riddles; I even doubt whether anyone ever saw a riddle here. One day Zarathustra severely determines his life-task, and it is also mine. Let no one misunderstand its meaning. It is a yea-saying to the point of justifying, to the point of redeeming all past things (*Ecce*, Zarathustra, 8)

Nietzsche saw his mother as "a poisonous viper,' and in this light, he remarked, "but I confess that the deepest objection to the 'Eternal Recurrence,' my real idea from the abyss, is always my mother and my sister" (*Ecce*, Wise, 3). This ironic statement suggests that his 'idea from the abyss," had a personal relevance and that he came to terms with a much more severe problem ("as my father I am dead") although his living mother's obnoxious behavior remained beyond managing in his life time.

Chapter 8

PAIN AND SUFFERING

Nietzsche usually wrote about pain and suffering as a subject of a psychological investigation, maintaining some personal distance from it, and he allowed himself to articulate his cries of pain only in letters to his close friends. I will first bring some expressions of raw pain, and in the next chapter describe Nietzsche's ways of coping with it. *Ecce Homo*, his autobiography, begins with an almost medical report "in my thirty-sixth year my vitality reached its lowest point I still lived, but I could not see three paces before me." In addition to an account of pain "the most profound bodily weakness, but also with an excess of suffering," it is also a report on living with an undiagnosed condition, one without remedy or symptomatic relief. And still, nevertheless, "In the midst of the agony caused by a seventy-two-hour headache and violent attacks of nausea," being productive and creative. His life became a series of recoveries and "relapses, breakdown, periods of decadence" (*Ecce*, Wise, 1). The mental anguish, described in this chapter, is not only a catalog of the consequences of abuse but also a description, by a sensitive and talented observer of psychological states, which enable us to see them in an unmediated personal way and not as impersonal diagnostic categories.

How Much Pain Can I Endure?

In a letter to Richard Wagner (September 27, 1876), Nietzsche described how on returning home it was necessary for him to sit in a darkened room for atropine treatment of his eyes "This neuralgia goes to work so thoroughly, so scientifically, that it literally probes me to find how much pain I can endure, and each of its investigations lasts for thirty hours." Such conditions recur every four to seven days, Nietzsche concludes "I have had enough of it, and I want to live in a state of good health or not at all."[109] Writing to Malwida von Meysenbug (May 13, 1877), he describes his "severe crippledom" accompanied with suicidal thoughts and the torments of violent stomach pains and headaches. Six weeks later Nietzsche wrote her "I do lie sick in bed here as in Sorrento and drag myself around in pain, day after day."[110] Two years later he had to resign from his university position, and he explained to the president and the university board (May 2, 1879) "All this time my headaches have increased so much that they are now scarcely endurable; there is also the increasing loss of time occasioned by my attacks of illness which last from two to six days."[111] This was followed by a letter to his publisher "I have resigned my professorship and am going into the mountains. I am on the verge of desperation and have scarcely any hope left. My suffering has been too great, too persistent." He signed the letter "A half-blind man."[112]

The pains were growing in intensity without any relief, and thoughts of death were abundant, at first fearing that he will die, later hoping that he will. In a letter to a long-time friend Heinrich Köselitz, nicknamed by Nietzsche Peter Gast (September 11, 1879), he wrote "Now I am in the middle of life and so 'encircled by death' that at any minute it can lay hold of me. From the nature of my sufferings, I must reckon upon a sudden death through convulsions."[113] The next week (September 18, 1881), he wrote Franz Overbeck "I am desperate. Pain is vanquishing my life and my will. What months, what a summer I have had! [...] Five times I have called for Doctor Death, and yesterday I hoped it was the end — in vain."[114]

The suffering continued year after year, growing in intensity. Again, writing to Overbeck, his devoted friend (March 24, 1883), Nietzsche describes a "Deep down, a motionless black melancholy, and fatigue." He was in bed, most of the time, lost much weight, but worst of all "I no longer see why I should live for another six months."[115] In a letter to Georg Brandes (April 10, 1888), Nietzsche summed up his desperate condition "There were extremely painful and obstinate headaches which exhausted all my strength. They increased over long years, to reach a climax at which pain was habitual so that any given year contained for me two hundred days of pain."[116] Three months later (July 20, 1888), Nietzsche was getting weaker, and he wrote Overbeck "My life force is no longer intact. [...] I am not suffering from headaches or from stomach troubles but under the pressure of nervous exhaustion."[117]

How can one cope with two hundred days of pain a year and with black melancholy and fatigue? How can one continue to live, rather than die and not suffer like that? Nietzsche's answers to these questions are the heart of his philosophy of living and coping psychology. The subtitle of Nietzsche's autobiography *Ecce Homo* is, *How one becomes what one is?* In Nietzsche's case, one becomes what one is by the manner one copes with his illness and suffering. More generally stated, by the way, one deals with one's unique life situation and constraints. What we do with what was fated, and how we do it determines who we become.

Nietzsche's Emotional Pendulum

Polarities, dualities, and extremes are abundant in Nietzsche's writings. Some of the contraries are low/high, ascending/descending, lofty/ base, hot/cold, north/south, light/darkness, strong/weak, healthy/sick, elite/rabble, heavy/light, abyss/peak, heaven/hell, noon/midnight, and manly/womanish. Zarathustra is repeatedly climbing mountains and eventually going down and eventually descending into the abyss. The three phases of lows, highs, and swaying between them appear in his writings quite often, and the following quotes attest to his experiences and suffering but also document poignantly universal emotional states. The theme of vacillation between going up and going down appears in the riddle opening *Ecce Homo,* which I tried to take on before. Now the second part of the riddle in which he described the origins of his character finds its solution. Allow me to quote again:

> This dual origin, taken as it was from the highest and lowest rungs of the ladder of life, at once a decadence and a beginning, this, if anything, explains that neutrality, that freedom from partisanship with regard to the general problem of life, which perhaps distinguishes me. I am more sensitive to the first indications of ascent and descent than any man that has yet lived. In this domain I am a master par excellence I know both sides, for I am both sides (*Ecce,* Wise, 1).

Nietzsche is divulging here that he is both sides, those of decadence and beginning, elation and dejection and high and low. In *Thus Spoke Zarathustra,* Nietzsche describes feelings of heaviness and lightness, and he wants to kill the spirit of gravity by laughter. He wishes to run and fly, and not having to push himself to move on. God is dancing, and the devil is heavy. The higher he shoots for, the lower he sinks and consequently loses faith, as the scornful dwarf whispered to him "You stone of wisdom! You threw yourself high, but every thrown stone must- fall!" *(Zarathustra,* The vision and the riddle, 1). He suffers from rapid transitions "I change too quickly: my today refutes my yesterday. When I ascend I often jump over steps, and no step forgives me that" *(Zarathustra,* I, The tree on the mountainside). The swaying between the two states is intense "The tension of my cloud has been too great: between laughter-peals of lightening I want to cast hail showers into the depth [...] truly, my happiness and my freedom come like a storm" *(Zarathustra,* II, The child with the mirror).

A Personal Heaven and Hell

Nietzsche was aware of this polarity and saw it as inevitable—"The path to one's own heaven always leads the voluptuousness of one's own hell" (*Gay,* IV, 338). He introduced his *The Gay Science* as "the gratitude of a convalescent" and a "saturnalia of the spirit intoxicated by hope." He felt optimistic again after a "stretch of desert, exhaustion, disbelief, icing up in the midst of youth, the interlude of old age at the wrong time." (*Gay,* Preface 2nd Ed., 2).

Describing Epicurus' happiness, which seems similar to his, Nietzsche noticed that it could have been found only by a person who suffered much "It is the happiness of eyes that have seen the sea of existence become calm" (*Gay,* I, 45). Similarly, he said that "The mother of excess is not joy but joylessness" (*Human,* Assorted, 77). For Nietzsche, the two emotional poles are interconnected, and no one of them could take place without the other "But what if pleasure and displeasure were so tied together that whoever wanted to have as much as possible of one, must also have as much as possible of the other—that whoever wanted to learn to 'jubilate up to heavens' would also have to be prepared for 'depression unto death'" (*Gay,* I, 12).

Two Struggling Wills

Living with an emotional seesaw is a demanding task and Nietzsche did his best to accept his psychological reality, with the help of his *Amor fati* battle cry. Ambivalence and anxieties could not be avoided as it turned out that his heart has its "double wills":

> Ah, friends, do you divine also my heart's double will? This, this is my abyss and my danger, that my gaze shoots towards the summit, and my hand would fain clutch and lean—on the depth! To man clings my will; with chains do I bind myself to man, because I am pulled upwards to the Superman: for there does mine other will tend. And *therefore,* do I live blindly among men as if I knew them not: that my hand may not entirely lose belief in firmness (*Zarathustra,* II, Manly prudence).

Nietzsche describes a struggle between these two powers: on one hand, there is "the spirit of Gravity, my devil and archenemy," this spirit is adept at promoting a hopeless, pessimistic outlook, and actually acts as described in the later cognitive-distortions theories of depression, by Aaron Beck, for example,[118] "the spirit that draws towards the abyss sitting upon him half dwarf, half a mole; crippled, crippling; pouring lead-drops into my ear, leaden thoughts into my brain" (*Zarathustra,* The vision and the riddle, 1). On the other hand, there is the opposite power of courage, which fights discouragement, by challenging "Dwarf! You or I." Humans are courageous animals, and their courage can attack pity, the deepest abyss and death itself. The abysmal thought (Eternal Recurrence) gets rid of the dwarf, that is, of depression (*Zarathustra,* The vision and the riddle, 2).

The struggle between the optimistic and pessimistic inner forces goes on, and it is impossible to run away from it. In the evening, when he returns home, the depressive cloud will wait for him "heavy and patient like a log."

Zarathustra believed that as a hermit, one who distances himself from human interaction, he could still find the blissful islands, but his alter-ego answered, in a typical depressive talk "But it is all one, nothing is worthwhile, seeking is useless, and there are no blissful islands anymore!" *(Zarathustra,* IV, The cry of distress). The same struggle is also described as one between Woe and Joy: "Woe" wishes him to fade and disappear, not liking itself hoping that things would have been different, wanting to go on living, be merry, passionate, with heirs and children. "Joy" wants none of these, but rather itself "wants eternity, wants recurrence, wants everything eternally the same" *(Zarathustra,* IV, The sleepwalker song, 9).

The Maps of Moods

Nietzsche localizes his moods geographically. Northern countries are cold, inhibited and gloomy (Germany); southern countries (Italy and France) are associated with liveliness, drives and colors, "Tigers and palm trees and rattlesnakes" *(Zarathustra,* II, Manly prudence). In addition to the blissful islands, he uses an image of the "the sorrowful black sea" and a mountain's summit "I must first descend deeper than I have ever descended [...] the mountains arise out of the sea" *(Zarathustra,* III, The Wanderer). His moods are also outlined chronologically. The time of "midnight dying happiness" sings "The world is deep: deeper than day can comprehend" *(Zarathustra,* IV, The sleepwalker song, 6). Here, midnight sings that what hurts the most can be the source of one's happiness, as happiness goes along with death "What has become perfect, everything ripe – wants to die! But everything unripe wants to live: alas!" *(Zarathustra,* IV, The sleepwalker song, 9). All along, Nietzsche remembered and could put into words, but not follow, the *Worldly wisdom,* expressed in his short poem (*Gay,* Prelude in rhymes, 6):

> Stay not where the lowlands are!
>
> Climb not into the sky!
>
> The world looks best by far
>
> When viewed from halfway high.

As much as dejection is painful and despairing "Not the height, it is the abyss that is terrible!" *(Zarathustra,* II, Manly prudence), it is the sudden elation that is dangerous. In the paragraph *On the last hour,* Nietzsche, like a prophet that he was, predicts his own demise "Storms are my danger. Will I have my storm of which I will perish...? Or will I go out like a light that no wind blows out but that becomes tired and sated with itself—a burned-out light? Or finally: will I blow myself out lest I burn out?" (*Gay*, IV, 315).

The Abyss

Nietzsche began his autobiography with "Not in vain have I buried my four-and-fortieth year today; I had the right to bury it; what was vital in it has been saved and is immortal" (*Ecce*, Preface, 1). These words were colored by gloom rather than by celebration. Zarathustra-Nietzsche describes himself as demoralized "Look here at this languishing man! He is only an inch from his goal, but from weariness, he has laid himself defiantly here in the dust: this valiant man! (*Zarathustra*, III, Old and new law-tables, 18). He needs rest, "My melancholy wants to rest in the hiding places and abysses of perfection: that is why I need music" (*Gay*, V, 368). Nietzsche uses similar terms to describe Wagner, who served as his mirror image "He knows that weariness of the soul which drags itself, unable to leap or fly any more, even to walk; he masters the shy glance of concealed pain, of understanding without comfort, of the farewell without confession—indeed, as the Orpheus of all secret misery he is greater than any" (*Contra*, 1).

Other people's gaiety accentuates Zarathustra's bleak mood. He could appreciate the dancing of sweet girls, but as for him "I am a forest and a night of dark trees." Looking at life, he felt like sinking into "the unfathomable" (*Zarathustra*, II, The dance song). He had no reason to go on living, asking himself in the evening whether it is not folly to go on like that, "Are you still living? Why, wherefore, whereby?" He felt bad about feeling bad and was unable to do anything about it. Realizing how unpleasant it all was for others, left him no options but to apologize "Forgive me my sadness!" (*Zarathustra*, II, The dance song) and even the few moments of gaiety in his life could not hide his essential bleak mood "Men of profound sorrow betray themselves when they are happy: they have a way of grabbing happiness as if they would like to overwhelm and strangle it from jealousy—alas, they know too well that it's running away from them!" (*Beyond*, IX, 279).

Nietzsche saw his sinking into depression as his fate "I too have been in the underworld, as was Odysseus, and I will often be there again" (*Human*, Assorted, 408). The figure of the prophet is the spokesperson of his depression. He speaks about the world but also about himself saying "And I saw a great sadness come over humankind. The best turned weary of their works. A doctrine appeared a faith ran beside it: 'All is empty, all is alike, all has been!' And from all hills there re-echoed: 'All is empty, all is alike, all hath been!'" (*Zarathustra*, II, The Prophet). The same doctrine appeared later as "But it is all one, nothing is worthwhile, seeking is useless…" (*Zarathustra*, IV, The cry of distress).

This "doctrine" expresses the cynical, pessimistic, over a generalized and hopeless way of thinking found in depression. The discourse went on to describe the gradual unfolding of a depressive episode: it started with a negative, pessimistic outlook, and continued with a death wish, which could not be carried out of weariness "Alas! Where is there still a sea in which one could be drowned?" changing into a state of stupor, in which Zarathustra was grieving for three days, without food or drink, without rest, unable to talk. Finally, he fell into a deep sleep full of nightmares, which left him in a daze, with an empty expression, as if returning from a strange land *(Zarathustra,* II, The prophet). This was apparently the land of death "The cold and quiet of the grave around us—this whole subterranean, concealed, mute, undiscovered solitude that among us is called life but might just as well be called death [...] it is only after death that we shall enter our life and alive, oh, very much alive, we posthumous people" (*Gay*, V, 365).

Zarathustra represented depression as evening and midnight, but also as winter time of the year "winter, an ill guest, sits in my house; my hands are blue from his friendly handshake" *(Zarathustra,* III, The Mount of Olives). Zarathustra liked winter, his guest, because it drives away flies (people), enabling him to mock his enemies freely. Winter makes it possible to lie in bed and enjoy a fantasy life, letting his "hidden happiness laugh and grow wanton." This wallowing in depression has its moments of vexation. He was preoccupied, in an almost paranoid manner of thinking, with what others were thinking about him. He felt that they were jealous, hateful or pitiful of him, which made him pity their pity and believe that it is their problem "For one person, solitude is escape of an invalid; for another, solitude is escape *from* the invalids." And yet, some doubt remained, and he could not deny that they thought that "he will yet *freeze to death* on the ice of knowledge" *(Zarathustra,* III, The Mount of Olives).

Depression mixed with traumatic memories of abuse, combined with difficulties in human relationships and defenselessness, resulted in pervasive feelings of contempt and disgust "Only my brothers, scare away the dogs from him [...] and all the swarming 'cultured' vermin who feast upon the sweat of every hero!" *(Zarathustra,* III, Old and new law-tables, 18). Again, the others are turned into evil wishers, vermin, parasites, and worms "that wants to grow fat on your sick, sore places [...] building its loathsome nest in your grief and dejection, in your tender modesty" *(Zarathustra,* III, Old and new law-tables, 19). Nietzsche knows that "My danger is the loathing of mankind" (*Ecce*, Destiny, 6) and this vulnerability is related to his sickness, which goes unnamed. The images Zarathustra use to describe depression are heart-rending "The human earth became to me a cave, its chest caved in, everything living became to me human decay and bones and moldering past." He could not find any saving grace in people, and felt disgusted at man and all existence "Ah, disgust! Disgust! Disgust! Thus spoke Zarathustra and sighed and shuddered; for he remembered his sickness" *(Zarathustra,* III, The convalescent, 2). The same motif found its way forcefully into his essay on Christianity "I cannot, at this place, avoid a sigh. There are days when I am visited by a feeling blacker than the blackest melancholy—contempt of man. Let me leave no doubt as to what I despise, whom I despise: it is the man of today, the man with whom I am unhappily contemporaneous. The man of today—I am suffocated by his foul breath!" (*Antichrist,* 38).

Near the Stars

Nietzsche asked in a poem "Who lives so near the stars? Who's so near the furthest reaches of the bleak abyss?" (*Beyond,* Aftersong, out of the high mountains). The answer is clear, and so is the psychological condition he described. In the aphorism *Belief in Inebriation,* Nietzsche demonstrates an uncanny insight into the state of intoxication, actually presenting an anatomy of a manic condition "sublime ecstasy," analyzed in terms of the self, attribution processes, and interpersonal effects. Nietzsche, defining himself as a fantastic enthusiast, a half-mad genius, was aware of the danger intoxication poses the "excessive wearing away of their nervous forces," and the miserable and desolate feelings afterward. He was also conscious of the advantages in operating vigorously with increased vitality and the achievements it holds for humanity, in being "insatiable sowers of the weed of discontent," thus stimulating individual and social changes. Intoxicated people are also an unsettling element, corrupting humankind with their supply of intoxicating "spiritual fire water":

> [They] come to consider such moments as the actual manifestation of their real selves, of their 'ego,' and their misery and dejection, on the other hand, as the effect of the 'non-ego!' This is why they think of their environment, the age in which they live, and the whole world in which they have their being, with feelings of vindictiveness. This intoxication appears to them as their actual life, their actual ego; and everywhere else they see only those who strive to oppose and prevent this intoxication, whether of an intellectual, moral, religious, or artistic nature (*Daybreak,* I, 50).

Nietzsche was enamored with his elevated moods and wished himself and others to persist in the state of "continual ascents as on stairs and at the same time a sense of resting on clouds" (*Gay,* IV, 288). Admittedly, "madness has a cheerful tempo," but Nietzsche is, all the same, cognizant of the danger involved in losing patience with conventions and the "arbitrariness in feeling, seeing, and hearing, the enjoyment of the mind's lack of discipline, the joy of human unreason." He concludes that such creative souls have to be watched over and protected (*Gay*, II, 76).

Despite the dangers, Nietzsche maintained that inebriation or intoxication is a necessary condition for creativity. In *Toward the psychology of the artist,* he ascertained "intoxication must first have enhanced the excitability of the whole machine; else there is no art." The consequent "feeling of increased strength and fullness" enables idealizing, that is to say, transforming things to reflect the artist's sense of perfection (*Twilight,* Skirmishes, 8-9). Nietzsche wants to stay near the stars, above the clouds "O pure, deep sky! You abyss of light! Gazing into you, I tremble with divine desires [...] my whole will desires only to fly, to fly into you!" *(Zarathustra,* III, Before sunrise). He preferred this to normal living "For I would rather have noise and thunder and storm curses than this cautious, uncertain feline repose," neither is he tolerant of overly careful people "I hate most all soft-walkers and half-and-halfers and uncertain, hesitating passing clouds." Storms without repose was indeed his life story.

The Birth of the Superman

The discourse on M*anly prudence* presents Nietzsche's dilemma: in states of decline he is grounded in the social reality but at the same time feels contempt and disgust towards people "and he who would keep clean among men, must know how to wash himself even with dirty water." In elated or frenzied states, in contradistinction, he is "pulled towards the Superman" and feels above and beyond others, well knowing that at the same time he becomes aloof and incomprehensible to others "And you wise and knowing ones, you would flee from the solar-glow of the wisdom in which the Superman joyfully bathes his nakedness!" *(Zarathustra,* II, Manly prudence).

Some of Nietzsche's most beautiful, enticing and memorable sayings, create in the reader a state of disarray, as despite being moved, it is unclear what is the lesson one should draw and how one is actually supposed to apply it. Such is the case with "I tell you: one must have chaos within oneself, to give birth to a dancing star" *(Zarathustra,* Prologue 5) and this is also true with "For believe me! The secret of harvesting from existence the greatest fruitfulness and the greatest enjoyment of existence is to live dangerously! Build your cities on the slope of Vesuvius! Send your ships into unexplored seas! Live in war with your equals and with yourselves!" (*Gay*, V, 283).

Nietzsche is singing an alluring Sirens' song. But we sailors, in order not to crash on the island's rocks, must realize that these words should not be taken as recommendations, but rather as evidence of his fortunate success in transforming involuntary states of mind and discordant manner of living into grand ideas and art. We should not forget that Nietzsche left out of these maxims the issue of talent and the many with chaos in their hearts and no stars at all. The idea of the Superman is truly a dancing star, born out of chaos "Lo; I teach you the Superman: he is that lightning, he is that frenzy!" *(Zarathustra,* Prologue, 3). Zarathustra described how the idea was born "Thus from out of me cried and laughed my wise desire, which was born on the mountains, a wild wisdom, in truth! – my great desire with rushing wings" *(Zarathustra,* III, Old and new law-tables, 2).

The birth of this idea was described again, and in this retelling, darker colors appeared along with the bright ones. Zarathustra "an arrow, quivering with sun-intoxicated rapture," is flying into a warmer south, where "all becoming seemed to me the dancing of gods and the wantonness of gods, and the world unrestrained and abandoned." This uplifting experience, turned out to be an instance of "Build your cities on the slope of Vesuvius," as he inevitably encountered the spirit of gravity—his old devil and arch-enemy "and all that he creates: compulsion, dogma, need and consequence and purpose and will and good and evil" *(Zarathustra,* III, Old and new law-tables, 2) and in the midst of this turmoil, he hit upon the idea "There it was too that I picked up the word 'superman' and that man is something that must be overcome, that man is a bridge and not a goal; counting himself happy for his noontides and evenings, as a way to new dawns" *(Zarathustra,* III, Old and new law-tables, 3).

Nietzsche recounted that the idea of Eternal Recurrence was conceived in the abyss. Our description so far, suggests the hypothesis that the theme of the Superman, was born in, and is colored by states of extreme elation or mania "Where is the lighting which licks you with its tongue? Where is the madness with which you should be injected? Behold, I teach you the Superman: he is that lightning, he is that madness!" *(Zarathustra,* Prologue, 3). The other side of the coin of the Superman is the last man *(Zarathustra,* Zarathustra's prologue, 5), portrayed contemptuously by Nietzsche, who had few good things to say about humanity in general (excluding ancient Greece and the Renaissance). Nevertheless, experiencing people as polluting and defiling "Truly, man is a polluted stream. One must be a sea, to receive a polluted stream and not become defiled," supports the hypothesis that sexual abuse occurred in his childhood. If this was the case, the idea of the Superman gained its impetus from rejection and intolerance of people and feelings of defilement, based on past trauma and present depression combined "Behold I teach you the Superman: he is that sea; in him can your great contempt be sunk" *(Zarathustra,* I, Prologue, 3).

Life is a Woman

Zarathustra described life as a dancing and laughing woman "Who would not hate you, great woman who binds us, enwinds us, seduces us, seeks us, finds us! Who would not love you, you innocent impatient, wind-swift, child-eyed sinner!" In this one sentence, Nietzsche vacillated between hate and love towards women and life alike. He is not up to life and he cannot dance "I am truly weary of being your shepherd, always sheepish and meek." One must approach life and take hold of it "To the rhythm of my whip you shall shriek and trot! Did I forget my whip? – I did not!" *(Zarathustra,* III, The second dance song).

The above line suggests a much more sympathetic reading of the discredited "You are going to women? Do not forget the whip!" *(Zarathustra,* I, Old and young woman). The whip here can be conceived not as an expression of aggression, but merely as a word of advice to an inhibited man, to be more direct and assertive in his dealings with women. The whip can be understood non-figuratively too, as Nietzsche quoted approvingly from an old Florentine novel "good women and bad women need a stick" (*Beyond,* IV, 147), and praised "the oriental approach," which sees women as possessions to be controlled (*Beyond,* VII, 238). Some readers find it their duty to launch a holy war on such "misogynistic and chauvinistic" ideas. Others are more understanding, seeing it not as recommendations, but rather as a reflection of attitudes prevailing at his times, or as a manifestation of his difficulties. If "life is a woman," delving into Nietzsche's ways with women, will teach us about his way with life.

Foolishness and Modesty in Love

Nietzsche was not secretive about his qualms with intimacy, women, and sexuality and he was also aware and wanted his readers to take into consideration, that his pronouncements about "woman as such" are only his truths (*Gay,* VII, 231). He was inhibited and awkward in love "Love is the danger for the most solitary man, love of anything, if only it is alive! Indeed my foolishness and modesty in love is laughable" *(Zarathustra,* III, The Wanderer). Love was not only dangerous for him, but it was also shameful "To a hard men intimacy is a matter of shame—and something precious" (*Beyond,* IV, 167).

I am going to base my reconstruction on Nietzsche's writings only, and my aim is not to label him in terms of this or that clear-cut sexual orientation, neither speculate on his presumed sexual encounters. This chapter is about Nietzsche's pain and suffering in life, and it will suffice to confirm that his complicated love-map contributed heavily to his loneliness and misery. His "foolishness and modesty," were, in other words, a combination of ambivalence, inhibition, and conflict about love. In other words again, in words used by the investigators of "adverse childhood experiences," he suffered from a "disorganized attachment style." What he believed and what he wished, and what he actually felt and did about women and love, did not go well with each other.

Nietzsche talked magniloquently about *Vita Femina* "Life is a woman, usually covered but unveiled in a moment of grace to see beauty" (*Gay*, IV, 339). He proudly acknowledged the feminine in him, and he saw himself pregnant with ideas, one who gives birth to books. In his writings, a woman appears as a symbol of life and as a symbol of everything that is good and beautiful in life: truth, wisdom, soul, creativity, eternity, and art. The truth is not only a woman to be courted; it is the sex organ of the goddess *Baubo* (*Gay*, Preface, 4). He compared music, which was dearer to him than life, to a woman. Music should be "unique, wanton, and tender, and like a dainty, sweet woman in roguishness and grace..." (*Ecce*, Clever, 7). In his moments of optimism and bliss, Nietzsche used female imagery to say a soft and peaceful "yes" to life "There are many excellent inventions on earth, some useful, some pleasant: the earth is to be loved for their sake. And there are many things so well devised that they are like women's breasts: at the same time useful and pleasant" *(Zarathustra,* III, Old and new law-tables, 17).

Nietzsche who declared "No new idols will be erected by me" who saw it his calling to overthrow them (*Ecce*, Preface), turned women into idols put on a pedestal, not as flesh and blood ones to be touched, but as idealized statues made of marble, to be admired from afar. Seen this way, he wrote, "The perfect woman is a higher type of human being than the perfect man" (*Human*, VII, 377). Real to life women, with bodies and feelings of their own, were an entirely different story, not an overly happy one. The story began with his mother, who as we saw in the preceding chapter, was experienced as poisonous "Everyone carries within him an image of woman that he gets from his mother; that determines whether he will honor women in general, or despise them, or be generally indifferent to them" (*Human*, VII, 380).

Nietzsche did mention one ideal enabling mother, the exact opposite of his own oppressing and guilt producing mother. He quoted in French, Madame de Lambert's advice to her son "My dear, never allow yourself anything but those follies which will bring you great pleasure." Nietzsche thought that it was "the most motherly and cleverest remark that has ever been directed to a son" (*Daybreak*, VII, 235). He could maintain prolonged positive and close relations with a few creative and independent-minded females, who to be on the safe side, were either older than him or unavailable romantically "Women are quite capable of entering into a friendship with a man, but to keep it going—that takes a little physical antipathy as well" (*Human*, VII, 390). The antipathy was not little, and it was supported by a dichotomous view of women.

Ambivalent Love

While Nietzsche condemned sexual repression, praised sensuality, sexuality and a marriage of equals, in practice he shunned them all. We saw that he had difficulties with touch, he also felt a particular revulsion towards female nudity, and sexual lust seemed to him deplorable. His avoidance of all intimate contacts was rationalized and portrayed as an artist's voluntary decision of choosing chastity for the sake of his art. He felt that lust must be excused "Love forgives the lover even his lust" (*Gay*, II, 62). Zarathustra loved the forest, because "in the towns, too many lustful people live." A woman's desire is dangerous "Is it not better to fall into the hands of a murderer than into the dreams of a lustful woman?" In his eyes, lust was bad, and intercourse was overrated "they know of nothing better on earth than to lie with a woman" *(Zarathustra,* I, Chastity). Not having an acceptable outlet, and feeling that passions were highly distracting "Such thoughts lead and mislead him, always further onward, always further away," he was stuck between the devil of loneliness which "surrounds him, curls round him," and the deep sea of threatening and constricting suppressed passions "that fearful goddess and *mater saeva cupidinum* [wild mother of the passions]" (*Human*, Preface, 3).

In a segment characterizing artists as ones who relate to appearances and meanings without regarding their biological basis, he used the following example "when we love a woman, we easily conceive a hatred for nature on account of all the repulsive natural functions to which every woman is subject. We prefer not to think of all this" (*Gay*, II, 59). Nietzsche who praised earthiness and wrote in favor of sexuality actually was revolted by the thought of seeing a nude woman, not to mention her sex organ. In the midst of a discussion of morality, using clothes as an analogy, the following appeared:

> A naked human being is generally a shameful sight. I am speaking of us Europeans (and not even of female Europeans!). Suppose that, owing to some magician's malice, the most cheerful company at table suddenly saw itself disrobed and undressed; I believe that not only their cheerfulness would vanish and that the strongest appetite would be discouraged (*Gay*, V, 352).

Interestingly, he did not take into account that not everyone would have felt like him and some would even find the experience enjoyable. Nietzsche we saw, loved women abstractly, but not when they were too close, and not when they expected to be touched or tried to kiss him. Lou Salomé wrote about her botched encounter with Nietzsche in *Sacro Monte di Orta* in Italy, which took place at the beginning of May 1882, as if not believing that it happened "Did I kiss him? —I no longer recall." When I visited the place and observed the serene and romantic view of the lake and the Isle of San Giulio, I could imagine, invent a story of what might have happened there: Nietzsche declared his love to her and perhaps proposed marriage without even getting physically closer. She, I guess, tried to kiss him; and he most probably was appalled. She, ultimately, wanted to forget that the encounter had ever happened.

The Temptress and the Housewife

In addition to women platonic friends, Nietzsche differentiated between two kinds of women, the temptress and the motherly housewife. His mother and sister represented the housewives and Lou Salomé was a personification of the temptress. In his eyes, women who started out as threatening though alluring temptresses, with shrewdness and art, grace, playfulness, lightness and a skill of enjoying and giving pleasure, could still end up as housewives. Such a catch precluded intimate relationships "A woman has so many reasons for shame; hidden in women is so much pedantry, superficiality, so many characteristics of the school teacher, petty arrogance, petty indulgence, and immodesty—just look at the way she interacts with children 'eternally boring in woman'—she is rich in that!" (*Beyond,* VII, 232).

The housewife is an unappreciated caretaker "the eternally boring," from whom it is almost impossible to take leave; the temptress is respected, desired and feared "the eternally feminine." The housewife is traditional and conventional, lacking in critical and original thinking. As old women, they are more skeptic than men, knowing that "superficiality is the essence, and that virtues and profundities are just a veil over this pudendum, a matter of decency and shame" (*Gay,* II, 64). Being afflicted with poverty of spirit, such females have only their virtue and shame to offer (*Gay,* II, 65). They "appear as utterly fragile ornaments who are hurt even by a speck of dust" and yet, they use their weakness to their advantage (*Gay,* II, 66). Unlike men, the temptress finds no interest in truth "her great art is the lie, her highest concern appearance and beauty." Men honor and love such women for this very art, and although it makes them suffer, they are happy to be associated with such beings "under whose hands, looks, and tender foolishness our seriousness, our gravity and profundity seem almost silly" (*Beyond,* VII, 232).

A Tragicomedy

It must have been important for Nietzsche to clarify that he made up his mind to give up intimate relations, not because he was an undesired man, but despite it. While discussing his crisis of relations with Wagner he added, as if bragging somewhat adolescently "Suddenly in the midst of everything, I left for a few weeks, despite the fact that a charming Parisian lady sought to console me; I excused myself to Wagner quite simply with a fatalistic telegram" (*Ecce*, Human, 2).

He called his hopeless entanglement about love "a comedy," and he made Zarathustra laugh at himself and say mockingly "Happiness runs after me. That is because I do not run after women. Happiness, however, is a woman" *(Zarathustra,* III, Involuntary bliss). Life is a woman, he said, and yet love is tied with perishing "The will to love: that is, also being willing to die" *(Zarathustra,* III, Immaculate perception) and "Women tear to pieces..." (*Ecce,* Books, 5). Writing about the aftermath of having to cope with trauma in life, Nietzsche revealed that what could be seen as a comedy is quite sad. A trauma-stricken person emerges changed, losing trust in life, seeing it as a problem, and although it is still possible to love life in certain ways "It is the love for a woman who raises doubts in us" (*Contra,* Epilogue, 1).

Zarathustra explained that he did not get married because he never met the woman by whom (and not with whom) he wanted to have children "unless it be this woman, whom I love: for I love you, O Eternity!" He emphasized and repeated this statement seven times, turning it into a symbolic ritual of vows taking "O how should I not lust for eternity and for the wedding ring of rings – the Ring of recurrence!" *(Zarathustra,* III, The seven seals, 2). Nietzsche the godless hermit is displaying here erotic feelings directed towards an abstract idea, similar to a Catholic nun, wearing a ring, a remembrance of her betrothal to the heavenly spouse.

Women are conceived as distractions, sidelining philosophers from their mission "We recognize a philosopher by the following: he walks away from three shiny and loud things—fame, princes, and women. That doesn't mean that they might not come to him." Nietzsche went on to explain that a philosopher is pregnant, with a strong maternal instinct, loving and dedicated himself to what grows in him. A philosopher's chastity is not due to "some ascetic scruple and hatred of the senses," but is rather a result of a calculated decision, similar to the one made by athletes and artists, not to spend energy on sexual intercourse, but use it to enhance their accomplishments (*Gay* , III, 8). Being married to eternity, finding women physically unappealing, feeling awkward with expressions of love, Nietzsche was left with admiration at a distance, and turning women into muses and benefactresses "The magic and the most powerful effect of women is, in philosophical language, *actio in distans* [action at a distance]: but this requires first of all and above all—distance" (*Gay,* II, 6).

Reenacted Abuse

Victims of childhood sexual abuse, experience an approach-avoidance conflict—they need and want to love and be loved, and are at the same time defensive, and afraid to get hurt again. They are, in other words, ambivalent about love. Ironically, when they find some human intimacy, it often turns out to be a mirror image of the traumatic experience. Judith Herman wrote that "Repetition is the mute language of the abused child"[119] and Bessel van der Kolk discussed the topic in terms of compulsion to repeat the trauma, re-enactment, re-experiencing, re-victimization, addiction to trauma and masochism.[120] The trauma can be then re-lived in any or both the roles of victims and victimizers. Michael Levi pointed out that the reenactment of past traumas is sometimes a way to master them; on other occasions, it occurs inadvertently and is the result of vulnerabilities, rigid defensive strategies, faulty affective regulation and cognitive distortions. He referred to studies that show that women who were sexually abused in childhood are more likely to be sexually and physically abused in their marriages.[121] Judith Herman characterized the re-enactments as uncanny; although they seem to be consciously chosen, they have a quality of inadvertence and involuntariness.

The abuse Nietzsche underwent was re-enacted in other adult relationships, sometimes hinted at; in other occasions revealed indirectly, not with concrete information about the concerned persons, but rather with a delineation of the feelings and forces involved. In these instances, the themes of inability to stay in a loving relationship along with a great yearning to have love, are intermingled with abusing and being abused, torturing and being tortured. Nietzsche mentioned on passing his sadistic fantasies "It is the most sensual men who need to flee women and torment their bodies" (*Daybreak*, IV, 294). He could fall in love, but not stay in love and not be loved, a situation he saw ironically as *Vivant comoedia*, a lively comedy "Now she loves him and looks ahead with quiet confidence—like a cow. Alas, what bewitched him, was precisely that she seemed utterly changeable and unfathomable" She should simulate a lack of love..." (*Gay*, II, 67).

I have mentioned Nietzsche's clue, that everything psychological in his writings is also about him (*Ecce*, Birth, 4) and that he used Dionysus, with whom he identified, as his mouth-piece (Chapter 4). Thus, his Night Song, usually understood as a meditation on Dionysian love,[122] can be understood as an expression of his own feelings "my soul too is the song of a lover [...] A craving for love is within me; it speaks the language of love [...] I do not know the happiness of those who receive, and I have often dreamed that even stealing must be more blessed than receiving." Following this frustrating dilemma, the theme of abuse resurfaces again "I should like to hurt those for whom I shine; I should like to rob those to whom I give; thus do I hunger for malice. To withdraw my hand when the other hand already reaches out to it; to linger like the waterfall, which lingers even while it plunges; thus do I hunger for malice. Such revenge my fullness plots: such spite wells up out of my loneliness" (*Zarathustra,* II, The night song).

Nietzsche had the same poem-lament appear twice: in *Thus Spoke Zarathustra,* voiced by a male, the magician; and in *Dithyrambs of Dionysus* voiced by a female, Ariande. Why was the lament repeated? Who is the magician? What does Ariande stand for? It is reasonable to assume that authors repeat messages that are significant to them, wishing to draw the readers' attention and make them wonder about their non-manifest meaning. Messages could also be repeated when they stand for different sides of one person. Most commentators assume that the magician (or Sorcerer in another translation) stands for Wagner and that the sermon is mostly about deception and art.[123] However, in Hellenic sources, Zoroaster was portrayed as magi, the ultimate sorcerer-astrologer. Pliny the Elder named Zoroaster, in the first century, as the inventor of magic and astrology (*Natural History,* 30, 2.3).[124] Hence, I suggest that the magician stands for Zarathustra, and the sermon is a confrontation between two parts in Nietzsche's soul. He felt that he knew Dionysus in a personal way, and he felt the same about Ariande "Who knows except me who Ariadne is! To all such riddles no one has ever found an answer; I doubt even whether anyone even saw a riddle here" (*Ecce,* Zarathustra, 8). The unhinged Nietzsche, wrote to Cosima Wagner, addressing her "Princess Ariande, my beloved," and signed the letter Dionysus. We do not know the nature of this "forbidden" love feelings towards another person's wife. In addition to being Dionysus' wife, there might have been a deeper significance to Ariande. In Greek mythology (*Britanica.com*) Ariande, the daughter of Pasiphae and Minos the Cretan king, fell in love with Theseus, the Athenian hero. After he slew the Minotaur (a half bull and half man beast), she helped him escape the Labyrinth, with a thread to mark the way. Theseus carried her later to the island of Naxos, and left her there to die. She lamented her bitter fate of exile and desertion and was rescued by the god Dionysus, who married her.

Ariande, exactly like the magician (Zarathustra's double), can thus be seen as a symbol of a person betrayed and abused in love. The magician was chastised by Zarathustra for lack of strength and resolve in stopping the cycle of abuse "he found a trembling old man with a fixed gaze; and as hard as Zarathustra tried to prop him up and stand him on his feet again, it was in vain [...] like someone who had been abandoned and left stranded by the whole world." The two identical laments reveal that pleasure can be found in abuse, that victims of abuse can be attracted to their abusers and even miss them. David Finkelhor and Kersti Yllo found that some women report that they had experienced pleasure when they were raped by their spouses, and especially in cases of repeated rape. They suggested that this is actually an "adaptive response" making the experience more survivable.[125] Children have a natural curiosity about their genitals and can derive pleasure from manipulating them already in infancy, a fact misused by child offenders, who are skilled at "grooming" children, arousing their trust and demanding secrecy, leaving them with the terrible, inexplicable concoction of pleasure, apprehension, shame, and guilt.[126]

If we do not opt for the obvious interpretation that the lament deals merely with Dionysus, the unknown feral god and lover, it is possible to see behind the following words, transcribed from a whole poem into discrete lines, a child abused by an adult he admired, loved and trusted. It is also possible to see here adult affairs, which reenact a childhood trauma. The lament-poem begins with a loveless person's need to be loved "Who will warm me, who loves me still? Give me hot hands! Give me braziers for my heart!" It continues with a mixture of excitability and dread "Laid out, shuddering, like something half-dead whose feet one warms – Racked, oh! by unknown fevers, shivering from pointy icy arrows of frost, hunted by you, thought! Unnamable! Disguised! Horrendous one!" A few lines later, a violent, destructive intrusion is described "Strike deeper, strike one more time! Skewer, smash this heart! Why this torment with blunt-toothed arrows? [...] You do not want to kill, only torment, torment? Why torment *me*, you gloating unknown god?" The poem goes on to graphically describe the physical act of (what I read as) an adult entering the child's bed, and the child's immediate revulsion "Aha! You sneak close? At such midnight, what do you want? Speak! You press me, squeeze me – Ha! Too close already! Away! Away!"

The victimizer is seen as a thief, shameless torturer, hunter, robber, an "executioner god," while the victim is described with self-loathing as passive and cooperating, unable to demand much and speak briefly "should I, like a dog, roll over before you? Devotedly, ecstatically beside myself wag love – to you?" [...] No, not dog, only your prey am I." The lament ends with a repetition of its opening lines "Give me *love* – who will warm me still? Who loves me still?" and with a yearning for the victimizing enemy "Give, yes give, cruelest enemy, give me – *yourself*! [...] Come back, with all your torments! To the last of all lonely ones. Oh, come back! (*Zarathustra,* IV, The Magician, 1). Incidentally, the shepherd who had a black snake penetrate his mouth (Chapter 6) also called himself "the lonesomest one" (*Zarathustra,* III, The vision and the riddle, 2).

Faults and Blunders

The list of difficulties in living continues. Nietzsche was aware of his problems in getting along with people. Seeing himself "so ill-attuned to life," he felt ridiculous, helpless and tormented "Here are my faults and blunders, here my delusion, my bad taste, my confusion, my tears, my vanity, my owlish seclusion, my contradictions. Here you can laugh. Laugh then, and be merry!" (*Gay*, III, 311).

Cleanliness and Solitude

Nietzsche's strong revulsion to people involved a heightened sensitivity to bad smells and dirt. In addition to this, or as a reaction to it, he demonstrated an excessive anxiousness about cleanliness "What most profoundly divides two men is a different sense and degree of cleanliness" (*Beyond*, IX, 271) and in his case "I am gifted with an utterly uncanny instinct of cleanliness." Nietzsche felt that with such developed "psychological antennae," he could sense physiologically the inner core, the "entrails," of people he encountered, their secrets, their inner filth and base blood. This, came with the high price of feelings of revulsion "This does not make them any more fragrant" (*Ecce*, Wise, 8). The extreme need for cleanliness, at first considered as "indescribable abundance of pleasure in the bath," and seen as a gift and sign of nobility, turned into an affliction, making him a saint-like person, separated and isolated from people (*Beyond*, IX, 271). The need to remain clean and avoid contamination with dirt grew in intensity "I would die in unclean surroundings" (*Ecce*, Wise, 8). Consequently, Nietzsche washed and swam frequently and climbed high mountains in search of light and fresh air. When these were not enough, he severed his relations and lived in solitude "For solitude is a virtue with us, as a sublime tendency and impulse for cleanliness, which senses how contact between one person and another—'in society'—must inevitably bring impurity with it. Every community somehow, somewhere, sometime makes people—'common'" (*Beyond*, IX, 284).

Nietzsche's feelings of being dirty and his need for self-purification, combined with seeing humans as "a polluted river," mentioned before, is not surprising, in light of the hypothesized sexual abuse in childhood. Given this, his lack of trust in people "accepting and eating a meal in whose cuisine one has no confidence" (*Gay*, V, 364), and his fear of getting hurt again in close relationships is understandable. Nietzsche compared "close proximity to a person" to touching a good etching with one's fingers, and by so doing, dirtying and losing its beauty "A human being's soul is likewise worn down by continual touching." It seemed to him that one always loses in being in too intimate a relationship with women and friends "sometimes one loses the pearl of his life in the process" (*Human*, VII, 428).

This trauma-ridden person was only defending himself. Adopting the role of a hermit, was one defense, but there were also others mentioned by him, such as using roles (dresses), disguise (masks) and disappearance. He put a chair at the door to avoid intrusions and played "ghost"— not responding, hiding, and making people afraid of him. He felt and played dead as if he was already posthumous (*Gay*, V, 365). Still being human (all too human), Nietzsche needed love too. Hence, his dilemma, which he called *from the land of cannibals* "In solitude the solitary man consumes himself, in the crowd the crowds consumes him, Now choose" (*Human*, Assorted, 348).

A Stranger in a Strange Land

Nietzsche described on many occasions his experience of being a misfit without roots in life: "I must keep tearing away and experience new bitterness" and "I often look back in wrath at the most beautiful things that could not hold me" (*Gay*, IV, 309). He divulged, "But nowhere have I found a home; I am unsettled in every city and I depart from every gate," and "I have been driven from fatherlands and motherlands" *(Zarathustra,* II, Immaculate perception). Nietzsche felt distant from other people "And that among men you will always be wild and strange," consequently crying out "O humankind, you strange thing" *(Zarathustra,* II, The Homecoming). He loved nature except for humans and loved art as an escape from them. However, closeness to others, in addition to the issue of cleanliness, made him uncomfortable "Every association with human beings makes us shudder slightly; that for all our mildness, patience, geniality, and politeness, we cannot persuade our nose to give up its prejudice against the proximity of human being" (*Gay*, V, 379).

A part of Nietzsche neither loved life did not particularly like other people nor loved itself. Nietzsche called the section describing his deep contempt of others *The fool interrupts* and he felt that he had to reassure himself "The author of this book is no misanthrope," and yet he went on to exclaim "Refined contempt is our taste and privilege, our art, our virtue perhaps, as we are the most modern of moderns" (*Gay*, V, 379). In a similar vein, he generalized, "Every superior human being will instinctively aspire after a second Citadel where he is set free from the crowd, the many, the majority." And yet, he admitted, that he "occasionally glisten with all the shades of distress, green and gray with disgust, satiety, sympathy, gloom and loneliness" (*Beyond*, II, 26). Christiane Sanderson, in *Counseling Adult Survivors of Sexual Abuse*, explains that in CSA "Another common defense against shame is contempt for the self, which is projected and relocated on to others. Such projections of contempt represent the externalization of perceived weakness in the self and manifest as hostility, ridicule and contempt for others, to make the other feel as small and shriveling as the survivor."[127]

Nietzsche lost his aplomb when he talked about the crowd, the rabble and the mob. The thinker who knew that there is no pleasure without displeasure or happiness without suffering; the stoically minded person who accepted the worst in life; the one who believed that every individual in unique, asked almost naively, "What does life have need of the rabble too?" *(Zarathustra,* II, The rabble). Nietzsche continued his diatribe "Truly, better to live among hermits and goat-herds than with our gilded, false, painted rabble [...] But there everything is false and rotten, most of all the blood, thanks to old, evil diseases and worse quacks" *(Zarathustra,* IV, Conversations with the kings). Here too, the triple mantra of disgust is repeated, as well as deriding prejudiced expressions such as "the stench of shopkeepers." Most of all Nietzsche could not stand those who possibly remind him of himself "What is it exactly that I find so totally unbearable? Something which I cannot deal with on my own, which makes me choke and feel faint? Bad air! Bad air! It's when something which has failed comes close to me when I have to smell the bowels of a failed soul" (*Genealogy*, I, 12).

We met the heightened feeling of disgust Nietzsche exhibited, many times before. I will consult Christiane Sanderson again, to get some insight into this feeling "Humiliation is a strong component in CSA, as is disgust, especially disgust at the self, the abuser, the sexual acts, and the child's own body and its response to the abuse."[128] At times, the reader suspects that this highly intelligent person is a stranger in a strange land, because he had a blind spot to the way others saw and experienced his words and actions, and therefore, he did not understand social nuances. About his short academic career, he wrote, "And when I lived among them I lived above them. They grew angry with me for that" *(Zarathustra,* II, Scholars) and one wonders, how exactly did he communicate his feelings of superiority to his colleagues? However, our evaluation is changed the moment we understand the meaning of his revelation "My humanity does not consist in the fact that I sympathize with the feelings of my fellows, but that I can endure that very sympathy. . . . My humanity is a continual self-mastery" (*Ecce*, Wise, 8). How could we expect a person who had to invest all his energies in basic survival and escape from trauma, to be attuned to social cues and the intricacy of human interaction?

Thus, Nietzsche did not use understatements and he said what was on his mind at any given moment or mood, without a second thought and without taking into consideration, or being aware at all of the impressions his extreme statements made on others. This is the case with his sweeping slanders of mobs, city dwellers and shopkeepers, as well as his self-praise and bragging. Eternal Recurrence is the "hardest of all thoughts to bear" and his *Thus Spoke Zarathustra* is "the greatest gift to mankind" and "the loftiest, deepest, full of gold" (and I am not saying that he was wrong).

Nietzsche summed up his life situation, saying "We are proper ne'er-do-wells and ne'er-do-ills," while life said to him "O Zarathustra, you are not faithful enough to me! You do not love me nearly as much as you say; I know you are thinking of leaving me soon." *(Zarathustra,* III, The second dance song). Zarathustra did not take good care of himself; neither was he a good actor. He was unaware of basic needs such as hunger and could not sleep at night *(Zarathustra,* Prologue, 8). He was oblivious to his surroundings "I live blindly among men as if I did not recognize them." He was defenseless "I let myself be deceived so as not to be on guard against deceivers." He was clueless "I have to be without foresight" *(Zarathustra,* II, Manly prudence). What was dryly described in the last chapter, as social difficulties following adverse childhood experiences, can also be described as problems in playing well the social game and enjoying the game:

> If life is to be pleasant to watch, its play must be well acted: for that, however, good actors are needed. I found all vain people to be good actors: they act and desire that others shall want to watch them — all their spirit is in this desire. They act themselves, they invent themselves: I like to watch life in their vicinity — it cures melancholy *(Zarathustra,* II, Manly prudence).

Nietzsche's life was not pleasant to watch, and he described his way of indecisive acting in two short, painful maxims. The first prod him in vain to behave otherwise; the second expresses resignation to his lack of assertiveness, his social anxiety, his shyness, his timidity, his inhibition, his pride and stiffness:

> *The maxim of the brute*
>
> Never ask! Why cry and shake?
>
> Please, I ask you simply take! (*Gay,* Prelude in rhyme, 17).

> *Principle of the Overly Refined*
>
> Rather on your toes high,
>
> Than crawling on all fours!
>
> Rather through a keyhole spy
>
> Than through open doors! (*Gay,* Prelude in rhyme, 42).

Chapter 9

SAGE, WARRIOR AND CREATOR

Beginning with his first book *The Birth of Tragedy*, suffering was a central topic in Nietzsche's teachings, an inherent part of life "Life itself, its eternal fruitfulness and recurrence, creates torment, destruction, the will to annihilation." (*Will*, IV, 1052). He explored pain first of all in his own life, wondering as we read in his letters "How can one cope with two hundred days of pain a year and with black melancholy and fatigue? How can one continue to live, rather than die and not suffer like that?". These questions relate to his physical pain and emotional suffering, which were only reinforced by a secret trauma, which we tried to elucidate. The answers-measures he tried, the ideas he put forward in his philosophy and psychology, and the inspiration he drew from his meta-psychological philosophy of life, the triad of the will to Power, the Superman and Eternal Recurrence, continued to shape each other reciprocally, throughout his life. He did not want his sickness and suffering to be in vain, and wished to share with his readers what he learned. Fortunately for us, undergoing many kinds of suffering was accompanied by different thought perspectives, which resulted in important insights about coping. He felt that a philosopher "simply cannot keep from transposing his states every time into the most spiritual form and distance: this art of transfiguration is philosophy" (*Gay*, preface, 3).

Nietzsche, the pastor's son and former student of theology, must have known the Biblical book of Job, an honest well-to-do man, who experienced consecutive dreadful disasters, losing everything he held dear, his children, his health and his possessions. Pain-ridden and heart-broken he tried to make sense of his suffering, its meaning and place in the divine plan of the world and life. Nietzsche entered a dialogue with four intellectual traditions about suffering: firstly, unlike Job, who justified God, he attacked the Christian-ascetic conception of suffering. Secondly, he acknowledged the ancient Greek wisdom of Silenus, the daemon companion of Dionysus, who was forced to reveal his secret to King Midas "Suffering creature, born for a day, child of accident and toil, why are you forcing me to say what would give you the greatest pleasure not to hear? The very best thing for you is totally unreachable: not to have been born, not to exist, to be nothing. The second best thing for you, however, is this — to die soon" (*Birth*, 3). Thirdly, although he did not agree with the Buddhist solution to the problem of suffering, he was acquainted with the first Buddhist noble truth, the principle of *Dukkha*, according to which life is full of suffering, associated with birth, growing old, illness and dying and the futility of the attempts to hold onto things that are constantly changing (*Will*, I, 1). Finally, he discussed Schopenhauer's pessimistic idea that suffering is an inherent feature of life, due to the cycle of constant dissatisfaction and continues striving. Life, like death, is the "swing of a pendulum between pain and ennui."[129]

At some point in their lives, people encounter a serious misfortune, a stressor, a trauma, or using a more optimistic term, a life challenge. The results of the encounter depend on the nature of the stressor, its intensity and circumstances (accident, terror, and abuse), characteristics of the victims (age, resourcefulness, prior experiences, dispositional optimism, resiliency and hardness), and the survivors' map of the world (system of meaning, philosophy of life). Survivors emerge out of traumatic events, different from what they were before, either maimed or strengthened. It is not always realized that the often quoted "what does not destroy me, makes me stronger" (*Twilight*, Maxims, 8), is a conditional statement, entailing also the possibility of destruction and disabling. The uncontrollable, irreversible and threatening features of such events are like an earthquake, which "can produce an upheaval in trauma survivors' major assumptions about the world, their place in it and how they make sense of their daily lives."[130]

In the present chapter, I will discuss Nietzsche's ways of coping with his many kinds of suffering, and in the next (and last) chapter I will consider his changed new and alternative perspectives to make sense of the world and life in the aftermath of trauma. The distinction I make here, between coping and finding meaning, is not clear-cut: cognitive measures are an important part of coping, and coping measures depend on a person's internalized map of the world.

The Great Suffering

Nietzsche wanted us to look at life with opened eyes, to see the whole picture, not as we wish it to be, and still realizing that our view is inherently limited. Thus, he argued that death is not unusual, but rather the rule in nature, while it is the phenomenon of life which is the exception "Let us beware of saying that death is opposed to life; the living is merely a type of what is dead and a very rare type" (*Gay*, III, 109). Similarly, psychological problems and depression should not surprise us, given the complexities of the human situation "The more normal this pathology is among human beings—and we cannot deny its normality—the higher we should esteem the rare cases of spiritual and physical power, humanity's *strokes of luck*" (*Genealogy*, III, 13). Suffering is the basic fact of existence, and moments of happiness are only short-lived exceptions. The question is how to do our best under this condition, live as passionately as we can, and not let it be a reason to reject life. Pain is a fact of life and not an objection to it: "If you have no more happiness to give me, well then! you still have suffering" (*Ecce*, Zarathustra, 1).

Nietzsche contrasted two approaches to suffering, the one typical of the "sick sheep" way of thinking (*Genealogy*, III, 15), endorsed by the Church, and espoused by the "last man," the product of conformist-consumerist modern culture. The other, the "discipline of the great suffering," is derived from the tragic Dionysian wisdom. The former wants to abolish suffering and pain in the name of pleasure and well-being; the latter, on the contrary, "would rather have it [suffering] higher and worse than ever." It conceives aiming solely for wellbeing, as a dangerous approach which will produce unworthy and preposterous human beings; it affirms that "only this discipline has created all enhancements of man so far" (*Beyond*, VII, 225). Unlike dichotomous approaches which see happiness as based upon minimal pain and maximal pleasure, typical of modern "positive psychology,"[131] Nietzsche suggested that the two are interconnected "that he who wants the greatest possible amount of the one must also have the greatest possible amount of the other" (*Gay*, I, 12). He saw the wish to abolish suffering as insanity leading the "sick sheep" to look for a reason for their misery "I suffer: it must be somebody's fault" (*Genealogy*, III, 15), which the Christian ascetic priests, hastened to supply, teaching that suffering was a heavenly deserved punishment for some offense (*Genealogy*, III, 20). Such explanations breed guilt, bitterness and resentment, and consequently paralyze the instinct of recovery (*Ecce*, Wise, 6).

The antithesis of the great suffering "the religion of smug ease," leads at best to comfortableness, as happiness can only come together with pain and misfortune (*Gay*, IV, 338). Art and philosophy are based on suffering and the suffering of their creators (*Gay*, V, 370). Nietzsche quoted approvingly Meister Eckhart's saying "The beast that bears you fastest to perfection is suffering" (*Untimely*, Schopenhauer, 4). Human suffering was behind the emergence of all gods and religious belief systems "It was suffering and incapacity that created all afterworlds—this, and that brief madness of bliss which is experienced only by those who suffer deeply" (*Zarathustra*, I, On the afterworldly).

Human achievements are due to the discipline of suffering, in which the tensions of unhappy souls, who confronted ruin courageously and inventively cultivated strength. These souls preserved their suffering, gave it meaning, and used it together with its accompanying "profundity, secret, mask, spirit, cunning, greatness." Such great suffering should be admired, as pitying would encourage indulgence and weakness and strangle creativity and integration (*Beyond*, VII, 225). Nietzsche even went one step further, wishing those he cared about "suffering, desolation, sickness, ill-treatment, indignities—I wish that they should not remain unfamiliar with profound self-contempt, the torture of self-mistrust, the wretchedness of the vanquished." Again, he had no pity for them "I wish them the only thing that can prove today whether one is worth anything or not—that one endures" (*Will,* p 481). Thus, the ability to bear one's pain and endure is a measure of greatness "I assess the power of a will by how much resistance, pain, and torture it endures and knows how to turn to its advantage" (*Will,* II, 382).

Writing about the great suffering, Nietzsche wished his disciples "suffering, desolation, sickness, ill-treatment, indignities," as well as self-contempt, self-mistrust and demoralization, and all that in order to discover their worth as ones able to endure (*Will,* IV, 910). We should not take this proclamation literally, as he usually wrote in absolute terms, without ifs or buts. Thus, despite his massive frontal attack on morality, he also said "It goes without saying that I do not deny – unless I am a fool – that many actions called immoral ought to be avoided and resisted or that many called moral ought to be done and encouraged" (*Daybreak,* II, 103). Not being a fool, he would have probably agreed that it would be better to take a pain reliever, rather than suffer a throbbing toothache. He thus referred to pain that cannot be avoided, not only current pain but also pain caused by the past encroaching on the present. He referred to mental pain, to post-traumatic suffering, to the pain of survivors of childhood sexual abuse included. The great suffering is thus not about annihilating suffering, but rather about endurance and living with it successfully, that is to say creatively. Nietzsche's means and principles of enduring and overcoming pain and suffering, dispersed throughout his writings, can be put together under three modes, the ways of the sage, the warrior and the creator, which I will delineate now.

The Way of the Sage

The highest wisdom teaches accepting and justifying "To think of one's self as a destiny, not to wish one's self 'different' this, in such circumstances, is the very highest wisdom" (*Ecce,* Wise, 6). This wisdom, which Nietzsche also calls the highest form of affirmation, recognizes that pain, suffering and sickness are an essential part of our life "I, Zarathustra, the advocate of living, the advocate of suffering, the advocate of the circuit—thee do I call, my most abysmal thought!" (*Zarathustra,* The convalescent, 1). Sickness is a fact of life "Even Socrates said, as he died: 'to live — that means to be sick a long time: I owe Asclepius the Savior a rooster'" (*Twilight,* Socrates, 1).

Love Your Fate

In addition to Socrates, Nietzsche conversed about radical acceptance with other thinkers in the "republic of geniuses" (*Untimely,* History, IX), and two

Stoic voices among them stand out, the first is Epictetus, who taught "Don't demand that things happen as you wish, but wish that they happen as they do happen, and you will go on well."[132] The second is the Emperor (Marcus Aurelius) who wrote:

> Whatever is agreeable to you shall be agreeable to me, O graceful universe! Nothing shall be to me too early, or too late, which is seasonable to you; whatever thy seasons bear, shall be joyful fruits to me, O nature! From you are all things; in you they subsist; to you, they return. Could one say, "you dearly beloved city of Cecrops!" And will you not say, "you dearly beloved city of God!"[133]

While both of them referred mainly to future events, Nietzsche, in his battle cry *Amor fati*, included the past too. He saw it as the core of his being (*Contra*, Epilogue), and as his formula for human greatness "that one wants nothing to be different, not forward, not backward, not in all eternity. Not merely bear what is necessary, still less conceal it—all idealism is mendacity in the face of what is necessary—but love it" (*Ecce*, Clever, 10). Like the Emperor, he wanted to learn to see the beauty in what is necessary, and by so doing make things beautiful:

Amor fati: let that be my love henceforth! I do not want to wage war against what is ugly. I do not want to accuse; I do not even want to accuse those who accuse. Looking away shall be my only negation. And all in all, and on the whole: someday I wish to be only a Yes-sayer (*Gay*, IV, 276).

In the next chapter, we will see that *Amor fati*, is tied in with the idea of Eternal Recurrence "the ideal of the most high-spirited, alive, and world-affirming human being." Adopting this idea means going beyond acceptance of reality and love of fate to coming to terms with what was, and wishing it to repeat into all eternity, shouting *da capo*, a music term in Italian, which indicates a repeat the previous passage from the beginning (*Beyond*, II, 56).

Redemption of the Past

In addition to the acceptance of present sickness, Nietzsche advised the acceptance of past abuse and violence which continues to intrude and taunt its victims. We are historical beings, whose memories can turn into "an invisible and dark weight," a painful burden. The "it was" can turn existence into trauma "a past tense that is never over and done with," that only death can terminate (*Untimely*, History, 1). Time cannot run backwards, and "that which was," becomes a stone we cannot roll. Nietzsche's idea of the Eternal Recurrence teaches how to accept and justify "what was," over and over again, redeem and integrate it "to compose into one and bring together what is fragment and riddle and dreadful chance in man – as poet, reader of riddles, and redeemer of chance" *(Zarathustra,* III, Old and new law-tables, 3). What was, is used to transform our life, by changing "every 'It was' into 'I willed it so!'" *(Zarathustra,* II, Redemption), until we can say, that we are willing to repeat it forever. In this redemption, one comes to terms with the past, the future, and the nature of time itself "I love him who justifies the future and redeems the past: for he wants to perish in the present" *(Zarathustra,* Prologue, 3).

Reversing of Perspectives

The "highest wisdom," is a comprehensive view, in which life is seen from many perspectives, always questioning the previous ways of understanding and interpretation of phenomena, enabling reformulations and reframing to suit one's life needs. Nietzsche learned to reverse perspectives in dealing with his sickness and suffering, where he discovered how to view values and ideas from the perspective of the sick, and see the working of an instinct for decadence, from the perspective of abundance and self-confidence (*Ecce,* Wise, 1). Rather than treating health and sickness as a dichotomy, he saw what is considered as health, as a relative health, a lower level of optimal health. Similarly, he saw the ability to tolerate pain and torture, and gain advantage from them, as indications of health and strength (*Will,* IV, 812).

If we cannot will things, it is possible to "lay some *meaning* into them" and believe that they thus obey our will (*Twilight,* Maxims, 18). If we cannot change reality, we can always change the way we see it, using what Nietzsche called the principle of belief "When a misfortune strikes us, we can overcome it either by removing its cause or else by changing the effect it has on our feelings, that is, by reinterpreting the misfortune as a good, whose benefit may only later become clear" (*Human,* III, 108). Thus, it is possible to posit that pain and pleasure cannot be separated, as pain and destruction are consequences of the will to pleasure and to create (*Will,* III, 853, 3). We can also argue, and hopefully be convinced, that pain is not a fact, but merely an interpretation of some complex physiological events "basically a fat word set in place of a spindly question mark" (*Genealogy,* III, 16). Besides, the problem is not a sickness, a normal essential phenomenon, but rather the wish to be healthy (*Gay,* III, 120). Actually our aim should be a new healthiness, encompassing sickness and health (*Ecce,* Thus, 2). Such a great health, with a great suffering "is the ultimate emancipator of spirit..." (*Contra,* Epilogue, 1). We can also turn pain into a lively image, a pet we can play with, "I have given a name to my pain and call it 'dog': it is just as faithful, just as obtrusive and shameless, just as entertaining, just as clever as any other dog—and I can scold it and vent my bad moods on it, as others do with their dogs, servants, and wives" (*Gay,* IV, 312).

Epictetus taught that people are not influenced by facts, but rather by the way they understood them[134], and Nietzsche likewise argued that it is not the very fact of physical or mental suffering which matters, but rather how they are understood "What really raises one's indignation against suffering is not suffering intrinsically, but the senselessness of suffering (*Genealogy*, II, 7). Similarly, "Man's problem is not suffering itself," but the lack of answer to the crying question "why do I suffer?" (*Genealogy*, III, 28). He certainly demonstrated a knack for reversing of perspectives, in describing how illness granted him freedom from abrupt changes, encouraged forgetting painful memories, and living at an easy relaxed pace. It saved him from bookishness and philology, forcing him to listen to his own voice and think. The period of sickness was a period of happiness, a return to himself and to creativity (*Ecce*, Human, 4). Illness enabled him to appreciate health, which is often taken for granted. It was an energizing self-restorative power that motivated him to live and create. Sickness increased his enjoyment of small things; and most importantly, with the instinct for self-healing, it cured him of his discouragement and philosophy of pessimism (*Ecce*, Preface, 2). The sage sees everything, and especially things like pain, which cannot be changed, as advantageous, as a blessing. Nietzsche described personal providence in the midst of "the beautiful chaos of existence," and how the playful chance sometimes leads to beautiful unexpected places, that we could not have found on our own. With a positive mindset, the sage believes that everything eventually works out for the best. Providence, however, needs our help in interpreting and rearranging events in a way that would benefit us (*Gay*, IV, 277).

The Benefits of Suffering

Not only is sickness an inherent part of life, it is often a beneficial one. Nietzsche found that the most brilliant parts of his writings co-occurred with bodily weakness and suffering (*Ecce*, Wise, 1). He felt that failures, anxieties, deprivations and mistakes, were necessary for him, just as their opposites "the path to one's own heaven always leads through the voluptuousness of one's own hell" (*Gay*, IV, 338). Those who cannot endure their suffering and try desperately to eliminate it, encourage neglectfulness remissness, and by their efforts rule out happiness "For happiness and misfortune are brother and sister, who grow tall together, or, as with you, remain small together" (*Gay*, IV, 338). The two, health and illness, cannot be separated; the ability to tolerate sickness defines health; and illness is a trigger for a new learning "as an instrument and fishhook of knowledge" (*Human*, Preface, 4). Pain is an important survival supporting signal, and hurt, conditions people to avoid dangers and protect themselves "some storm is approaching, and we do well to 'catch' as little wind as possible" (*Gay*, IV, 318). Moreover, "illness may even act as a powerful stimulus to life, to an abundance of life," exemplified by

Nietzsche, who after a prolonged sickness, rediscovered life, enjoyed it even more, and transformed his suffering into his new philosophy (*Ecce*, Wise, 2).

Nietzsche rejected the conception of suffering as an argument against existence, and pointed out that there were ages in which people tolerated suffering "and saw in it an enchantment of the first order, a genuine seduction to life. Perhaps in those days [...] pain did not hurt as much as it does now" (*Genealogy*, II, 7). Furthermore, for healthy people, "being sick can even become an energetic stimulus for life, for living more." His long period of sickness seemed to him "as it were, I discovered life anew, including myself; I tasted all good and even little things, as others cannot easily taste them. I turned my will to health, to life, into a philosophy" (*Ecce*, Wise, 2). Nietzsche felt that he owed his philosophy and the idea of *Amor fati*, to a higher kind of health, to his prolonged illness "It is great pain only which is the ultimate emancipator of the spirit." Pain teaches a strong suspicion which enables seeing things from different perspectives, seeing them as different from what they seem to be. A great torturing long pain "compels us, philosophers, to descend into our ultimate depths, and divest ourselves of all trust, all good-nature, veiling, gentleness, and mediocrity" (*Gay*, Preface to 2nd edition, 3).

Having to live with pain and suffering, Nietzsche tried not only to persevere, but to turn it into a great suffering, thus turning a constraint into an opportunity, and the list of advantages is telling: "Prophetic human beings are afflicted with a great deal of suffering [...] it is their pain that makes them prophets" (*Gay*, III, 316). Pain and sickness do not necessarily make people any better, but they do make them deeper, and without them the great suspicion which liberates the spirit and a philosophical examination of life will probably be lost "Only great pain is the ultimate liberator of the spirit" (*Gay*, Preface to the 2nd Edition, 3). Persons who experienced severe suffering become ones who know much about a terrifying world, about which others have no clue "Deep suffering makes noble; it separates" (*Contra*, The Psychologist Speaks Up, 3). The ability to discover happiness in the midst of "weariness, in the old illness, in the convalescent's relapses," is a sign of the free spirit, who can remain grateful, see the bright side of things and furthermore, after some periods of sickness get cured of pessimism (*Human*, Preface, 5).

Suffering well, is a suffering that motivates, arouses appreciation and not pity "I love him whose soul is deep even in the wounding, and whom a little thing can ruin: thus he gladly goes across the bridge" (*Zarathustra*, Prologue, 4). Suffering and illness lead to deep solitude and release from habits and duties, which aid the search for knowledge "The man who suffers severely looks forth with terrible calmness from his state of suffering upon outside things: all those little lying enchantments, by which things are usually surrounded when seen through the eye of a healthy person, have vanished from the sufferer" (*Daybreak*, II, 114).

Digesting and Forgetting

When Nietzsche wrote in his notebook "Kant says: 'Two things remain forever worthy of reverence [the starry heaven and the moral law]' — today we should sooner say: 'Digestion is more venerable'" (*Will*, 331), he used digestion as a metaphor for the critical function of assimilating life's experiences. He had this meaning in mind when he bade his readers "Good teeth and a digestion good; I wish you — these you need, be sure!" (*Gay*, Prelude in Rhymes, 54). An ability to digest one's experiences, positive and negative alike "just as he digests his meats, even when he has some tough morsels to swallow," is a sign of strength and health (*Genealogy*, III, 16). In a letter to Franz Overbeck from December 25, 1882, Nietzsche wrote, "The last morsel of life was the hardest I have yet had to chew, and it is still possible that I choke on it. I have suffered from the humiliating and tormenting memories of this summer as from a bout of madness."[135]

Psychological indigestion is a major problem of modern culture, in which people are imploded with an overload of disintegrated and unassimilated information and changing fashions (*Will*, I, 71). Digestion is a metaphor of the minds' way of operation, aiming at mastery. It acts like a stomach, digesting the external world and assimilating it into existing schemes; and like a stomach, it can in certain cases prefer ignorance, refusing to digest what seems unfavorable to it (*Beyond*, VII, 230). Hence, mental suffering is not due to a person's soul, but to a person's stomach, a weak digestive system (*Genealogy*, III, 16). Individuals can avoid and overcome suffering with the help of an active process of selection, setting limits, assimilation and forgetting. Forgetting, that is usually conceived as undesirable and automatic, is considered by Nietzsche as desirable, serving health, and leaving room for the important functions of self-directing and planning "if forgetfulness were not present, there could be no happiness, no cheerfulness, no hoping, no pride, no present" (*Genealogy*, II, 1). The feeling of remorse, guilt and the accompanying rehashing of past events is a form of decadence "This reopening of old wounds, this wallowing in self-contempt and contrition, is one more illness, out of which no 'salvation of the soul' can arise but only a new form of soul sickness." In such cases, when these negative feelings hinder recovery "one must try counterbalancing it all by new activities, in order to escape from the sickness of self-torture as quickly as possible" (*Will*, II, 233).

Individuals and cultures need a plastic force, or resilience, to enable growth in different directions and "reshaping and incorporating the past and the foreign, of healing wounds, compensating for what has been lost, rebuilding shattered forms out of one's self." Human beings have to digest the new unfamiliar stimuli impinging on them, but they must also deal with "the large and ever-increasing burden of the past, which pushes them down or bows them over." The dark heavy burden of the past, invisible to others, slows them down, removing them from the children's "blissful blindness between the fences of the past and future." The words "It was," brings with it suffering, struggles and weariness, turning human existence into "a never completed past tense." Thus, being happy and making others happy, is possible, when a plastic force exists, mainly through forgetting, seeing things un-historically, and living in the present. Forgetting is an essential condition for having trust in one's capabilities and effective action. Without forgetting, the past becomes "the gravedigger of the present." However, both remembering and forgetting are needed, and one must be wise, a sage, with a clear horizon, to know which of them to choose at a given situation "for the health of a single individual, a people, and a culture the unhistorical and the historical are equally essential." A person's horizons enable a constructive use of the past, drawing from the roots, taking advantage of one's personal, familial and cultural history; absorbing and transforming the past for one's benefit (*Untimely*, history, 1).

Nietzsche hypothesized that behavioral and cognitive means are two different and contradictory ways of coping with trauma "When we are assailed by an ill we can dispose of it either by getting rid of its cause or by changing the effect it produces on our sensibilities: that is to say by reinterpreting the ill into a good whose good effects will perhaps be perceptible only later." He went on to explain that metaphysical philosophy, art, and religion, do not try to change the causes of suffering, but rather change people's understanding and attitudes, actually effecting "momentary amelioration and narcoticizing." This investment precludes attempts to change the reasons for suffering and doing away with it (*Human*, III, 108). In the case of past trauma, however, when things cannot be undone, neither be forgotten, behavior, and especially avoiding situations and conditions associated with it, will be the wrong step to take, and acceptance the preferred option to pursue.

The Way of the Warrior

The metaphors of war and warrior can be found in many domains, among them business, sports, public policy, health and religion. Life can be conceived as a war, and indeed, one American hardcore punk band is called *Modern Life Is War*. Lawyers fight against injustice, politicians fight against inequality, physicians fight against diseases, teachers fight against ignorance, not to mention firefighters. The fighting metaphor plays a role in the conduct of life. A sick person, we believe, is fighting to stay alive, and a depressed person feels defeated, losing the fighting spirit. Unlike war (for or against someone or something), warriors are not defined by whom they fight, but rather by how they do it, by their traits and behaviors. A warrior, such as a Samurai, stands for tradition, determination, resourcefulness, bravery, sacrifice, strength and loyalty.

War is a metaphor that must be used judiciously, as everything else is liable to become secondary to winning: it can arouse hate of the enemy, neglect of other issues and concerns, and overriding of ethical considerations "everything is fair in love and war." On the other hand, it is a fruitful metaphor which suggests ways and means to cope with adverse life conditions: guerrilla warfare rather than a frontal onslaught, information gathering, deception and surprise attacks. Nietzsche's use of the hero-warrior-soldier images stemmed from his knowledge and love of the Hellenic ancient culture, which adored heroism, and life of combat and victory, as described in his early essay *Homer's Contest.* He identified with Odysseus and was a devotee of Heraclitus, who taught that everything is strife and endless contest (*Agon*). His service in the army, as a young man, who was still a Prussian patriot with a love of discipline, sword and uniform, must have contributed to his self-image as a soldier.

A Soldier and Warrior

Nietzsche did not wish to eradicate suffering nor fight against it. His challenge was endurance, living to the best of his ability, with suffering, pain and sickness, without surrendering to them. He wanted to be a hero, a person who is "Going out to meet at the same time one's highest suffering and one's highest hope" (*Gay,* III, 268). Heroism is thus, overcoming resistance and going on with one's life's mission. He described how he had to be hard, push himself out of bed, take a walk in the snow-capped mountains, and sit down later to write, despite terrible eye-strain. This was a way to reach freedom, not by release from pain, but by overcoming it. Fighting to survive without losing ground, was a lesson he learned "Out of life's school of war: What does not destroy me, makes me stronger" (*Twilight,* Maxims, 8). In the same spirit he declared that war is the profound persons' great wisdom "through a wound the spirits increase, and vigor grows" (*Twilight,* Preface), and he recommended accordingly "In times of painful tension and vulnerability, choose war: it hardens, it produces muscles" (*Will,* IV, 1040).

Nietzsche wrote to his friend Heinrich Köselitz (April 6, 1883) "You would not believe, dear friend, what an abundance of suffering life has unloaded upon me, at all times, from *early* childhood on. But I am a soldier—and this soldier, in the end, did become the father of Zarathustra!" He declared in his autobiography "At heart I am a warrior. Attacking belongs to my instincts," and he added that such strong natures need "the pathos of aggression," overcoming resistance in order to thrive (*Ecce*, Wise, 7). I will dwell now, on some aspects of the warrior image: training, discipline, bodily fitness and hardness; love of confrontation, a goal dearer than life, and an ability to command and obey.

Respecting the Body

Nietzsche advocated staying in a good physical shape "My most creative moments were always accompanied by unusual muscular activity. The body is inspired: let us waive the question of the 'soul'" (*Ecce*, Thus) and also "Remain seated as little as possible; trust no thought that is not born in the open, to the accompaniment of free bodily motion nor one in which your very muscles do not celebrate a feast" (*Ecce*, Clever, 1). Incidentally, Nietzsche's recommendation was confirmed almost 130 years later, in a large medical study that found that too much sitting is linked to heart disease, diabetes, and premature death.[136] Nothing much can be accomplished without proper care "the right place is the body, the gesture, the diet, physiology; the rest follows from that" (*Twilight*, Skirmishes, 47). Life habits, proper diet, rest, and fresh air are important "To counter any kind of affliction or distress of soul one ought in the first instance to try a change of diet and hard physical labor" (*Daybreak*, IV, 269). The body must be studied, and one must know even "the size of one's stomach," in order to preserve mental functioning and creativity (*Ecce*, Clever).

In order to stay fit, people must take into consideration their special needs and characteristics "Each one has his own standard, often between the narrowest and most delicate limits" (*Ecce*, Clever, 1). Nietzsche highlighted the importance of proper nutrition "All prejudices may be traced back to the intestines" (*Ecce*, Clever, 1). He also mentioned the importance of the adequate place of residing "None of us can live anywhere" (*Ecce*, Clever, 2) and of recuperation after a stressful effort, by means reading, listening to music and enjoying intimacy (*Ecce*, Clever, 3). The voice of the healthy body is honest and pure and "it speaks of the meaning of the earth" (*Zarathustra*, I, The afterworld). Zarathustra asked us to listen to this voice and liberate ourselves from inhibitions set upon sensuality, lust for power, and selfishness "these three have hitherto been the best cursed, worst slanted and slandered, — these three I will weigh in a humanly good way" (*Zarathustra*, III, The three evils, 1).

Instincts and Training

Warriors and other noble types, listen to their instincts and behave like an animal risking its life to protect its young, or an animal following a female in heat, without thinking about danger or death. Being blind to our instincts, we seek moderation in pleasures, but miss intensity "that pleasure of the rider on a fiery steed!" (*Gay*, IV, 870). I hope that my readers will close their eyes for a moment, imagine this beautiful and inspiring image, and let it sink in. Nietzsche commended daring and adopting "the life of wild animals, for the forests, caves, steep mountains, and labyrinths" *(Zarathustra,* IV, Science). A warrior is trained to respond swiftly with pre-rehearsed routines, without too much deliberation "We must in fact seek the perfect life where it has become least conscious (i.e. least aware of its logic, its reasons, its means and intentions, its utility) the demand for a virtue that reasons is not reasonable" (*Will*, II, 439).

The will must be continuously trained in order to respond appropriately, and in order to maintain a joyful sense of self-mastery "Every day on which we have not at least once denied ourselves some small thing is turned to bad use and a danger to the next day" (*Human*, Wanderer, 305). An experience and a perception of commanding and obeying is established by such training "one is a cause oneself, only when one knows that one has performed an act of will" (*Will*, II, 136). Habits are built through training, but it is important to leave room for spontaneity, thus "I love brief habits" (*Gay*, IV, 295). In order to maintain a sense of efficacy, it is also important not to demand what cannot be guaranteed to happen (*Beyond*, I, 19). A soldier must be prepared to persevere under harsh conditions. Discipline is translated into routines, which are typical of barracks living, like habits of posture, cold showers and daily physical exercises. Sermons on morality are not needed to create strong and hard persons "But to *create conditions that require stronger men* who for their part need, and consequently will have, a morality (in other words, a physical-spiritual discipline) *that makes them strong*" (*Will*, IV, 981). Strength necessitates being hard and the rejection of softness, pity and self-pity "This new law-table do I put over you, O my brothers: Become hard!" (*Will*, I, 231).

Confrontation and Opposition

Nietzsche saw himself, as one of the "opposite men," persons who realize that opposition encourages human development. The higher the danger and pressure one is exposed to, the more powerful, inventive and resourceful will the person be, acquiring "stoicism, the art of the tempter and devilry of every kind, that everything evil, terrible, tyrannical, like beasts of prey and snake-like in man" (*Genealogy*, II, 44). For such opposite persons, pain and suffering constitute a resistance that must be overcome "I assess the power of a will by how much resistance, pain, and torture it endures and knows how to turn to its advantage" (*Will*, II, 382). This is also a measure of their freedom "The highest type of free man must be sought where the highest resistance is constantly overcome: five steps away from tyranny, close to the threshold of the danger of servitude" (*Twilight*, Skirmishes, 38). The courageous warrior, who is willing to take risks, cares about higher goals than self-survival and happiness (*Gay*, III, 268). Having a mission and goal in life, makes it easier to fight "If we have our own why of life, we shall get along with almost any how. Man does not strive for happiness; only the Englishman does" (*Twilight*, Maxims, 12).

Russian Fatalism

A warrior, keeps on fighting and does not lose hope, which is the most powerful stimulant to life "Man must be sustained in suffering by a hope so high that no conflict with actuality can dash it—so high, indeed, that no fulfillment can satisfy it: a hope reaching out beyond this world" (*Antichrist*, 23). Yet, sometimes it is advisable to dance rather than fight, and one must choose wisely between the two paths "How poisonous, how crafty, how bad, every long war makes one, which cannot be waged openly by means of force!" (*Beyond*, Chapter II, 25). We should also avoid "The Appearance of Heroism—throwing ourselves in the midst of our enemies may be a sign of cowardice" (*Daybreak*, IV, 299). Using the dancer metaphor, rather than the warrior, is suitable especially when lightness, flexibility, spontaneity and lack of seriousness are called for.

Sometimes, though, inactivity, which is inexpensive and even enjoyable, is the best treatment for sicknesses of the soul (*Human*, Assorted, 361). The same warrior metaphor can be used, not only to fight and resist, but also for letting go in the manner of "Russian fatalism." Instead of feeling helplessness and resentment, it is preferable to adopt the stance of "the Russian soldier, when a campaign becomes unbearable, finally lies down in the snow." This is also the way of the fakir; and hibernation, rather than continuing fighting in vain, reduces activity, saves energy, supports survival, and in the worst case, accepts death. Nietzsche described how he used "Russian fatalism" to survive unbearable situations, rather than give them his attention, try to change them, and blame himself for failing "To accept one's situation as destiny, not to wish one's self 'different'—this in such circumstances is sagacity itself" (*Ecce*, Wise, 6).

♦

We should be mindful of the limitations of the "school of war." In the midst of painful conditions, when suffering is unavoidable, the warrior takes over, and endurance becomes the goal. The warrior metaphor is beneficial in encouraging mental and physical fitness, recommending rehearsal and preparation in advance. Staying fit necessitates overcoming resistance, and it is reasonable that people, who exercised their determination a few times a week, will later cope better with pain and recuperate faster. However, endurance is possible with manageable intensities of pain, beyond which, a breakdown is unavoidable. In such cases, and when pain comes in waves time after time, serene acceptance is almost inconceivable and fighting is futile. The war rhetoric of being brave, not giving in, maintaining hopes, and going on "one day at a time," is usually conjured at times of anguish. It is used by people to prep themselves up, or to encourage others undergoing a tough condition. After the death of a person, who was sick for a while, it is usually said that she fought for her life until the very end.

Apparently, such phrases are comforting and express good intentions, but it is still an open question what fighting for life entailed and how those who were seen as fighting, differed from those who were not. It is quite possible, that what decided our interpretation was the independent progress of the disease: if she made it to her granddaughter's birth we say that she fought; if he died a few days earlier, we say that his spirit was broken and he did not fight hard enough. Do we really get stronger, when advised to be strong? Or perhaps, in some crisis situations, unexpected resources are found, and then are attributed to strength and bravery.

The Way of the Creator

Zarathustra dedicated entire discourses to the warrior and to the creator. Creators are persons with a ruling idea, who understands that "the question is not free from what, but free for what," ones who determine their own values; who are their own rule-makers, judges and punishers *(Zarathustra,* I, The way of the creator). They transform their suffering into pieces of art; like God they create the world in their own image "you want to create yourself a god from your seven devils, and like God they can create as well as destroy." Adopting a cause, involves painful concessions and giving up other interests "no one can spend more than he has" (*Twilight,* Germans, 4). They must be dedicated, in Zarathustra's words, "I love him who does not hold back one drop of spirit for himself" *(Zarathustra,* Prologue, 4) and "Ready must you be to burn yourself in your own flame; how could you become new if you have not first become ashes!" *(Zarathustra,* I, The way of the creator). Living with a mission is a mark of greatness, and Nietzsche's answer to the question of human greatness was "I always see only the actor of his own ideal" (*Beyond,* IV, 97). Being a creator, one who has a mission in life, one who has a significant project to accomplish, be in science, politics, business or art, is the individual's answer to the question "why I am here." It is the person's justification for existence and establishing a purpose, a high and noble goal "To this end" (*Untimely*, History, 9).

The creator, like a warrior, needs discipline, which entails limiting horizons and narrowing of perspectives "stupidity is a condition of life and development." All significant achievements were made possible by a prolonged obedience to an idea and a mentor (*Beyond*, V, 188). All significant contributions which make it "worthwhile to live on earth," in the fields of virtuousness, thought, art, music, dance, and war, require the ability to command and obey oneself over "a long period of time and in a single direction" (*Beyond*, II, 188). Creating is a demanding activity, which requires self-tyrannizing (*Philologists*, 6), being on guard against the waste of time and disturbances (*Zarathustra*, IV, The higher man). Creators, like warriors, should not hold on to happiness, knowing that the few moments of bliss are the result of their activity and overcoming resistance (*Philologists*, 181). Like warriors, who are always ready for the next war, creators do not seek satisfaction in the present, but aim to advance their creation "Existence really is an imperfect tense that never becomes a present" (*Untimely*, History, 1). The work of creation is bigger than themselves "A vocation is the backbone of life" (*Human*, IX, 575) and "He who has a why to live can bear almost any how" (*Twilight*, Maxims, 12). In other words, although creators suffer like anyone else, they have something more important than themselves. Hence, their pain is moved to the background and their creation is positioned in the front of the stage.

The Poets of our Lives

The highest wisdom of acceptance, love of fate, reversing perspectives and reframing, supplied the first answer to the question of how is it possible to go on living with debilitating pain and suffering. The school of war's second answer taught us how to confront them bravely like a warrior. Creation is the third answer, a way of going beyond this sorry reality by investing ourselves in artistic-aesthetic activity, and by this very creative activity, transform life into a piece of art "Without art we would be nothing but foreground and live entirely in the spell of that perspective which makes what is closest at hand and most vulgar appear as if it were vast, and reality itself" (*Gay*, II, 78). Art is the justification of life "Without music, life would be an error" (*Twilight*, Maxims, 33) and "Art is the fundamental metaphysical activity of Man; art is the highest form of human activity" (*Birth*, Preface). This is the heart of the ancient Greek culture, which invented Olympian gods and goddesses to make the world more beautiful and interesting. The sublime is "the artistic taming of the horrible" (*Birth*, 60). Thus, art is a veil that covers a harsh reality, an idea which appears also in Nietzsche's notes "Truth is ugly: *we possess art* lest we perish of the truth" (*Will*, III, 22).

Zarathustra taught that the answer to suffering is creation "Creation—that is the great redemption from suffering and life's growing light. But that the creator may be, suffering is needed and much change. Indeed, there must be much bitter dying in your life, you creators" *(Zarathustra,* II, in the happy isles). The child is the third metamorphosis, or stage, preceded by the other needed conditions of the camel (endurance and bearing) and lion (courage). The child is the paragon of the creator, and it is necessary to regain its spirit in order to create "The child is innocence and forgetting, a new beginning, a game, a self-propelled wheel, a first movement, a sacred 'Yes'" *(Zarathustra,* I, On the three metamorphoses).

When pain becomes a salient feature of our life, art can help us make sense of it. Nietzsche suggests that if we want to be "the poets of our lives," we should learn from artists, how to turn ugly, repulsive and undesired things into their opposite of the beautiful, attractive and desirable, by changing perspectives, distancing and framing (*Gay*, IV, 299). Thus, the creator and the sage join hands, as finding a productive interpretation is actually an artistic activity. When we suffer, art makes it possible to continue living, giving us a break to recuperate "preventing the bow from snapping." It makes the inconceivable human reality simpler, offering solutions to the riddles of life (*Untimely*, Wagner, 4).

A Will to Appearance

Art is a child of the Dionysian "with its primordial joy experienced even in pain, is the common source of music and tragic myth" (*Birth*, 24), and of the Apollonian, the "primordial pleasure of mere appearance," giving birth to beauty "just as roses burst from thorny bushes." Nietzsche felt "ultimate gratitude to art" calling it "cult of the untrue" and "the good will to appearance" (*Birth*, 49). It is this will to appearance, which helped David Bowie, with his last album *Blackstar*, turn his illness and approaching death into a piece of art. With this will, we can play a part, pretend that nothing is wrong with us, avoid the pity of others and feel a little better for having the show go on. Art gives us a possibility of choice in situations that do not depend on us "this triumphant state is what the tragic artist chooses, what he glorifies." (*Twilight*, Skirmishes, 24). Art offers consolation by its power of illusion "when I could not find what I *needed*, I had to gain it by force artificially, to counterfeit it or create it poetically" (*Human*, Preface, 1). Art can redeem illness and suffering by turning an unfortunate person into a heroic tragic figure, living in a "states in which suffering is willed, transfigured, deified, where suffering is a form of great delight" (*Will*, III, 853, 2).

Tragicomedy

Life and suffering can be seen as lamentable or as amusing, and sometimes the two can co-exist. In ancient Greece, tragedies had the role of giving "metaphysical solace," having the spectators feel "that despite every phenomenal change, life is at bottom indestructibly joyful and powerful" (*Birth*, 7) and again "we may see the artistic buoyancy and creative joy as a luminous cloud shape reflected upon the dark surface of a lake of sorrow" (*Birth*, 9). Nietzsche described the power of art, to offer solace in dealing with hardships, already in his early, unpublished essay *The Greek State*, in which he argued that art enables life under the harshest conditions and offered an escape from the snare of "practical pessimism." This medicine, he found, can only work for those who "can emerge from this horrifying struggle for existence," people who are also "preoccupied with the fine illusions of artistic culture" (*Greek*).

Humor is a creative act, a form of art, which looks at things from a different unexpected perspective. Humans invented laughter as a response to their deep suffering "The unhappiest and most melancholy animal is as fitting, the most cheerful" (*Will*, I, 91). Rather than sink into suffering we should take a rest from ourselves "by looking down upon, ourselves and, from an artistic distance, laughing over ourselves or weeping over ourselves. We must discover the hero no less than the fool in our passion for knowledge; we must occasionally find pleasure in our folly, or we cannot continue to find pleasure in our wisdom" (*Gay*, II, 107).

Aesthetic considerations can be our guiding principle in coping with pain, making us ask if the way we cope is beautiful and graceful, or not. Making something beautiful or seeing it as such, is again a human quality, implying a choice, and one can carry her burden in an inspiring uplifting manner, or in an unworthy demoralizing one "Physiologically, everything ugly weakens and saddens man. It reminds him of decay, danger, impotence; it actually deprives him of strength." The way persons cope with pain, sickness and anticipated death, impact their own feelings and the feelings of others, their Will to Power, courage and pride, "all fall with the ugly and rise with the beautiful" (*Twilight*, Skirmishes, 20).

♦

We must be realistic and admit that art is not a solution for everyone, it is not a fast cure, and it does not guarantee health, happiness or release from pain. And yet, "the slow arrow of beauty" offers something intangible, a longing, a wish to do something with one's pain and life, the satisfaction of shaping, at least what is up to us, in our own style. Nietzsche described this sad beauty as noble and serene, one that develops slowly and is found in our hearts "What do we long for when we see beauty? To be beautiful" (*Human*, IV,

149). One of the most moving examples of such moments is the traditional *Jisei* the short death poems written by samurai and sages upon their death in Japan.[137]Another inspiring achievement is *The Diving Bell and the Butterfly,* Jean-Dominique Bauby's memoir of life after a massive stroke that left him with locked-in syndrome.[138]

The attribution of creativity to a successful coping with pain (*Will,* II, 382), is open to other interpretations, namely, that the ability to endure, existed already before the tribulations took place, and that it is this trait and not the suffering that correlates with creativity. It is arguable that if a person is not creative, pain and suffering will not change much; if she is, she might have managed to create in any case. It should not be forgotten that the discovery and production of fleeting moments of beauty, and the enjoyment of non-materialistic aesthetic experiences necessitate a release from economic hardship and worries, and an upbringing and culture that encouraged this aspect in life.

Post-Traumatic Growth

We saw (Chapter 3) that the responses to trauma, are neither permanent, nor universal, and that they kept changing in different periods of history. In other words, the societal expectations, and especially those of the mental health caretakers, tend to be internalized and fulfilled. Just for this reason, the idea of post-traumatic growth (PTG) is welcomed. PTG does not cancel the negative psychological consequences of trauma, but rather can coexist with it.[139] In the last two decades, reports of experiencing growth following trauma, are more common than reports of psychiatric disorders.[140] Such reports come from people who experienced bereavement, life endangering medical condition, severe accidents, assault and injury.[141] People have an implicit (human beings are basically good or evil) and explicit (such as religion or political affiliation) map of the world, a global belief system, which guides their decisions and helps them interpret what transpires in life. When disasters, personal and collective hit suddenly and without any preparation, the belief systems are shaken or crumbled, and the world cannot be experienced anymore as good, safe and predictable. Usually, but not always, people resort then to a search for meaning, an attempt to make sense of the traumatic event and maintain or design a map of the world in tune with the new reality. This search is adaptive when it achieves some resolution, quite early in the process. When the trauma is perceived as very unfair, the resolution is more difficult to achieve, and the repeated attempts and failures to do so, increase the person's distress.[142]

Richard Tedeschi and Lawrence Calhoun proposed a model of post-traumatic growth, based on interviews with trauma survivors who reported desirable changes in five domains: improved relationships, new possibilities for one's life, a greater appreciation for life, a greater sense of personal strength and spiritual development. These achievements did not preclude statements such as "I am more vulnerable, yet stronger." Actually, we should talk about post-coping growth as the gains described are the result, not of the trauma itself, but of grappling with it successfully "in coping with the losses and rebuilding their lives, some individuals may unexpectedly arrive at a new level of meaning, a changed philosophical stance that represents a renewed and valued purpose, a redefined sense of self, and a changed relationship with the world."

A massive trauma upsets the victims' fundamental belief and value systems, schemes and goals, and their concept of their life and themselves. They experience then emotional distress, flashbacks, intrusive memories and involuntary ruminations which occur frequently in different situations. These can be construed as a prolonged attempt to cognitively process the events, trying to make sense and draw conclusions.[143] Wishing to reduce their emotional distress and gain support from close persons, survivors tend to disclose their pain, in talking, praying, and writing, such as in a diary or other literary forms. This continuous process eventually enables the creation of new schema, perspectives and narratives, the building blocks of the post-traumatic growth. From a different perspective, the cognitive engagement can be conceptualized as an intrinsic motivational drive towards authenticity or consistency. Traumatized persons effect changes in their worldview to accommodate their hurt and loss, thus reaching a new meaning and significance.[144]

In a study, incorporating in its title a quote from Nietzsche *whatever does not kill us,* the effect of adverse life events on mental health was examined with a large sample of trauma survivors, who were interviewed during four years. The results confirmed that indeed such past events can foster adaptability, resilience, and feelings of well-being, only if the events were significant enough, were not too prolonged or severe, and permitted coping. Lower levels of adversary had no impact, and higher ones were associated with impairment, post-traumatic stress symptoms and lower life satisfaction. Persons with a prior positive coping with trauma, fare better in a later trauma, compared with those who did not have such an experience.[145]

♦

The concept of PTG can be criticized for being "an appealing but poorly understood construct." On one hand, it is based on accepting statements of interviewees as reflecting real practical behavioral changes, while in fact they can be only post-trauma "cognitive maneuvers." On the other hand, it disregards the more significant variable of resilience, of which PTG is only one possible component. It is questionable whether PTG can occur without a resilient return to the pre-trauma level of functioning.[146]

Nietzsche saw himself as a doctor of the soul and his own patient as well (*Human*, Assortment, Preface, 5). If the Hippocratic dictum proclaimed "To cure sometimes, to relieve often, to comfort always," his medicine for suffering substituted cure with understanding and interpreting, relief with fighting and persevering, and comfort with artistic creation and appreciation. His approach can be seen as a forerunner of PTG, although the literature dealing with this topic, besides quoting one line of his, does not recognize his contribution.

Nietzsche reminds us that there is no universal remedy for pain and that the means chosen must suit the person "One temperament finds it useful to be able to give vent to its disgust in words, being made sweeter by speech. Another reaches its full bitterness only by speaking out" (*Human*, Assorted, 44). People can be sages, warriors and artists combined or emphasize one role according to temperament and circumstances. However, both PTG and Nietzsche's teachings are not for everyone, as it takes some mental strength, and an ability to distance one's self from an aching body and an agonized soul, to see the whole picture, to think about the meaning of pain, rather than yell, cry or curse. While the PTG literature sees self-reports as an indication of growth, with no regard to the quality and originality of the intellectual product, Nietzsche considers only the minority of creators with outstanding achievements. He differentiated between the minority of individuals who treat their experiences, even the prosaic ones, in a way that makes them a "plot of ground that bears fruit three times a year," and the majority of individuals who "always stay lightly on the surface, like cork" on top of the currents of their life. The former "create a world out of nothing"; the latter "create nothing out of the world" (*Human*, IX, 627).

Nietzsche used, on three separate occasions, the metaphor of a tree, to express, what will be conceptualized later as PTG. He invited his readers to examine the lives of the best creative persons, and consider whether a tree could grow high without bad and stormy weather "misfortune and external resistance, some kinds of hatred, jealousy, stubbornness, mistrust, hardness, avarice, and violence." For a tree that can survive these conditions, they are ultimately necessary and favorable conditions for growth "The poison, of which weaker natures perish, strengthens the strong—nor do they call it poison" (*Gay*, I, 19). Zarathustra expressed the same idea "For a tree to become tall it must grow tough roots among the rocks" *(Zarathustra,* Virtue That Diminishes, 3). Nietzsche suggested again, contrary to what is usually assumed, that in order to grow and reach their highest talents, human plants need enormous dangerous "opposite conditions" to stimulate their spirit's power of will, refinement, audacity, and "power of invention and simulation."

However, Nietzsche the "opposite man," believed that trauma and pressures are not sufficient conditions for enhancement and growth, and that other resources such as talents, hardness, resilience (which he described as surviving "danger in the alley and the heart"), stoicism, life in hiding (being able to keep one's trauma a secret) and the art of experiment and delivery, are needed as well. He concluded his discussion, with a reference to serpents, which according to the reading offered here, symbolize his own hidden trauma "everything evil, terrible, tyrannical in man, everything in him that is kin to beasts of prey and serpents, serves the enhancement of the species 'man' as much as its opposite does" (*Beyond,* II, 44).

Chapter 10

THE THREE OVERCOMINGS

We have arrived at this book's last chapter, and it is time to log the path we have taken until now. Trauma, according to Charles Figley, is as an injury that may be physical or psychological, that involves the features of suddenness and lack of anticipation; violence, mutilation, and destruction; randomness; and lack of preventability."[147]I suggested that Nietzsche underwent a severe trauma and subsequently suffered from what is called now Post-Traumatic Stress Disorder. This trauma was rooted in a suffocating religious upbringing lacking in love, and most probably in being a victim of childhood sexual abuse. In the last chapter, I reviewed Nietzsche's approach to understanding and coping with mental suffering. The theory of posttraumatic growth implies that with the collapse of their initial assumptions about the self and the world, individuals attempt to make sense of what happened to them, tending to be "more likely to become cognitively engaged with fundamental existential questions about death and the purpose of life." This spiritual-existential quest occurs in the context of their culture and former belief systems, leading to changes in values and preferences, as well as changes in the religious, spiritual and existential components of their philosophies of life. Many survivors enter a process of self-questioning, attempting to find out why traumatic events happen, what does it say about the world and other people, what is the goal of their life now, and why continue to struggle. The new intellectual structure can accommodate the trauma, serves life better, and often turns out to be more satisfying, elucidating, and meaningful.[148]

The Search for Meaning

Nietzsche realized that the problem of humans "was *not* suffering itself, but that there was no answer to the crying question, '*why* do I suffer?'[...] the meaninglessness of suffering, *not* suffering itself, was the curse that lay over mankind so far—" (*Genealogy*, III, 28). His view was echoed by Viktor E. Frankl who wrote in *Man's Search For Meaning* "In some way, suffering ceases to be suffering at the moment it finds a meaning, such as the meaning of a sacrifice [...] that is why man is even ready to suffer, on the condition, to be sure, that his suffering has a meaning."[149] Lack of such meaning creates a suffocating void, opening the door to suicidal nihilism, thinking that since there is no meaning, reason or purpose to one's suffering, death is just as welcome (*Ge-*

nealogy, III, 28). When removing the cause of misfortune is not possible, people are left with overcoming it "by changing the effect it has on our feelings, by reinterpreting the misfortune as good, whose benefit may only later become clear" (*Human,* III, 108). They then have to choose between adopting a ready-made philosophy, as found in religions or doctrines such as Marxism, and creating their personal system of meaning. This choice, in the case of Christianity, is between "confession, the conjuring of souls, and forgiveness of sins" and a new sun, a new justice and a new watchword, which he urged his readers to find:

> Consider how every individual is affected by an overall philosophical justification of his way of living and thinking: he experiences it as the sun that shines especially for him and bestows warmth, blessings, and fertility on him; it makes him independent of praise and blame, self-sufficient, rich liberal with happiness and good will; incessantly it refashions evil into good, leads all energies to bloom and ripen, and does not permit the petty weeds of grief and chagrin to come up at all (*Gay,* IV, 289).

Nietzsche signed *Ecce Homo,* his autobiography, with the sentence "Have you understood me? Dionysus versus the Crucified" (*Ecce,* Fatality, 9). He returned to this motto in one of the last comments that were written in his notebooks, where he suggested that both types, Dionysus and the Crucified, are "The type of a spirit that takes into itself and *redeems* the contradictions and questionable aspects of existence!" Dionysus of the Greeks, however, stands for a religious affirmation of the whole life, without rejection and condemnation of sexuality and the worldly, with a tragic acceptance of life's destruction and torment. The meaning of their martyrdom is different: in Christianity, suffering is the path to holy existence; in the Dionysian-tragic approach, life is holy enough to justify even suffering "The god on the cross is a curse on life, a signpost to seek redemption from life; Dionysus cut to pieces is a *promise* of life: it will be eternally reborn and return again from destruction" (*Will,* IV, 1052).

The two figures represent two philosophies of life, two systems of meaning. One, including Christianity, morality, and asceticism, was ingrained in his culture and family and was installed in him from birth, by pious parents: his father was a pastor and son of a pastor, and his mother was a daughter of a pastor too. The other, following a traumatic juncture, emerged gradually in a protracted process, accompanied by grappling with many kinds of suffering (Chapter 8), wandering, solitary walks in nature, and extensive writing in books and personal notebooks. This outgrowth went side by side with the collapse of his old worldview, in the process of growing reservations, criticism, loss of faith, ultimately identifying himself as the anti-Christ, concluding his virtually last book with an exclamation which goes beyond rational criticism, revealing a personal hurt and pain:

> Wherever there are walls; I shall ascribe this eternal accusation against Christianity upon them—I can write in letters which make even the blind see… I call Christianity the one great curse, the one great intrinsic depravity, the one great instinct for revenge for which no expedient is sufficiently poisonous, secret, subterranean, petty—I call it the one immortal blemish of humankind… (*Antichrist*, 62).

As an adult, remembering his childhood, he wrote "God, the immortality of the soul, salvation, the beyond'—even as a child I had no time for such notions, I do not waste any time upon them—maybe I was never childish enough for that?" (*Ecce*, Clever, 1). The child's intuitions were put into words in 1862 when he was seventeen years old and free of the "yoke of habit and prejudice." He concluded then, in the essay *Fate and History*, that the central teachings of Christianity were discredited by historical research. His views were reinforced by reading David Strauss's *Life of Jesus*, and eventually, he gave up his faith, and in 1865 terminated his theology studies.[150] Perhaps, this was the moment when like many other moderns he killed God. There was a hefty price to pay for losing the spiritual ground "what were we doing when we unchained this earth from its sun? Where is it moving to now? Where are we moving to? Away from all suns? Are we not continually falling?" (*Gay*, III, 125). Before the "killing of God," Christianity instructed him how to live (love thine neighbor), gave him counsel about the fear of death (immortality of the soul) and offered a meaning to life (attaining salvation and heavenly bliss). What would be the answers now? Zarathustra conveyed Nietzsche's state of mind at this point "Here do I sit and wait, old broken tables around me and also new half-written tables. When comes mine hour?" (*Zarathustra*, III, Old and New Tables, 1). Because he was "Against meaninglessness, against value judgment" (*Will*, I, 4), he had to inscribe his new tables.

Sooner or later (and for some never), people ask themselves questions about the nature of the world, life, and the meaning or goal of their existence. They wonder what the right way to conduct their life is, why bad things happen to them, how to overcome despair and achieve happiness, and what will happen to them after they die. Often, the quest begins when they feel burdened with uncertainties, usually after the bankruptcy of an older belief system. They need to understand themselves and the world because the answers to these questions are necessary for the construction of a rudimentary map for life; and living without answers, that is to say, lacking a personal philosophy of life, is unsettling. Nietzsche's search began with the realizations that meaning does not exist in the world; it is we who create it; and that it cannot be judged in terms of truth or lie:

> There is only one world, and this is false, cruel, contradictory, seductive, without meaning—A world thus constituted is the real world. Living with this reality needs lying and invention of truths. Metaphysics, religion, morality, science are all faith and confidence enabling lies. The ability to so lie is based on the will to art, to lie, to flight from 'truth,' to the negation of 'truth' and the successful application of this art, the installation of belief in life is an exhilarating feeling and experience of mastery, 'What delight! What a feeling of power!' (*Will*, III, 853, 1).

Nietzsche's New Sun

The present chapter suggests that Nietzsche's meta-psychology, his triad of the themes of the Will to Power, the Eternal Recurrence, and the Superman, is his "new sun, a new justice and a new watchword" (*Gay*, IV, 289), the fruit of his intellectual engagement and coping with his trauma and suffering. It would be preposterous to claim a direct causal link between the two domains. Nietzsche would be the first to assert that we cannot know the reasons for our activities, and furthermore, there are always a plethora of reasons for everything we do, besides chance, temperament and talents. Thus, finding Schopenhauer's tomes in a used books store, and getting to know Wagner personally, significant events in his intellectual development, took place merely by chance. Besides, he was usually not a systematic, linear writer. He wrote about the same topics, on different occasions, in different styles, from different perspectives, and with different conclusions and implications. Hence, he invites different selections and interpretations, and not surprisingly, various commentators understand the triad differently. For this reason, no comprehensive and definitive treatment is possible, and these ideas can be perceived from a particular points of view only. I will examine, from the angle of Nietzsche's life, how these ideas grew out of his anguish, and how they were used as self-healing.

The decision to relate to this particular set of ideas, and not to others, is open to criticism. It can be shown that other themes, such as his cognitive, personality, social and moral psychologies are also part of his new psychology and philosophy, the opposite of *psychologica,* psychology serving particular ideologies and interests.[151] Nietzsche did not write about a unified triad of ideas, and yet, these three are his most famous concepts. Unlike the core of his psychological and psychotherapeutic work, the three central themes are much loftier and abstract, being actually a system of beliefs, in other words creative lies, which cannot be proven or disproven, a set of ideas, albeit with a practical ends in mind, as beliefs are something which helps us evaluate facts of life and directs our behavior. The three themes are interconnected, and do not stand separately alone; they are changing as they relate to each other as if they take part in a conversation. They connect human life, time and the universe; they constitute a composite, approachable from numerous perspectives and extending its arms in many directions: Nietzsche's psychology and psychotherapy, other themes in his oeuvre, his means of coping with suffering in particular, and other giants in the republic of geniuses (*Untimely*, History, IX), and unfortunately also some fiends in the republic of evil, who arrived after his demise.

From Trinity to Triad

Rather than offering objective easily accessible propositions, Zarathustra (representing Nietzsche) offered an esoteric teaching and his words are "subtle, remote things," that will not be understood by all people *(Zarathustra*, IV, The higher man, 5), aimed not to promote survival and happiness, but rather to enable the readers to understand their life's challenges in a new light. He felt that books, his included, are dangerous in the wrong hands, and he wrote for the select "very few" (*Gay*, IV, 381; *Human*, Assorted, 158). The triad of ideas is a response and an antithesis, to Christianity with its morality and asceticism, which he rejected, and it is tempting to speculate that it is a mirror image of the holy trinity. *Amor Dei* is forsaken in favor of *Amor fati*. Instead of God, we have the Will to Power, that is to say, life and self-emergence. Instead of Christ and the Son of man, we have Zarathustra and the Superman; the Holy Ghost, Resurrection, and the Second Advent are transformed into the Eternal Recurrence.

Do we have here a secular religion? Nietzsche himself was aware that he opened himself to such an interpretation, and his very denial in his autobiography begs the question "Yet for all that, there is nothing in me of a founder of religion—religions are affairs of the rabble" (*Ecce*, Destiny, 1). If the Will to Power and the Superman take the place of God and Christ, or if we become Gods ourselves, God, in this form or another, is still alive "All gods are dead; now we want the Superman to live" *(Zarathustra*, I, Bestowing of virtues, 3) and also "Once you said 'God' when you gazed upon distant seas; but now I have taught you to say 'superman'" *Zarathustra*, I, Happy Isles). In fact, after Zarathustra's declared "Away with *such* a God! Better to have no God, better to set up destiny on one's account, better to be a fool, better to be God oneself!" the old pope responded "O Zarathustra, you are more pious than you believe, with such an unbelief! Some God in you has converted you to your ungodliness" *(Zarathustra*, IV, Retired from service). Instead of establishing the Kingdom of God on Earth, Nietzsche suggested in the name of the Will to Power and the Superman, the creation of his millennium, which must come and remain "our great, remote human kingdom, the Zarathustra-kingdom of a thousand years" *(Zarathustra,* IV, The honey offering).

We concluded that Nietzsche himself is the type of the overcomer and survivor. Each element in the triad is closely tied with overcoming: overcoming helplessness and lack of control (the Will to Power), overcoming societal conventions and personal limitations (the Superman); and overcoming life's misfortunes and traumas (Eternal Recurrence). These ideas inspired the ways of overcoming trauma, the ways of the sage, the warrior and the creator, described in the previous chapter. They were founded upon Nietzsche's life and upon his answers to personal pain and suffering, as he declared in a statement, used as a motto of this book, "My writings speak only of my overcomings: 'I' am in them, together with everything that was hostile to me" (*Human,* Assorted, 1). These themes, as we saw (Chapter 8), were most emphatically expressed by Zarathustra in an emotionally loaded passage, moving from states of extreme elation, in which the idea of the Superman was born, to dejection, falling into the abyss, where the Eternal Recurrence was conceived. Nietzsche became the personification of these ideas: he stated that *Amor fati* was "the core of my nature" (*Ecce,* Contra Wagner, 4) and that he had a Will to Power "such as no man has ever possessed" (*Ecce,* Birth of Tragedy, 4). The three constructs are not only connected, they are one thing and they are a secret "To be sure, you call it will to procreate or impulse towards a goal, towards the higher, more distant, more manifold: but all this is one and one secret" *(Zarathustra,* II, Self over-coming).

Dionysian Holism

Religions, we saw, offer their answers to the question of meaning of life, in a one-size-fits-all format, but since "the death of God" they lost their grip on believers. Philosophers usually posit their solutions with a more systematic worldview. Nietzsche, however, thought that modern philosophy became irrelevant to life, and aspired, with his "will to art" to fill the void with his triad of ideas, at the same time knowing that these questions are not really answerable: we cannot conceive the world as it really is; nor can we understand ourselves. We all have our mirrors, in which we can see our interpretations of our sensations and experiences, or differently phrased our artistic creations. Nietzsche asked "And do you know what 'the world' is to me?" and the image he saw in his mirror can be understood in present-day terms of emergence and complexity, and it contained the three themes in a rudimentary form:

> A sea of forces flowing and rushing together, eternally changing, eternally flooding back, with tremendous years of recurrence, with an ebb and a flood of its forms; out of the simplest ways striving toward the most complex, out of the stillest, most rigid, coldest forms toward the hottest, most turbulent, most self-contradictory, and then again returning home to the simple out of this abundance, out of the play of contradictions back to the joy of concord (*Will*, IV, 1067).

The three themes, I suggested, share the common denominator of overcoming, and they can also be conceived as stemming from a common root. The above quote could be a perfect poetic epigraph for a book on the "big bang" cosmological model of the universe. Nietzsche held two complementing perspectives; one is psychological multiplicity according to which, things are not one solid unity as they seem to be, but rather an ensemble of multiple interacting or struggling units. The second is of nonduality, wholeness, interconnectedness, and unity, positing that things are not discrete and cannot be isolated from others. The first perspective was analytic and rational; the second was a revelation, deep conviction, a sudden understanding that mystics experience, and charlatans like to call "enlightenment." It is not knowledge based on objective observation, but "The world viewed from inside" (*Beyond*, II, 36). Nietzsche felt that the individual and the world are not discrete independent entities, but rather one thing; that life and death are one, and he wrote in his notes "If becoming is a great ring, then everything is equally valuable, eternal, necessary" (*Will*, II, 293). Nietzsche's conception of wholeness and the unity of opposites resonate with religious, pantheistic and mystical thinkers, who taught that reality and life are non-dual: there are "no two things," there is no separation between people and things, no separation between the self and the world. We are all one, and in other words, there is no room for a subject-object relationship.

The idea that the world is an integral whole appeared already in his *The Birth of Tragedy*, where Dionysus was the main protagonist "Nothing in existence should be excluded, nothing is dispensable" (*Ecce*, Birth, 2). The Dionysian is "the religious affirmation of life, life whole and not denied or in part" (*Will*, IV, 1050), and "the great pantheistic sharing of joy and sorrow that sanctifies and calls good even the most terrible and questionable qualities of life" (*Will*, IV, 1057). Thus, the three themes of the Nietzschean meta-psychology are interconnected as different faces of the whole: the Will to Power is one law about one world; Recurrence is the wholeness of time, the past, present, and future; the Superman is the one who encompasses the whole in one's self. He connected the idea of holism with joy and acceptance "All is redeemed and affirmed in the whole; Joy of perishing in life, part of the whole" (*Will*, IV,

1066). Zarathustra pronounced "Said you ever *Yes* to one joy? O my friends then said you *Yes* also to all woe. All things are enlinked, enlaced and enamored!" (*Zarathustra*, IV, The drunken song, 10), and he continued "Pain is also a joy, curse is also a blessing, night is also a sun—go away! Or you will learn that a sage is also a fool" (*Zarathustra*, IV, The drunken song, 10). Wishing for happy moments, one must accept all bad ones too. This kind of joy, wanting to repeat itself, loves eternity (*Zarathustra*, IV, The sleepwalker song, 10). The acceptance and the joy of wholeness and interconnectedness, the cardinal ingredient of Eternal Recurrence and *Amor fati*, are reflected in the notion of the unity of opposites and the ideal of the synthetic person.

Coincidentia Oppositorum

Everything is included in wholeness, life as well as death, statements as well as their opposites. In wholeness, contradictions disappear, and dualities disintegrate. The idea of unity of opposites was also derived from Nietzsche's analysis of language and morality "There are no opposites: only from those of logic do we derive the concept of the opposite—and falsely transfer it to things" (*Will*, III, 552). Nietzsche doubted "whether there are any opposites at all" and suggested that opposite values are "merely foreground estimates," that is to say, no more than one of many possible perspectives, one that is seen not from above, but from below, or as painters call it a "frog perspective" (*Beyond*, I, 2). Considering opposites as moral constructs, Nietzsche posited that "Between good and evil actions there is no difference in type; at most, a difference in degree." Good actions are a sublimated form of evil ones, and evil ones are distorted good actions (*Human*, II, 107).

The unity of contradictions is also the hallmark of personal merit: in his autobiography, Nietzsche described Zarathustra, and by implication the Superman and himself, as a unity of contradictions, integrating opposing forces, base as well as high powers "He contradicts with every word that he utters this most affirmative of all spirits. Through him, all contradictions are bound up into a new unity" (*Zarathustra*, Zarathustra, 6). Zarathustra described himself as "If I myself am a grain of that redemptive salt which ensures that all things in the mixing—jug are well mixed: for there is a salt that binds good to evil; and even the most evil is good for spicing and for the ultimate foaming over" (*Zarathustra*, III, The seven seals, 4). He contended that inability to understand "the necessity for the reverse side of things" is typical of mediocre minds. Such persons want to fight and eradicate evils, without realizing that they are an integral part of what they wish to preserve. Instead, he offered a different insight "that with every growth of man, his other side must grow too," and the higher a person, the higher is the ability to accept and express the "antithetical nature of existence." Commonplace persons live and show only a limited part of their drivers and cannot cope with the tension of a multiplicity of drives and conflicts, the very thing that makes the higher type the "synthetic person" stronger (*Will*, IV, 983).

The Will to Power

Zarathustra and Jesus saw everything in terms of one principle "All fundamentally one law, all consequences of one instinct" (*Antichrist*, 33), and what was love for Jesus, was power for Zarathustra. In this respect, Nietzsche was also close to Heraclitus, who presumably said *Panta rhei*, everything flows. In his psychology, Nietzsche taught that many factors and a significant portion of chance influence human behavior; in his meta-psychology, he offered a one explain-all tendency-principle-drive-instinct "All events that result from intention are reducible to the intention to increase power" (*Will*, III, 663). Nietzsche even went beyond meta-psychology to suggest "a unified theory of everything," according to which, everything in the universe flows, everything is part of a totality, with different and changing degrees of power; and that one principle, the Will, is intrinsic to all ranks and levels of organization in a hierarchy "The will to accumulate force is special to the phenomena of life, to nourishment, procreation, inheritance — to society, state, custom, authority. Should we not be permitted to assume this will as a motive cause in chemistry, too? — and in the cosmic order?" (*Will*, III, 663).

Nietzsche believed that psychology before him was constrained by moral prejudices and fears, and it did not dare to delve into the depth, "the morphology and doctrine of the development of the Will to Power" (*Beyond*, I, 23). A doctrine is "belief (or system of beliefs) accepted as authoritative by some group or school" (*Wordweb.com*), although in this case, the authority and the school are the same, those of Nietzsche. Morphology will ask how the will is established, what are its benefits and how can it be enhanced. He described the "Dionysian world of the eternally self-creating, the eternally self-destroying" as equal to the Will to Power "and nothing besides! And you yourselves are also this Will to Power—and nothing besides!" (*Will*, IV, 1067). In introducing this quote he emphasized that this is how the world seems to him, how it is reflected in his mirror, but in other formulations he relinquished this qualification "There is nothing to life that has value, except the degree of power, assuming that life itself is the Will to Power" (*Will*, I, 55). Using the voice of Zarathustra, he taught that life, truth, overcoming, freedom, responsibility and the Will are equal to each other (*Zarathustra*, II, *Self-overcoming*). Thus, he spoke about the Will in two voices: one recognizes that it is his subjective view, a "faith and confidence enabling lie" or "invented truth," a product of his "will to art" (*Will*, III, 853, 1); the other declaratory, a statement of a real fact; as if he forgot that it was his invention.

The Will is a primary universal quality of all humans and animals "people are willing to give up everything but power" (*Daybreak*, IV, 262). Nietzsche added facetiously that all animals, including the "philosophical animal," strive instinctively "for the optimal beneficial conditions in which it can let out all its power and attain the strongest feeling of its strength" (*Genealogy*, III, 7). All living creatures seek first of all to discharge their strength "life itself is Will to Power," and self-preservation is only one of its possible indirect results (*Beyond*, I, 13). Life and the living body are incarnated Will "it will strive to grow, spread, seize, become predominant." Hence, the Will is the accumulation of power (*Will*, III, 663), and the Will is the will to life (*Beyond*, VII, 259). The Will is an umbrella concept, as there is nothing that is not subservient to it: procreation, aspirations, and destruction "perishing and the falling of leaves, behold, there life sacrifices itself—for the sake of power." The will includes struggles, inner conflicts, death, decline, and loss. In short, the Will is behind every development which takes place, desirable as well as undesirable (*Genealogy*, II, 12). Nietzsche elaborated on the many faces of the Will throughout his writings, sometimes repeating the same arguments, as if wanting to convince us that it is a valid and beneficial idea. Let us examine now the Will in the life of individuals, as the leading force in creation, and its expression in society as a whole. We will complete the cycle by returning somehow to God.

The Demon of Will

Nietzsche conceived the Will as his psychology in a nutshell "Neither necessity nor desire, but the love of power is the demon of mankind." Humans are addicted to the feeling of power. Therefore pleasures and fulfillment of basic needs and even luxuries are not going to suffice, as long as the demon is not satisfied (*Daybreak*, IV, 262). The Will, our demon, specializes, or is manifested as a will to food, property, and tools; it is the will to master, and the will to serve; it is evident in the clash of wills, in the workings of the body and in the spiritual functions of willing to assimilate and shape reality (*Will*, III, 658). It is the central motivation, the "basic will of the spirit," which commands one's dealing with the self and the environment "It possesses the will from multiplicity to simplicity, a will which ties up, tames, desires to dominate, and truly does rule." It aims to grasp and organize the outside world in ways which encourage growth, a feeling of development and increased power (*Beyond*, VII, 230).

The Will is the need for truth, and living according to one's values (*Beyond*, VI, 211), it makes us examine our own lives, and it serves as the very standard for judging our achievements so far "A table of excellencies hangs over every people. Lo! It is the table of their triumphs; lo! It is the voice of their Will to

Power" *(Zarathustra,* I, Thousand and one goals). The Will is the criterion for making decisions, asking whether a contemplated action would increase or decrease our power and sense of power "Your will and your valuations have ye put on the river of becoming" *(Zarathustra,* II, Self-overcoming). In light of the rejection of the absolute morality of commandments, the Will becomes the criterion of what is genuine and right "the 'sense of truth' will have to legitimize itself before another tribunal—as a means of the preservation of man, as *Will to Power.*" Thus, the doctrine posits the Will as an outstanding universal force, and as a measure and standard of value of everything there is. The motif of overcoming, we saw, was central in Nietzsche's own life and became the common denominator of his metapsychology. The Will grows by many instances of overcoming, and life itself told Zarathustra its secret "I am that *which must overcome itself again and again*" *(Zarathustra,* II, Self-overcoming). Self-overcoming means a continuous process of self-creation and change, setting goals and attempting to attain them "Truly, I say to you: Unchanging good and evil does not exist! From out of themselves, they must overcome themselves again and again" *(Zarathustra,* II, Self-overcoming).

The Will to Create

Zarathustra taught his disciples "Willing liberates: for willing is creating: thus I teach. And you should learn only for creating!" *(Zarathustra,* II, Blessed Isles), and Nietzsche wrote in his notes that "our love of the beautiful: it also is our shaping will." The Will is the will to create, to design the self and one's world "To impose upon becoming the character of being—that is the supreme Will to Power" and the process of becoming demands perseverance, invention, effort, courage, and patience (*Will,* III, 617). We cannot do otherwise because of "the joy in shaping and reshaping—a primeval joy! We can comprehend only a world that we have made" (*Will,* III, 495). Shaping one's life according to self-selected values is willing in action, which is not a simple task at all. It demands openness, enthusiasm, and creativity, a "Will to the conceivability of all being." The goal selected must be suited for the person, as a cause must be "smooth and subject to the mind as the mind's mirror and reflection.' Not only that, the person must find it to be highly significant "You want to create the world before which you can kneel: this is your ultimate hope and intoxication." To create, one needs the ability to master the self and carry out the roles of "judge and avenger and victim of his own law." Creating would be impossible without taking risks "The devotion of the greatest is to encounter risk and danger and play dice for death" *(Zarathustra,* II, Self-Overcoming). Finding a cause is only the first step, followed by the more complicated steps of overcoming resistance and continued renewal, as revealed by life "I am that *which must overcome itself again and again*" (*Twilight,* Skirmishes, 38).

The Will in Society

The art of building a manageable picture of the world, which can be seen as the art of lying in the name of the Will, also extends to the social realm. People will say things, deceive, pretend and manipulate others, to enhance their own sense of mastery and power. The spirit (that is the Will) enjoys its "capacity for adopting multiple masks and shiftiness" and enjoys its protean hidden powers "to appearances, to simplification, to masks, to cloaks, in short, to the surface—for every surface is a cloak." The spirit also enjoys the opposite of such will—to acquire knowledge, comprehend the complexity of things, achieve intellectual conscience and taste; and it is willing to pay the price of strict discipline, extreme self-honesty and hardship (*Beyond*, VII, 230).

The Will is expressed differently in different situations, as Zarathustra said, "Where I found a living creature, there I found Will to Power; and even in the will of the servant I found the will to be master" (*Zarathustra*, II, Self-overcoming). The weak have their indirect ways of mastery, which can be seen already in small children who weep and cry until they are pitied and consoled. This is also the case with adults who complain and lament to be noticed and compensated or at least find satisfaction in inconveniencing and hurting others "despite all their weakness, they still *have* at least one *power*: *the power to hurt*. Thus, the craving for pity is a search for "self-enjoyment, and at the expense of one's fellow men" (*Human*, I, 50). Benefiting as well as hurting others, are motivated by the need to gain power. Inflicting pain establishes power; giving pleasure maintains power over those already dependent on us, and even self-sacrifice can be a means to gain the upper hand. In other words, every action defines power relations and the ways we try to achieve power reveal and shape the kind of person we are (*Gay*, I, 13).

Imitatio Dei

I claimed before, that Nietzsche's meta-psychology could be conceived as a secular religion, a claim which is reinforced by Nietzsche conception of the Will as the one all-encompassing force, a tyrannical impulse to create the world in one's own image "the will to the *causa prima*" (*Beyond*, I, 9). Wishing to become the primary cause is a clear allusion to God, who is conceived as the creator of the world and living things, in his own image. However, wishing to be creators, humans are liable to fall into the trap of *causa sui* [cause itself] and start believing in freedom of will, that they are entirely in charge of their actions absolving "God, the world, ancestors, chance, and society for them" (*Beyond*, I, 21). In his notes, Nietzsche jotted down Plato's remark in *Theages* "Every one of us would like if possible to be master of all men and above all to be God," and added that "This attitude must return" (*Will*, IV, 958). He brought back this attitude indeed, with the idea of the Will to Power, and his many statements boil down to saying that humans wish to be, should be, and everything they do is motivated by the desire to be like God— most powerful, unique and eternal. Unlike the Christian God, who is conceived idealistically as loving merciful entity, the Will, being a demon, is closer to the Gnostic traditions, where God was also portrayed as a naked, arbitrary destructive power.

Superman and Higher Persons

What is the Superman, and, of course, the Superwoman? Is it a personal goal, or a social ideal; a personality-type or a rank on a scale ranging from "little man" to "higher man"? With Nietzsche, the answer to such questions is "all of the above" and much more. Many rivers go to the sea of the Superman, and the sea itself is described in many voices and from different perspectives. One feels that the Superman is the result of the encounter between repeated experiences of heightened feelings, sometimes frightening, of strength and energy, and a magical word, an idea, a slogan that was fermenting in the background, resulting in a revelation. These very feelings, one can feel, are the opposite, the reaction, or the negation of the painful feelings of weakness, victimhood and helplessness. Only later, in his notes and other essays did he try repeatedly to understand the meaning and significance of the word and the experience.

Zarathustra's first discourse to the people begins with the words: "I teach you the Superman. Man is something that should be overcome. What have you done to overcome him?" *(Zarathustra,* Prologue, 3). In this sentence "Man" refers to humanity at large, to his listeners and readers, men and women, but also to each one of us individually. Thus, the Superman can be seen from the perspectives of individuals and society. It can also be conceived as a human, mythological representation of the Dionysian-tragic religion, a counter-ideal of the ascetic one (*Ecce,* Genealogy). Not only that, the Superman can be conceived as a complementing concept to Eternal Recurrence, being ascending and not cyclical; aspiring and not resigning. Lastly, the Superman is the medicine prescribed for the cure of the social illness of nihilism; not a onetime pill, but rather a goal to look up to, a perpetual dream never to be fully materialized, as Zarathustra's proclaimed, "Never yet has there been a Superman. I have seen them both naked, the greatest and the smallest men:— and they are still all—too similar to one another. Verily, even the greatest I found to be—all-too-human" *(Zarathustra,* II, On Priests).

Overcoming

Nietzsche realized that the ultimate importance he gave to the production of great men, closer than others to the Superman, is not readily acceptable, "It is sometimes harder to agree to a thing than to understand it" (*Untimely,* Schopenhauer, 6). He also realized that the idea of the Superman invites misinterpretations. The word designates a type of "supreme achievement" which is the opposite of what modern "good" Christian and nihilistic persons stand for. The idea, declared by Zarathustra, the "annihilator of morality," is misunderstood as referring to an idealistic type of higher individuals, a mixture of a saint and a genius. Understanding the Superman in terms of Darwinism and "hero worship" as the "scholarly oxen" do, is an equally a wrong reading (*Ecce*, Books, 1).

The Will to Power, we said, emerges through overcoming resistance. The Superman, also translated as Overman, is one that overcomes "A table of virtues hangs over every people. Behold, it is the table of its overcomings; behold, it is the voice of its Will to Power" (*Zarathustra,* Thousand and One Goals). Self-overcoming means a continuous process of self-creation and change, setting goals and attempting to attain them "a mightier power and a new overcoming grow from out your values" (*Zarathustra,* II, Self-overcoming).

Most people are concerned with coping, persevering and surviving, finding answers to the question "How is man to be maintained?" Zarathustra, unlike them, posed another question, "How is man to be *surpassed*?" and the answer is the way of the Superman, which must be held more important than any social obligations and pleasures held by petty people. In this way, individuals move from being "masters of the day," to becoming "masters of the future" (*Zarathustra,* Prologue, 3). Overcoming is thus a process of self-overcoming combined with overcoming the inhibitory forces, the main one being the state "There, where the state ceases—there only commences the man who is not superfluous." Where the state ceases commences the "the rainbow and the bridges of the Superman" (*Zarathustra,* I, The new idol).

As was quoted before "Never yet has there been a Superman" (*Zarathustra,* II, The Priests), and all we can therefore get are approximations, and the best of them is "Nature's most excellent human products." Nietzsche wrote admiringly about Zarathustra "excellent man of this sort gladdens our senses; he is carved from a single block, which is hard, sweet, and fragrant." He described a person strong enough to make everything turn to her or his own advantage, in other words, a survivor, one who overcomes. Being self-directed, such a person sets limits and horizons, able to affect self-healing and turn severe accidents into advantages. He or she feel self-respect and honor their choices, reject "bad luck" and guilt, and know how to process and forget painful experiences. These traits are certainly commendable. However, Nietzsche added somewhat surprisingly "Lo then! I am the very reverse of a decadent, for he whom I have just described is none other than myself" (*Ecce*, Wise). Is he saying that there was not a Superman as yet, because only now did the teacher of the Superman materialize "Behold I teach you the Superman" (*Zarathustra,*

Prologue, 3), or is he implying that he Zarathustra-Nietzsche himself, is the one? He also believed that the exposure of the ills of Christian morality had already elevated him "above all mankind" (*Ecce*, Destiny, 6). Thus, The Superman is Zarathustra; and Zarathustra is Nietzsche, and in the following quote we find again that Nietzsche is also Dionysus:

> The soul which has the longest ladder and can descend the deepest, The most spacious soul that can run and stray and rove furthest in its own self, The most necessary soul that out of desire hurls itself into chance. The stable soul that plunges into Becoming, the possessing soul that has to taste of willing and longing— The soul that flies from itself and overtakes itself in the widest sphere, The wisest soul to which foolishness speaks most sweetly, The most self-loving soul in whom all things have their rise and fall, their ebb and flow— But this is the very idea of Dionysus. (*Ecce*, Zarathustra, 6).

Higher Persons

In a summing up statement, Nietzsche described higher persons who, in comparison with other human beings, can be considered as Superman, as "synthetic, summarizing, and justifying." They emerge in different places and cultures, and they grow up in different conditions from those of the average person (*Antichrist*, 4). A review of the many references to the Superman and the various varieties of higher characters, suggests the following clusters of attitudes and traits:

Powerfulness: higher persons possess physical, mental and creative "overflowing power" and these resources are controlled (*Will*, IV, 966), in other words, they know "how to press these magnificent monsters into service" (*Will*, IV, 933). Nietzsche saw power as an essential trait of the Superman "What determines your rank is the quantum of power you are: the rest is cowardice" (*Will*, IV, 898). Zarathustra clarified the importance of power using a comparison between different types "More Caesar Borgia then Parsifal, a type opposed to 'modern' men, 'good' men, Christians, nihilists, not an 'ideal type'" (*Ecce*, Books). The strength of the Will is manifested in the ability to create some meaning of life in a meaningless world (*Will*, III, 585). Zarathustra, the harbinger of the Superman, wished to have "laughing lions" as sons, who will be "higher, more victorious, more joyful men, such as are square-built in body and soul" (*Zarathustra*, IV, The greeting).

Independence: they determine their own values independently, and live according to their own laws and standards (*Untimely*, Schopenhauer, 1). Being one's own legislator, necessitates an ability to stay on one's own, which is a part of the idea of greatness "the sense of being noble, of willing to be for oneself, of being able to be different, of standing alone, and of having to live by one's own initiative." The more a person can be solitary, beyond good and evil, master of his or her virtues, the greater the person (*Gay*, VI, 212). Higher persons are ones who swim against the current, who "do it their way," who decide and create their own values, laws, pleasures and rights, metaphorically becoming creating Gods (*Gay*, III, 143). By so doing, and not necessarily in being useful, they become "the pinnacle of the whole species of man," who without intending it, have a strong and lasting impact on their human environment (*Will*, IV, 877; *Will*, IV, 999).

Synthesis: higher persons can control and coordinate conflicting drives and are tolerant of contradictions in general "The highest man would have the greatest multiplicity of drives, in the relatively greatest strength that can be endured" (*Will*, IV, 966). They welcome and embrace contradictions "Eternal contradiction, begetter of all things" (*Birth*, 4), and can contain the tension of different drives (*Will*, IV, 967). They are masters of the earth "as much a totality as something multifaceted, as wide as it is full" (*Gay*, VI, 212); synthetic persons and rulers "The Roman Caesar with Christ's soul" (*Will*, IV, 983).

Creativity: they are creators, a special type of a barbarian, who like Prometheus "comes from the heights: a species of conquering and ruling natures in search of material to mold" (*Will*, IV, 900). They are not merely practical role-playing cogs in the machine, and have a full inner world with more pleasures and interests. They are better at perceiving and observing "Spectators in the spectacle, of life" and poets of their life; creators of their own evaluations, perspectives, scales, affirmations and negations (*Gay*, IV, 301). Nietzsche mentioned Caesar, Homer, Aristophanes, Leonardo and Goethe as examples, persons who were great creators, skeptic immoralists, who could will and did not need faith (*Will*, II, 380).

Commitment: they are dedicated to the goal of the Superman and the value of overcoming as the ultimate value "Not 'mankind,' but Superman is the goal" (*Will*, IV, 1001), obeying the call to "Create beyond itself" *(Zarathustra*, I, On the despisers of the body). They wish to transcend the lowly "human all too human" and the more they promote the goal of the higher person, the higher they are themselves (*Will*, IV, 999). They are "true men" in the sense of going beyond sheer animality to become "philosophers, artists and saints," enlightened "as to the character of existence" (*Untimely*, Schopenhauer, 5).

Higher and Above

Up to this point in the discussion of higher persons and the Superman, we could say that persons who overcome their trauma following the ways of the sage, the warrior and the creator, share many features with this exclusive group, and that people who cope with trauma have what to learn from this elevated echelon. However, there is one aspect of the idea that they can do without. Nietzsche also saw the Superman as someone who not only overcomes himself or herself, but rather as someone who overcomes and masters other people, lower in his scale of virtues. Nietzsche would not have been an admirer of the post-modernistic "everything goes" slogan and the view that there is no high or low in culture or art. He represents the opposite view, that there is an order of rank; there are highs and lows; and there are differences in value among humans, as well as among music compositions, literary pieces and paintings, "I teach that there are higher and lower men" (*Will*, IV, 997).

The Superman, as the very word indicates, is obviously above the low, regular and average; something at the top of a hierarchy or metaphorically at the summit of a mountain. Overcoming thus becomes, for those who can, the act of a continuous climbing along the different ranks of a ladder. On the lowest rank, Nietzsche positioned the last man and the small people, together with invalids, ascetics and apostates, all those who make up life in the big city. On the next rank are found average, mediocre, good people (in the negative sense of the word), Christians and nihilists. Above this grade, in a transitional stage, the climbers free themselves of their restraining chains, to finally reach the realm of higher persons, which puts them closer to the goal of the Superman. The ascent is not for all: one must believe in higher persons, look up to them and reject in practice the assumption of equality of people and notions of "happiness for the greatest number," typical of the "market's place" (*Zarathustra*, IV, The higher man, 1). One must also accept the fact of uncertainty in life without definitive guidelines, and also surpass "the petty virtues, the petty policy, the sand-grain considerateness, the ant-hill trumpery, the pitiable comfortableness" (*Zarathustra*, IV, The higher man, 3), which gets dangerously close to contempt and hate of others.

Nietzsche described different types of higher persons who represent the promise of a "higher form of being," symbolized by the Superman (*Will*, IV, 866). In the gallery are included "modern persons," who tolerate ambiguities, change habits easily and design their own moralities (*Gay*, VII, 215), and "Good Europeans," who overcame nationalism and strive to become "legislators of the future, the masters of the earth" (*Will*, I, 132). The "Europeans of the day-after-tomorrow" are highly individualistic, looking for their virtues in the depth of their soul (*Gay*, VII, 214), and they are close to the "children of the future," untimely, beyond a particular locale, who refuse to "compromise, to be captured, reconciled and castrated" (*Gay*, V, 377).

At a certain point, the music changes and the higher persons are transformed into fierce, threatening warriors, heralding not the Superman, but rather the super race. They are "the redeeming man," also called the man of the future "sublime maliciousness, an ultimate self-conscious willfulness of knowledge" (*Genealogy*, II, 24). The preparatory human beings "which will restore honor to courage above all," who will fight and destroy "the sand and slime of present day civilization and metropolitanism," are warriors "who know how to be silent, lonely, resolute, and content and constant in invisible activities" (*Human*, IV, 283). They will be joined by the new barbarians, cynics, experimenters, conquerors who achieve "union of spiritual superiority with well-being and an excess of strength" (*Will*, IV, 899). With these additions to the gallery of higher persons, Nietzsche the critic of society moved to uncurbed adoration and hero worship of warriors-destroyers and their depiction as posters and not as real persons. He admitted that his enthusiasm got out of hands, describing "a world so over-rich in the beautiful, the strange, the questionable, the frightful, and the divine" (*Gay*, V, 382; *Ecce*, Zarathustra, 2). Yet, it got much worse, continuing with plans to breed the Superman (*Untimely*, Schopenhauer, 6; *Antichrist*, 3; *Will*, IV, 877) and a "stronger race" (*Will*, IV, 898), culminating in putting the value of barbarism, strength and cruelty at the top of the pyramid and in his call to annihilate inferior races in favor of a master domineering one.

At this point, it becomes apparent that of the three meta-psychological themes, the Superman turned out to be the most problematic, if not offensive way of coping with the consequence of abuse. It encourages hate of weakness, adoption of a rigid male identity and adoration of power. Fortunately, the next theme in the triad is much easier to appreciate.

Eternal Recurrence

The idea or an image of Eternal Recurrence and the slogan of *Amor fati* could serve as a battle-cry, a heraldic motto, to which the symbol of Zarathustra's two friends, an eagle carrying a snake around its neck, could be added. This pair symbolizes spirituality, the world of ideas, and earthiness adorned with a pinch of shrewdness (*Zarathustra*, Prologue, 1). Eternal Recurrence and *Amor fati* are associated concepts and intimately connected with Nietzsche's life, and other themes in his oeuvre. These ideas link together human life, time and the universe, and promoting the idea of interconnectedness; they are joined with other thinkers in the republic of geniuses.

Nietzsche talked about Eternal Recurrence in four voices, those of a biographer (*Ecce Homo*), an artist-poet (*Thus Spoke Zarathustra*), a psychologist-philosopher (in the rest of his writings) and a scientist-logician, who, according to his notes, planned to write a book dedicated to further elaboration and substantiation of the idea (*Will*, IV, 1057). This motif, like themes in a symphony's first movement, appeared in his early writings in an embryonic-suggestive form, and its different aspects were gradually elaborated and interwoven until they appeared full-blown in one particular moment.

Epiphany in Lake Silvaplana

Nietzsche, who found the idea of Eternal Recurrence to be of tremendous importance (*Will*, IV, 1053), shared with us exactly where he was when it came to him: it was on August 1881 "Six thousand feet beyond man and time," walking beside Lake Silvaplana, that "The fundamental idea of the work, the Eternal Recurrence, the highest formula of a life affirmation that can ever be attained was first conceived" (*Ecce*, Zarathustra, 1). In retrospect, Nietzsche, his own biographer, saw a parallel between the Eternal Recurrence and "the Phoenix music," where tunes and themes return, and described the inspiration and revelation in both cases, as "second birth." I used the word "epiphany," having in mind St. Paul's vision on the way to Damascus, to describe the moment, where after a long process of searching, a solution is suddenly found, things look different, and the person feels changed. It seems that out of the three themes, and due to the dramatic circumstances of its birth, Eternal Recurrence was closest to his heart. I would even say that the three topics can be characterized by different temperatures. The Will to Power is cold and analytic; the Superman is hot and passionate; Eternal Recurrence is warm and comforting.

Nietzsche described how the figure and type of Zarathustra, the epitome of Eternal Recurrence, came to him, or "waylaid" him as if it was ready and waiting, perhaps in his soul (*Ecce*, Zarathustra, 1), where the figure of Dionysus already resided, making him identify himself as "I, the last disciple of the philosopher Dionysus—I, the teacher of the Eternal Recurrence" (*Twilight*, Ancients, 5). Like Dionysus, Zarathustra could contain in his soul the ebb and flow of life; like Dionysus, he found a solution to the psychological problem of being skeptical and critical, a nihilist who "says no and acts no" about conventions, and at the same time, maintaining an affirming spirit and remaining light-footed like a dancer. The two figures, mythological and poetical also stand for Nietzsche, the person, and they all exemplify Eternal Recurrence in action, as they also exemplified the Superman. They show how despite life's difficulties and the burden of one's destiny, these things are not taken as an objection to existence, and how one can still say "Yea and Amen" to life (*Ecce*, Zarathustra, 6).

The theme of Eternal Recurrence is directly connected with Nietzsche's traumatic memories and states of despair and dejection. It appeared first in the vision of a snake entering a young shepherd's mouth, when in response to the dwarf, the symbol of the negative "spirit of gravity," Zarathustra declared "*Was that life*? Well! Once more!" (*Zarathustra*, III, The vision and the riddle, 1). The scene continued with Zarathustra's elaboration of this "abysmal thought," the present, the moment, is a gate where two eternal, endless antithetical roads forward and backward, past and future, meet. Accordingly, what happens, already happened, and what will happen has already happened before; all things are connected, and the present moment draws after it all coming things "This moment, and we wish it existed already, and we must eternally return and run it" *(Zarathustra,* III, The vision and the riddle, 2). In a second instance, the idea of Eternal Recurrence was voiced by the animals, trying to encourage Zarathustra, who experienced severe emotional paralysis, memory flashbacks and hopelessness "Things all dance themselves: they come and hold out the hand and laugh and flee—and return. Everything goes, everything returns; eternally rolls the wheel of existence. Everything dies, everything blossoms forth again; eternally runs on the year of existence" *(Zarathustra,* III, The Convalescent, 2). Finally, the theme appeared for the third time, in a tone of reconciliation, resolution and even victory, although the chapter's title *The drunken song,* suggests that this closure could also be understood as a pipe dream, in which even the ugliest man (discussed in chapter 6) adopted, or imitated Zarathustra's teachings of earth-loving acceptance, '"Was *that*—life?' will I say unto death, 'Well! Once more!'" *(Zarathustra,* IV, The drunken song, 1).

The Eternal Recurrence is not a guarantee of bliss and happiness. Moreover, realizing that it also implies that whatever we do, our problems, pain, and shortcomings will return, can stir up disgust at all existence "Eternally he returns, the man of whom you are weary, the small man." There is no way out, and even death cannot release us "But the plexus of causes returns in which I am intertwined—it will again create me!" Thus, for Zarathustra, there is one option left, to eternally return, not to a different or better life, but rather, "to teach the eternal return of all things" again (*Zarathustra,* III, The Convalescent, 2). Zarathustra was not a teacher of hope and optimism, one who promises that things will be better in the future; he gave no comfort to sufferers who could not tolerate their given situation and did not accept themselves and wished instead for descendants and "the further, the higher, the brighter." Nietzsche taught the very opposite: affirmation and joy which wants itself "it wants eternity, it wants recurrence, it wants everything eternally-like-itself" *(Zarathustra,* IV, The drunken song, 9).

Straight Lines and Circles

In his psychology, Nietzsche's formula for happiness, in the conduct of life was "a Yea, a Nay, a straight line, a goal" (*Antichrist,* 1). Indeed, when it comes to action, one must be rational and decisive. However, understanding the world and life is a different matter altogether, in the words of the dwarf, "Everything straight lies [...] all truth is crooked, time itself is a circle" (*Zarathustra,* I, The riddle and the vision). We can understand the dwarf (a person who sees the world from a different point of view) as if saying that our concept of time, like all concepts, is a lie and that reality is not as unequivocal as our notions and abstractions lead us to believe. Is it possible at all to see the world and ourselves without the customary conceptual scaffoldings? Can anyone do it? What would we see then? What would be the consequences of such a viewpoint?

Nietzsche is the teacher of nonlinear, circular thinking. Eternity and recurrence are opposites of the straight line and the "either or" (Aristotelian) logic. They are without beginning or end, and in them, every point does not follow the preceding one. They are rather multi-dimensional, a totality of time and space, in which everything, the good and the bad, is connected, and in which everything returns. In this perspective, there is no uni-directional time at all, and the world becomes "a monster of energy," where the Will, waves of force, play recurrently in an eternal sea of change, moving from contradictions to concord and back again; changing joyfully and eternally without disgust or weariness. This is the Dionysian world "of the eternally self-creating, the eternally self-destroying," beyond moral evaluations, without a goal, being solely a Will. Recurrence implies that there are no fixed states, no pauses, no being; but only eternal becoming (*Will*, IV, 1062). The ever repeating strife of blind forces is the essence of the world and the nature of us humans as well, and if we must have a goal, it will have to be "the joy of the circle is itself" (*Will*, IV, 1067).

Nietzsche tried to help us do the impossible, embrace a circular mode of thought, by offering thinking or imagining experiments, using invigorating vocabulary with words like eternity and recurrence, and by divulging his own vision. His words were intended only for a select group of people, and it takes readiness and maturity to endure the idea of Recurrence (*Will*, IV, 1058). Maturity implies freedom from morality, enjoyment of uncertainty, having an experimental mindset, and abolishing the concepts of free-will and "knowledge-in-itself" (*Will*, IV, 1060). It takes people who can seek the eternal pleasure of existence "not within the appearances, but rather behind the appearances." In other words, such persons can see the eternal in changing and passing appearances, in an artistic, poetic way (*Birth*, 17). Mindfulness, a psychologically detached observation, is closely related to this comforting creative perspective. The art of meditation on human phenomena eases life's burden, gives presence of mind in dealing with challenges, adds some humor to boring moments, and supplies beneficial lessons from the unhappiest phases of life (*Human*, I, 35).

Can the idea of Eternal Recurrence be proven? At times, Nietzsche tried to claim that his meta-psychology is scientific and logically valid, and he even intended to write an essay to develop his argument. Thus, he argued that, "The law of conservation of energy demands Eternal Recurrence" (*Will*, IV,

1063), and determined, in the role of a physiologist, that the Will to Power can be found already in essential living organisms "This is the primeval tendency of the protoplasm when it extends pseudopodia and feels about" (*Will*, III, 656). These attempts, like all attempts to prove the correctness of belief, the existence of God, for example, are unconvincing. I prefer to listen to the poet, who in the role of Zarathustra believed that explanations are unnecessary and realized that poets are liable to take their own metaphors too seriously.

The Experience of Time

Recurrence and the Will, to my taste, can and should be understood figuratively; Recurrence is merely an abstract formulation of the poetic "the eternal sand-glass of existence will ever be turned once more, and you with it, you speck of dust!" (*Gay*, IV, 341). In this case, we should ask what associations and implications do these images suggest. This is in fact what Nietzsche did, when he initially presented the idea of Recurrence as a conjecture, inviting his readers to participate in a thinking experiment "What, if some day or night a demon were to steal after you into your loneliest loneliness and say to you: 'This life as you now live it and have lived it, you will have to live once more and innumerable times more'" (*Gay*, IV, 341).

You the reader must examine your own reactions, and your answer to Nietzsche's thought experiment will be the correct one for you. Do you see this conjecture as a menace or as an opportunity? He suggested an additional thinking experiment, again not as a geophysicist, but as a poet contemplating the fleeting moment, who wondered, "Whether some beings might be able to experience time backward, or alternately forward and backward (which would involve another concept of cause and effect)" (*Gay*, V, 374). Nietzsche did not tire of reminding us, that we know only words, how things are called, and not the things themselves. We have invented words and concepts because they support daily functioning and survival: time, the past, present, future, before and after, are such words. However, "Through words and concepts, we are still continually misled into imagining things as simpler than they are" (*Human*, Wanderer, 11). We live in our interpretations and words, which are limitless and yet, "We cannot look around our own corner." Mind you, Nietzsche time conjectures are not about physics, but rather about experience, and in fact, we can all experience time in different manners: passing slowly when young, and quickly when old, or standing still when dancing or in severe pain. From this perspective, Eternal Recurrence is understood as Nietzsche's interpretation, his own example of a different experience of time. His point of departure, like one of his genius confreres Qohelet and Schopenhauer, was the fleeting of time; the vanishing of days and consequently death.

Examining the uses of history for life, pondering the passing of the present and the moment, into the past, Nietzsche was moved to say "It is something amazing: the moment, in one sudden motion there, in one swift motion gone, before nothing, afterward nothing." Our own life is but a moment, and in this context, Nietzsche mentioned an emperor (the stoic Marcus Aurelius) who to come to terms with the fleeting moment, made it a point to always remember the transitoriness of all things (*Untimely*, History, 1). His own solution to the dilemma was different and consisted of finding a new kind of eternity "Everything seems far too valuable to be so fleeting: I seek an eternity for everything: ought one to pour the most precious salves and wines into the sea?—My consolation is that everything that has been, is eternal: the sea will cast it up again" (*Will*, IV, 1065).

Eternity is the opposite of a linear dimension with a beginning and end; it is multi-dimensional, a totality of time and space in which everything, the good and the bad, is connected, "entangled, ensnared, enamored"; in which everything returns. Adopting this interpretation, turns persons into ones who love the world, love eternity, becoming eternal themselves *(Zarathustra,* IV, The drunken song, 9). Zarathustra, the lover of eternity, the teacher of recurrence, exclaimed: "Oh, how should I not lust after eternity and after the nuptial ring of rings, the ring of recurrence?" However, when Nietzsche described a nuptial ring, worn with almost erotic yearning, he did not talk solely about time, but also about his issues and difficulties "Never yet have I found the woman from whom I wanted children, unless it be this woman whom I love: for I love you, O eternity. For I love you, O eternity!" *(Zarathustra,* III, The seven seals, 1).

How does the idea of the Eternal Recurrence contribute to life? Recurrence is a supposition, a worthy attitude, the "heaviest burden" which is the highest criterion, the "ultimate sanction and seal." It supports life in two ways: the first is retrospective, in coping with what already happened, affirming the past as a necessity. The second, is prospective, relating to current decisions, replacing the Categorical Imperative with a Dionysian one, suggesting that we ask how we would feel about repeating forever a particular value setting decision "Do you want this once more, and also for innumerable times?" (*Gay*, IV, 341). If we can desire such a commitment, the decision was a good one. This question adds a second criterion to the Will question, as to whether a contemplated choice will increase or decrease power.

Affirmation and Human Greatness

Eternal Recurrence and *Amor fati* are closely related. The former is an idea, a belief about the nature of the world and change processes; the latter is a formula, a dictum of appropriate attitude and behaviors to uphold when faced with fate's bad turns. In discussing the way of the sage, we understood the "highest wisdom" of acceptance, in coping with illness and suffering, as the application of these idea and rule (Chapter 9). Eternal Recurrence was revealed in Lake Silvaplana, and *Amor fati* appeared for the first time in an aphorism about his new-year wishes "I want to learn more and more to see as beautiful what is necessary for things; then I shall be one of those who makes things beautiful." He wished that *Amor fati* will be his love; that positive outlook will be his manner; and that he will not fight what is ugly, neither accuse anymore (*Gay*, IV, 276). In other words, the full acceptance of a given reality, without condemnation, will enable creating art out of it, and at the same time effect personal change "My formula for greatness in man is *Amor fati*: that a man should wish to have nothing altered, either in the future, the past, or for all eternity." One should accept necessity; avoid covering it up with idealistic false notions, and love it (*Ecce*, Clever, 10). Nietzsche's formula *Amor fati* is the culmination of extreme pessimism and radical nihilism combined "that one wants nothing to be different, not forward, not backward, not in all eternity." This greatness is "the ideal of the most high-spirited, alive, and world-affirming human being." Such a person comes to terms with what was, and moreover, wants it to repeat for all eternity, "shouting insatiable *da capo* [a musical term in Italian, meaning repeat the previous part from the beginning]." With such an attitude, a guideline for bearing with others, one turns one's self into a necessity (*Beyond*, II, 56).

The Dionysian affirmation of the world, repeatedly referred to as the *Amor fati* dictum, is comprehensive, without selection or exception, "it wants the eternal circulation—the same things, the same logic and illogic of entanglements" (*Will*, IV, 1041). Affirming one moment is affirming ourselves and all existence. Things in the world are interconnected and all eternity is needed to produce one happy event, and thus by the very affirmation of the moment "all eternity was called good, redeemed, justified, and affirmed" (*Will*, IV, 1032). Nietzsche saw such affirmation as his life task, both as an individual and as a teacher "On one occasion Zarathustra sets out his life-task—and it is also mine. Let no one misunderstand its meaning. It is an affirmation to the point of justifying, to the point of redeeming even the entire past" (*Ecce*, Zarathustra, 8). The highest form of *Amor fati* is a will to affirm even the Eternal Recurrence "the unconditional and infinitely repeated circular course of all things" (*Twilight*, Ancients, 5). The notions of the Eternal Recurrence, the Dionysian, *Amor fati* and affirmation, are interrelated and sometimes equivalent "The highest state a philosopher can attain: to stand in a Dionysian relationship to existence – my formula for this is *Amor fati*" (*Will*, IV, 1041).

Innocence and Irresponsibility

Affirmation, in Nietzsche's view, implies seeing life events as necessity and fatality, presuming that everything is the way it is because it had to be so and could not have been otherwise. Necessity and fatality, affecting human behavior and decisions, are directly related to his doctrine of innocence and irresponsibility, which he saw as his new gospel, new knowledge and new habit. Such a gospel is, of course, the opposite of the old gospel of sin and guilt. In this new gospel all evaluations, distinctions, dislikes and appreciations are worthless, as there is no place for blaming or praising nature and necessity. Human behavior is the result of "chemical processes, and the clash of elements"; people are torn between different motives, and it is one of them, and not us, which wins and takes control. We are in the hands of our abilities and drives "man may act as he can, that is, as he must," although our intelligence (if we are not stupid) has some role in deciding how far the wish for pleasure will carry us (*Human*, II, 107).

Nietzsche took into consideration that the idea that people are not responsible for their actions and nature will meet adamant resistance, as it goes against their socialization and customary ways of thinking and seeing the world. Nevertheless, "the sun of the new gospel," can offer consolation, affirmation and wisdom, and he tried to help us swallow the bitter pill arguing that "a sense of true and just knowledge" and some degree of "self-illumination and self-redemption" are often achieved by means of pleasure, egoism, vanity as well as errors and illusions. Besides, everything in the field of morality has evolved, is mutable and vacillating, "everything is fluid" and hence, rather than judging, Nietzsche called for a different kind of knowledge "that of understanding, non-loving, non-hating, surveying," in other words, he was commending mindfulness, a habit with which we can hopefully become wise and innocent ourselves (*Human*, II, 107). Ten years later, Nietzsche's "new gospel," appeared as the answer to the question "What alone can be our doctrine?" and the principles of irresponsibility, innocence and necessity were put forward in forceful words:

> That no one gives man his qualities—neither God, nor society, nor his parents and ancestors, nor he [...] No one is responsible for man's being there at all, for his being such-and-such, or for his being in these circumstances or this environment. The fatality of his essence is not to be disentangled from the fatality of all that has been and will be (*Twilight*, The four great errors, 8).

The doctrine reaffirmed that humans do not exist for some purpose, are not here because of some will, are not intended to attain any ideals of happiness and morality "We have invented the concept of 'end': in reality, there is no end." We cannot be held responsible, as there is no *causa prima,* an independent primary cause for actions "One is necessary, one is a piece of fatefulness, one belongs to the whole, one is on the whole." It follows that there is nothing that could judge, measure, or compare our actions, as they are an integral part of everything there is. This perspective, together with the denial of a creator and judging God, is the "great liberation; with this alone is the innocence of becoming restored" (*Twilight,* The four great errors, 8).

Nietzsche's doctrine is reinforced by additional considerations. Responsibility assumes free will and a soul or an ego making conscious decisions. These terms are according to him, only grammatical fictions, or constructions. The very word "I" is only "a synthesis which is itself *created* by thinking" (*Beyond,* III, 54). To think that the will is an effective capacity and not merely a word is a similar mistake (*Twilight,* Reason, 5). Semantics aside, an individual is "the entire single line of humanity up through himself" (*Twilight,* Skirmishes, 33). In other words, we are not responsible for our traits and dispositions, no one asked us into what family we wish to be born, and we are in the hands of our genes and human evolution. We are a result and not a cause, but we are also a cause of what comes after us, a link and bridge into the future. We are hence a fatality in two senses, in our misfortunes and in the way we deal with them. Nietzsche, thus teaches us acceptance blended with hope, a fitting lesson with which to end my book:

> You yourself, poor, fearful man, are the implacable *Moira* [fate] enthroned even above the gods that govern all that happens; you are the blessing and the curse and in any event the fetters in which the strongest lies captive; in you the whole future of man is predetermined: it is of no use for you to shudder when you look at yourself (*Will,* I, 61).

END

ENDNOTES

[1] Ed Diener, Shigehiro Oishi, and JungYeun Park, “An Incomplete List of Eminent Psychologists of the Modern Era,” *Archives of Scientific Psychology* 2 (2014): 20, DOI: 10.1037/arc0000006

[2] Uri Wernik, *Nietzschean Psychology, and Psychotherapy: The New Doctors of the Soul* (Lanham, MD: Lexington Books, 2016).

[3] See, Curtis Cate, *Friedrich Nietzsche* (Woodstock, NY: Overlook Press, 2005), Lesley Chamberlain, *Nietzsche in Turin: An Intimate Biography* (New York: Picador USA, 1998), Ronald Hayman, *Nietzsche, a Critical Life* (New York: Oxford University Press, 1980), and Janko Lavrin, *Nietzsche: A Biographical Introduction* (New York: Scribner, 1971).

[4] See, Rüdiger Safranski, *Nietzsche: A Philosophical Biography*, trans., Shelly Frisch (London: Granta Books, 2002), Thomas H. Brobjer, *Nietzsche's Philosophical Context: An Intellectual Biography* (Urbana: University of Illinois Press, 2008), Gary Elsner, *Nietzsche: A Philosophical Biography* (Lanham, MD: University Press of America, 1992), Reginald John Hollingdale, *Nietzsche The Man and His Philosophy* (Baton Rouge: Louisiana State University Press, 1966), and Julian Young, *Friedrich Nietzsche: A Philosophical Biography* (Cambridge: Cambridge University Press, 2010).

[5] See, Joachim Ko¨hler, *Zarathustra's Secret: The Interior Life of Friedrich Nietzsche*, trans., Ronald Taylor (New Haven: Yale University Press, 2002), and Jim Miller, *Examined Lives: From Socrates to Nietzsche* (New York: Farrar, Straus and Giroux, 2011).

[6] Italo Calvino, trans., Patrick Creagh, “Why Read the Classics?”*New York Review of Books*, October 9, 1986, accessed May 1, 2017, http://www.nybooks.com/articles/1986/10/09/why-read-the-classics/

[7] Margaret Sanger, "Frederick Nietzsche," in *Margaret Sanger Papers, Library of Congress* (LCM, November 1914): 130:356, accessed May 1, 2017, https://www.nyu.edu/projects/sanger/webedition/app/documents/show.php?sangerDoc=143705.xml

[8] Richard Lowell Howey, “Some Reflections on Irony in Nietzsche,” *Nietzsche-Studien* 4 (1975): 36.

[9] Anacleto Verrecchia, “Nietzsche's Breakdown in Turin,” in *Nietzsche in Italy*, ed. Thomas Harrison (Stanford, CA: Stanford University: ANMA Libri, 1988)), 105-112.

[10] Will Durant, *The Story of Philosophy: The Lives and Opinions of the Greater Philosophers, rev. ed.* (New York: Simon & Schuster, 1933).

[11] Ibid, 559.

[12] Ibid, 560.

[13] William James, *The Will to Believe, and Other Essays in Popular Philosophy, and Human Immortality, 1896 Reprint* (New York: Dover Publications, 1960), 92.

[14] William James, *Pragmatism: A New Name for Some Old Ways of Thinking, 1907 reprint* (New York: Dover Philosophical Classics, 1995), 6.

[15] Ibid, 19.

[16] Johann Gottlieb Fichte, *Science of Knowledge, 1794 reprint*, trans., Peter Heath and John Lachs (Cambridge: Cambridge University Press, 1982), 16.

[17] Thomas Mann, *A Sketch of My Life,* trans., H. T. Lowe-Porter (New York: Alfred A. Knopf, 1960), 44.

[18] Oscar Wilde, *The Artist as Critic; Critical Writings of Oscar Wilde,* ed. Richard Ellmann (New York: Random House, 1969), 410.

[19] See, for example, William Todd Schultz, Handbook *of Psychobiography* (Oxford: Oxford University Press, 2005), and Dan P. McAdams and Richard L. Ochberg, *Psychobiography and Life Narratives* (Durham: Duke University Press, 1988).

[20] James William Anderson, "Psychobiography Column – June 2014," *The Society for Qualitative Inquiry in Psychology.* Accesses September 18, 2015, http://qualpsy.org/psychobiography-column-june-2014.

[21] Wernik, *Nietzschean Psychology,* 4-7.

[22] William Schaberg, *The Nietzsche Canon* (Chicago: University of Chicago Press, 1996), 32.

[23] Verrecchia, *Nietzsche's Breakdown.*

[24] Eva M. Cybulska, "Nietzsche: Madness as Literature," *Psychiatric Bulletin* 21 (1997): 510-511.

[25] Wernik, *Nietzschean Psychology,* 11-12.

[26] Thomas Szasz, *The Myth of Mental Illness: Foundations of a Theory of Personal Conduct* (New York: Harper & Row, 1974).

[27] Robert Whitaker, *Anatomy of an Epidemic: Magic Bullets, Psychiatric Drugs, and the Astonishing Rise of Mental Illness in America* (New York: Crown Publishers, 2010).

[28] Max Nordau, "Degeneration, 1895," in *Encyclopedia of Disability,* Vol. 5, ed. Gary L. Albrecht (Thousand Oaks, CA: SAGE Publications, 2006), accessed October 1, 2015, DOI: http://dx.doi.org/10.4135/9781412950510.n1015.

[29] William W. Ireland, "Friedrich Nietzsche: a Study in Mental Pathology," *The Journal of Mental Science* 47 (1901): 10.

[30] PJ Möbius, *Ueber das Pathologische bei Nietzsche* (Wiesbaden: J F Bergmann, 1902), quoted in Leonard Sax, "What Was the Cause of Nietzsche's Dementia?" *Journal of Medical Biography* 11 (2003): 51.

[31] Eva M. Cybulska, "Were Nietzsche's Cardinal Ideas – Delusions?" Indo-Pacific Journal of Phenomenology 8, (2008): 1-13, accessed October 1, 2015, http://www.ajol.info/index.php/ipjp/article/viewFile/65432/53122

[32] Eva M. Cybulska, "The Madness of Nietzsche: a Misdiagnosis of the Millennium?" *Hospital Medicine* 61 (2000): 571-75.

[33] Richard Schain, "Nietzsche's Visionary Values - Genius or Dementia?" *Philosophy Pathways,* 42 (2002). Accessed, September 25, 2015, http://rschain1.tripod.com/ Nietzsches_Values.htm

[34] Malek K. Khazaee, "The Case of Nietzsche's Madness," *Existenz* 3 (2008): 40, accessed September 25, 2015, http://www.bu.edu/paideia/existenz/volumes/Vol.3-1Khazaee.pdf

[35] Lynn Margulis, "On Syphilis and Nietzsche's Madness: Spirochetes Awake!" *Dædalus* (Fall 2004): 118-125.

[36] Leonard Sax, "What was the cause of Nietzsche's dementia?" *Journal of Medical Biography* 11 (2003): 47–54.

[37] M. Orth and M.R Trimble, "Friedrich Nietzsche's Mental Illness--General Paralysis of the Insane vs. Frontotemporal Dementia," *Acta Psychiatrica Scandinavica* 114 (2006): 439-44.
[38] C.M. Owen, C. Schaller and D.K. Binder," The Madness of Dionysus: A Neurosurgical Perspective on Friedrich Nietzsche," *Neurosurgery* 61 (2007): 626-32.
[39] Jean-Paul Marat, "A Stroke of Bad Luck: CADASIL and Friedrich Nietzsche's 'Dementia' or Madness," accessed September 25, 2015, http://tipsdiscover.com/health/stroke-bad-luck-cadasil-friedrich-nietzsche-s-dementia-madness/#ixzz3iJ6HseAl
[40] Brian Domino, "The Legend of Nietzsche's Syphilis," review of *The Legend of Nietzsche's Syphilis,* by Richard Schain. *Journal of Nietzsche Studies* 35/36 (2008): 191, accessed September 26, 2015, http://www.hunter.cuny.edu/jns/reviews/richard-schain.-the-legend-of-nietzsches-syphilis.
[41] Lucien R. Karhausen, "Weeding Mozart's Medical History," *Journal of the Royal Society of Medicine* 91 (1998): 547.
[42] Lucien R. Karhausen, "Mozart's 140 Causes of Death and 27 Mental Disorders," *BMJ,* 341 (2010): 1329.
[43] Maxine Harris, *The Loss that is forever: The Lifelong Impact of the Early Death of a Mother or Father* (New York: Penguin Books, 1995).
[44] Köhler, Zarathustra's Secret, 210.
[45] Eva Cybulska, "Nietzsche's Eternal Return: Unriddling the Vision: A
Psychodynamic Approach," *Indo-Pacific Journal of Phenomenology* 13 (2013): 5-6, DOI: 10.2989/IPJP.2013.13.1.2.1168.
[46] Eva Cybulska, "Nietzsche's Übermensch: A Glance behind the Mask of Hardness," *Indo-Pacific Journal of Phenomenology* 15 (2015): 1.
[47] Kyle Arnold and George E. Atwood, "Nietzsche's Madness" in *Handbook of psychobiography,* ed. W. Schulz (New York: Oxford University Press, 2005), 228.
[48] Friedrich Nietzsche, "Out of My Life, 1895," quoted in Arnold and Atwood, *Nietzsche's Madness.*
[49] Friedrich Nietzsche, "My Life," in *The Nietzsche Reader,* Eds. Ansell Pearson and Duncan Large (Oxford: John Wiley & Sons, 2005).
[50] Alfred C. Kinsey, Wardell Baxter Pomeroy and Clyde E. Martin, *Sexual Behavior in the Human Male* (Philadelphia: W.B. Saunders, 1948).
[51] Uri Wernik, "Will the Real Homosexual in the Bible Please Stand Up?" *Theology & Sexuality* 11 (2005): 47-64, DOI:10.1177/1355835805054345.
[52] Uri Wernik, "The Nature of Explanation in Sexology and the Riddle of Triolism" *Annals of Sex Research* 3 (1988): 5-20, DOI:10.1007/bf00849719.
[53] Hollingdale, *Nietzsche.*
[54] Kaufmann, Walter. *Nietzsche: Philosopher, Psychologist, Antichrist,* 4th ed. (Princeton, New Jersey: Princeton University Press, 1974), 34.
[55] Köhler, *Zarathustra's Secret.*
[56] Ibid, 172-3.
[57] Safranski, *Nietzsche: A Philosophical Biography,* 245-48.

[58] Norma Procopiow, "The Poetics of Riddle in W.S. Merwin's Poetry" *Flashpoint,* Web Issue 16 (Spring 2014), accessed September 22, 2015, http://www.flashpointmag.com/Procopiow_Merwin.htm

[59] Northrop Frye, *Anatomy of Criticism: Four Essays* (Princeton, NJ: Princeton University Press, 1957), 280.

[60] Procopiow, *The Poetics.*

[61] W.S. Merwin, "Preface to Asian Figures," quoted in Procopiow, The Poetics.

[62] Procopiow, *The Poetics.*

[63] Carl. G., Jung, *Memories, Dreams, Reflections,* ed. Aniela Jaffé (New York: Pantheon Books, 1963), 102.

[64] Wernik, *Nietzschean Psychology,* 5-7.

[65] Alfred Korzybski, *Science, and Sanity* (Lancaster, PA: International Non-Aristotelian Library, 1933), 747–61.

[66] Frank M. Ochberg, "Posttraumatic Therapy" in *International Handbook of Traumatic Stress Syndromes,* Eds. John P Wilson and Beverley Raphael (New York: Plenum Press, 1993), 734.

[67] Menachem Ben-Ezra, "Traumatic Reactions from Antiquity to the 16th Century: Was there a Common Denominator?" *Stress and Health* 27 (2011): 223–40.

[68] Edward Tick, *War and the Soul: Healing Our Nation's Veterans from Post-Traumatic Stress Disorder* (Wheaton, IL: Quest Books, 2005).

[69] Jason Crowley, "Beyond the Universal Soldier: Combat Trauma in Classical Antiquity," in *Combat Trauma and the Ancient Greeks,* Eds. Peter Meineck and David Konstan (New York: Palgrave Macmillan, 2014), 106.

[70] "Post Traumatic Stress Disorder," American Psychiatric Association, accessed October 18, 2015, http://www.dsm5.org/Documents/PTSD%20Fact%20Sheet.pdf

[71] "Post Traumatic Stress Disorder," *Medical News Today,* accessed 20 October 2015, http://www.medicalnewstoday.com/articles/156285.php

[72] Ludovici and Levi, *Selected Letters,* 64-70.

[73] Euripides, *The Bakkhai,* trans., Robert Bagg (Amherst: University of Massachusetts Press, 1978).

[74] Sander J. Breiner, *Slaughter of the Innocents: Child Abuse Through the Ages and Today* (New York: Plenum Press, 1990).

[75] David Bakan, *Slaughter of the Innocents* (San Francisco: Jossey-Bass, 1971).

[76] Kenneth V. Lanning, "1992 FBI Report: Satanic Ritual Abuse," last updated on November 11, 2011, http://www.skeptictank.org/fbi1992.htm

[77] Stephanie J. Woods, "Normative Beliefs Regarding the Maintenance of Intimate Relationships Among Abused and Non-abused Women," *Journal of Interpersonal Violence* 14 (1999): 479-491.

[78] Barry A. Farber, Rachel Khurgin-Bott, and Sarah Feldman, "The Benefits and Risks of Patient Self-Disclosure in the Psychotherapy of Women with a History of Childhood Sexual Abuse," *Psychotherapy: Theory, Research, Practice, Training* 46 (2009): 52-67, DOI:10.1037/a0015136.

[79] Walther Helmut, "The Young Nietzsche," accessed October 28, 2015, http://www.f-nietzsche.de

[80] Anthony M. Ludovici, trans. and Oscar Levi, ed., *Selected Letters of Friedrich Nietzsche* (N.Y: Garden City and Toronto: Doubleday Page & Company, 1921), 159.
[81] Ludovici and Levi, *Selected Letters.*
[82] Alice Miller, *For Your Own Good: Hidden Cruelty in Child-Rearing and the Roots of Violence,* 3rd ed. (New York: Farrar, Straus & Giroux, 1990).
[83] Gertrude Jobes, *Dictionary of Mythology, Folklore, and Symbols* (New York: Scarecrow Press, 1962), 434-71.
[84] Klaus Vollmar, *The Little Giant Encyclopedia of Dream Symbols,* tr. Elisabeth E. Reinersmann (New York: Sterling Publishing, 1997), 401-3.
[85] Anthony M. Ludovici, Notes to *Thus Spake Zarathustra* by Friedrich Nietzsche, trans., Thomas Common (Edinburgh: T. N. Foulis, 1909), 405–58.
[86] Laurence Lampert, *Nietzsche's Teaching: An Interpretation of Thus Spoke Zarathustra* (New Haven: Yale University Press, 1986), 170-1, 297.
[87] Rene Fredrickson, *Repressed Memories: A Journey to Recovery from Sexual Abuse* (New York: Simon and Schuster, 1992), 129-130.
[88] Christine Landis and Maxine Harris, Eds. *Sexual Abuse in the Lives of Women Diagnosed with Serious Mental Illness* (Amsterdam, the Netherlands: Harwood Academic Publishers, 1997), 205-6.
[89] B. D. Perry et al., "Childhood Trauma, the Neurobiology of Adaptation, and 'Use-dependent' Development of the Brain: How 'States' Become 'Traits,'" *Infant Mental Health Journal* 16 (1995): 271–291, DOI: 10.1002/1097-0355(199524).
[90] M.J., Dorahy and K. Clearwater, "Shame and Guilt in Men Exposed to Childhood Sexual Abuse: A Qualitative Investigation," *Journal of Child Sex Abuse* 21 (2012):155-75, DOI: 10.1080/10538712.2012.659803.
[91] Christopher Middleton, ed. and trans., *Selected Letters of Friedrich Nietzsche* (Chicago: University of Chicago Press, 1969), 3.
[92] O. Hobart Mowrer, "Integrity Groups: Principles and Procedures," *The Counseling Psychologist* 3 (1972): 7–33, DOI:10.1177/001100007200300203.
[93] N. Rodriguez et al., "Posttraumatic Stress Disorder in a Clinical Sample of Adult Survivors of Childhood Sexual Abuse," *Child Abuse & Neglect* 20 (1999): 943–952, DOI:10.1016/0145-2134(96)00083-X.
[94] C. H. Kempe et al., "The Battered-child Syndrome," *JAMA.* 181 (1962): 17-24, DOI:10.1001/jama.1962.03050270019004.
[95] V.J. Felitti and R.F. Anda, "Origins and Essence of the Study," *The ACE Reporter* 1 (2003). Accessed November 13, 2015, http://www.acestudy.org/files/ARV1N1.pdf
V.J. Felitti and R.F. Anda, "The Relationship of Adverse Childhood Experiences to Adult Health, Well-being, Social Function, and Healthcare," in Ruth A. Lanius, Eric Vermetten, and Clare Pain, eds., *The Impact of Early Life Trauma on Health and Disease: The Hidden Epidemic* (Cambridge: Cambridge University Press. 2010).
[96] V.J. Felitti and R.F. Anda, *The Relationship.*
[97] E. A. Walker et al., "Psychosocial Factors in Fibromyalgia Compared with Rheumatoid Arthritis: II. Sexual, Physical, and Emotional Abuse and Neglect," *Psychosomatic Medicine* 59 (1997): 572–77.

[98] Lu Weili et al., "Correlates of Adverse Childhood Experiences among Adults with Severe Mood Disorders," *Psychiatric Services* 59 (2008): 1018-26.
[99] M. George, "Listening and Hearing: Child Sex Abuse," *Nursing Standard 10* (1996): 22–23.
[100] K. Freshwater, C. Leach, and J. Aldridge "Personal Constructs, Childhood Sexual Abuse, and Revictimization, *British Journal of Medical Psychology* 74 (2001): 379–397.
[101] P. O'Leary, and N. Gould, "Men Who Were Sexually Abused in Childhood and Subsequent Suicidal Ideation: Community Comparison, Explanations, and Practice Implications," *British Journal of Social Work* 39 (2009): 950-68.
[102] J. M. Golding, S. C. Wilsnack, and M. L. Cooper, "Sexual Assault History and Social Support: Six General Population Studies," *Journal of Traumatic Stress 15* (2002): 187–197, DOI: 10.1023/ A:1015247110020.
[103] D. DiLillo and P. J. Long, "Perceptions of Couple Functioning Among Female Survivors and Child Sexual Abuse," *Journal of Child Sexual Abuse 7* (1999): 59–76.
[104] V. E. Whiffen, J. M. Thompson, and J.A. Aube, "Mediators of the Link Between Childhood Sexual Abuse and Adult Depressive Symptoms," *Journal of Interpersonal Violence 15* (2000): 1100–1120.
[105] Perry, B. D., et al., *Childhood Trauma.*
[106] Allan N. Schore, "Dysregulation of the Right Brain: A Fundamental Mechanism of Traumatic Attachment and the psychopathogenesis of Posttraumatic Stress Disorder," *Australian and New Zealand Journal of Psychiatry* 36 (2002): 9-30, accessed November 13, 2015, http://www.trauma-pages.com/a/schore-2002.php
[107] Erwin R. Parson and Luerena K. Bannon, "Stress Responses in Sexual Trauma Victims and Others Experiencing Overwhelming Events," *PTSD Resources for Survivors and Caregivers,* accessed January 6, 2016, http://www.giftfromwithin.org/pdf/strategy.pdf
[108] Erwin R. Parson, Dawn M. Brett, and Alan S. Brett, "Childhood and Adult Sexual Victimization: Living in the Aftermath of Transgression and Quest for Restoration of the Self, *PTSD Resources for Survivors and Caregivers,* accessed, January 6, 2016, http://www.giftfromwithin.org/pdf/chldhood.pdf
[109] Middleton, *Selected Letters* 147.
[110] Middleton, Selected Letters, 156.
[111] Ludovici and Levi, *Selected Letters,* 119f.
[112] Ibid, 121.
[113] Ibid, 122f.
[114] Middleton, *Selected Letters,* 178.
[115] Ibid, 209.
[116] Ibid, 292.
[117] Ibid, 299.
[118] Aaron T. Beck, *Depression: Causes and treatment* (Philadelphia, PA: University of Pennsylvania Press, 1972).
[119] Judit Herman-Lewis, *Trauma and Recovery: The Aftermath of Violence-from Domestic Abuse to Political Terror* (New York: Basic Books, 1992), 80.
[120] Bessel A. van der Kolk, "The Compulsion to Repeat the Trauma: Re-enactment, Revictimization, and Masochism," *Psychiatric Clinics of North America* 12 (1989): 389-411.

[121] Michael S. Levy, "A Helpful Way to Conceptualize and Understand Reenactments," *The Journal of Psychotherapy Practice and Research* 7 (1998): 227–235.
[122] Claudia Crawford, *To Nietzsche: Dionysus, I Love You! Ariadne* (Albany: State University of New York Press, 1995), 55.
[123] Peter J. Burgard, *Nietzsche and the Feminine*. (Charlottesville: University Press of Virginia, 1994), 87.
[124] Roger Beck, "Zoroaster, as Perceived by the Greeks," *Encyclopaedia Iranica* (New York: Encyclopædia Iranica Online, 2003), last Updated, July 20, 2002, http://www.iranicaonline.org/articles/zoroaster-iv-as-perceived-by-the-greeks.
[125] D. Finkelhor and K. Yllo, *License to Rape: Sexual Abuse of Wives* (New York: The Free Press, 1985), 125.
[126] V. Petraitis, and C. O'Connor, *Rockslide: The Danger of Paedophiles – Untold Stories*, (Melbourne: Hybrid Publishers, 1999), 196.
[127] Christiane Sanderson, *Counseling Adult Survivors of Sexual Abuse*, 3rd ed. (London and Philadelphia: Jessica Kingsly Publishers, 2006), p.340.
[128] Ibid, 337.
[129] Arthur Schopenhauer, *The World as Will and Representation*, trans. E. F. J. Payne (Dover Publications, 1966), p.132.
[130] Richard G. Tedeschi and Lawrence Calhoun, "Posttraumatic Growth: A New Perspective on Psychotraumatology" *Psychiatric Times*, 21 (2004): 1-4.
[131] Martin, .E.P., Seligman and Mihaly Csikszentmihalyi, "Positive Psychology: An introduction," *American Psychologist* 55 (2000): 5–14, DOI:10.1037/0003-066x.55.1.5. PMID 11392865. See critique of positive psychology, closer in spirit to Nietzsche, in Barbara Ehrenreich, *Bright-Sided: How the Relentless Promotion of Positive Thinking has Undermined America* (New York: Metropolitan Books, 2009).
[132] Epictetus, *Enchiridion*, trans., Elizabeth Carter, para. 8, accessed, January 6, 2016, http://classics.mit.edu/Epictetus/epicench.html
[133] Marcus Aurelius Antoninus, *The Meditations of the Emperor Marcus Aurelius Antoninus*, trans. Francis Hutcheson and James Moor, ed. and intro., James Moore and Michael Silverthorne (Indianapolis: Liberty Fund, 2008), IV, 23, accessed February 12, 2016, http://oll.libertyfund.org/titles/2133.
[134] Epictetus, *Enchiridion*, para. 5.
[135] Middleton, *Selected Letters*, 197.
[136] A. Biswas et al., "Sedentary time and its association with risk for disease incidence, mortality, and hospitalization in adults: a systematic review and meta-analysis," *Annals of Internal Medicine*, 162 (2015):123-32, DOI: 10.7326/M14-1651.
[137] Yoel Hoffmann, *Japanese Death Poems: Written by Zen Monks and Haiku Poets on the Verge of Death* (Boston, MA: Tuttle Publishing, 1986).
[138] Jean-Dominique Bauby, *The Diving Bell and the Butterfly: A Memoir of Life in Death*, trans. Jeremy Leggatt (New York: A.A. Knopf, 1997).
[139] S. Cadell, C. Regehr and D. Hemsworth, "Factors Contributing to Posttraumatic Growth: A Proposed Structural Equation Model," *American Journal of Orthopsychiatry* 73 (2003): 279-287.

[140] Richard G. Tedeschi, "Violence Transformed: Posttraumatic Growth in Survivors and their Societies," *Aggression and Violent Behavior* 4 (1999): 319-341.
[141] Tedeschi and Calhoun, *Posttraumatic Growth,* 1-4.
[142] Roxane Cohen Silver and John A. Updegraff, "Searching for and Finding Meaning Following Personal and Collective Traumas," in *The Psychology of Meaning, eds.* Keith D. Markman, Travis Proulx, and Matthew J. Lindberg (Washington, DC: American Psychological Association, 2013), 237-255.
[143] Tedeschi and Calhoun, *Posttraumatic Growth,* 1-4.
[144] Alia I. Sheikh, "Posttraumatic growth in trauma survivors: Implications for practice" *Counselling Psychology Quarterly,* 21 (2008; 21): 85–97.
[145] Mark D. Seery, Alison E. Holman and Roxane Cohen, "Whatever Does not Kill us: Cumulative Lifetime Adversity, Vulnerability, and Resilience," *Journal of Personality and Social Psychology,* 99 (2010): 1025-1041, accessed February 12, 2016, http://dx.doi.org/10.1037/a0021344.
[146] Maren Westphal and George A. Bonanno, "Posttraumatic Growth and Resilience to Trauma: Different Sides of the Same Coin or Different Coins?" *Applied Psychology* 56 (2007): 417–427, DOI: 10.1111/j.1464-0597.2007.00298.x
[147] Charles .R. Figley, "Forward," in *International Handbook of Trauma and Stress Syndrome,* Eds. J. Wilson and B. Raphael (New York: Plenum, 1993), xvii-xx.
[148] Tedeschi and Calhoun, *Posttraumatic Growth,* 1-4.
[149] Viktor E. Frankl, *Man's Search for Meaning* (Boston: Beacon Press, 2006), 117.
[150] Elisabeth Förster-Nietzsche, *The Young Nietzsche,* trans., Anthony Mario Ludovici (London: W. Heinemann, 1912). 135-7.
[151] Wernik, Nietzschean Psychology, 4-7.

SELECTED BIBLIOGRAPHY

Aschheim, Steven E. *The Nietzsche Legacy in Germany, 1890-1990.* Berkeley: University of California Press, 1992.

Aurelius, Marcus. *The Emperor's Handbook: A New Translation of The Meditations.* Translated by David Hicks and Scot C. Hicks. New York: Scribner, 2002.

Beck, Aaron T. Depression: Causes and treatment. Philadelphia, PA: University of Pennsylvania Press, 1972.

Brobjer, Thomas H. Nietzsche's Philosophical Context: An Intellectual Biography. Urbana: University of Illinois Press, 2008.

Cate, Curtis. *Friedrich Nietzsche.* Woodstock, NY: Overlook Press, 2005.

Carter, Elizabeth. *The Enchiridion.* South Bend, in Infomotions, 2001.

Chamberlain, Lesley. Nietzsche in Turin: An Intimate Biography. New York: Picador, 1998.

Crowley Jason. "Beyond the Universal Soldier: Combat Trauma in Classical Antiquity." In *Combat Trauma and the Ancient Greeks,* edited by Peter Meineck and David Konstan, 105-130. New York: Palgrave Macmillan, 2014.

Durant, Will. *The Story of Philosophy: The Lives and Opinions of the Greater Philosophers.* Rev ed., New York: Simon & Schuster: 1933.

Elsner, Gary. Nietzsche: A Philosophical Biography. Lanham, MD: University Press of America, 1992.

Euripides. *The Bakkhai.* Translated by Robert Bagg. Amherst: University of Massachusetts Press, 1978

Felitti Vincent J. and Robert Anda F. "The Relationship of Adverse Childhood Experiences to Adult Health, Well-being, Social Function, and Healthcare." In Ruth A. Lanius, Eric Vermetten, and Clare Pain, *The Impact of Early Life Trauma on Health and Disease: The Hidden Epidemic.* Cambridge: Cambridge University Press. 2010.

Frankl, Viktor E. *Man's Search for Meaning.* Boston: Beacon Press, 2006.

Fredrickson, Rene. *Repressed Memories: A Journey to Recovery from Sexual Abuse.* New York: Simon and Schuster, 1992.

Freud, Sigmund. "A Short Account of Psycho-analysis." In *Standard Edition Complete Psychological Works of Sigmund Freud (SE), vol. 19.* Edited and translated by James Strachey. London: Hogarth, 1953.

____________ "New Introductory Lectures on Psychoanalysis." In *SE, vol. 22.* Edited and translated by James Strachey and Anna Freud. London: Hogarth, 1964.

____________ "The Interpretation of Dreams" *SE, vols. 4 and 5.* Edited and translated by James Strachey. London: Hogarth Press, 1958.

____________"The Psychopathology of Everyday Life." *SE, vol. 6.* Edited and translated by James Strachey. London: Hogarth Press, 1958.

Frye, Northrop. *Anatomy of Criticism: Four Essays* (Princeton, NJ: Princeton University Press, 1957.

Golomb, Jacob. *Nietzsche's Enticing Psychology of Power.* Ames, Iowa: Iowa State University Press, 1989.

___________ *Nietzsche and Depth Psychology.* Albany: State University of New York Press, 1999.

Griffith, Samuel B. *The Art of War by Sun Tzu.* London: Oxford University Press, 1971.

Harris, Maxine. *The Loss that is Forever: The Lifelong Impact of the Early Death of a Mother or Father.* New York: Penguin Books, 1995.

Hayman, Ronald. *Nietzsche, a Critical Life.* New York: Oxford University Press, 1980.

Hoffmann, Yoel. *Japanese Death Poems: Written by Zen Monks and Haiku Poets on the Verge of Death.* Boston, MA: Tuttle Publishing, 1986.

Hollingdale, Reginald John, Ed. *A Nietzsche Reader.* Harmondsworth: Penguin, 1977.

___________ *Nietzsche the Man and his Philosophy.* Baton Rouge: Louisiana State University Press, 1966.

James, William. "The Sentiment of Rationality." In *The Will to Believe.* 1897 Reprint. New York: Dover Publications, 1956.

James, William. *Pragmatism.* 1897 Reprint. New York: Dover Publications, 1995.

Jung, Carl. G., and Aniela Jaffé. *Memories, Dreams, Reflections.* New York: Pantheon Books, 1963.

Karhausen, Lucien R. *The Bleeding of Mozart: A Medical Glance on his Life, Illness, and Personality.* Bloomington, Indiana: Xlibris, 2011.

Kaufmann, Walter, trans. *Basic Writings of Nietzsche.* New York: Random House, 2000.

___________ *Nietzsche, Philosopher, Psychologist, Antichrist.* 4th ed. Princeton, N.J.: Princeton University Press, 1974.

Kaufmann, Walter Arnold, ed. *The Portable Nietzsche.* New York: Penguin Books, 1976.

Kinsey, Alfred C., Wardell Baxter Pomeroy, and Clyde E. Martin. *Sexual Behavior in the Human Male.* Philadelphia: W.B. Saunders, 1948.

Köhler, Joachim. *Zarathustra's Secret: The Interior Life of Friedrich Nietzsche.* New Haven: Yale University Press, 2002.

Korzybski, Alfred. *Science and Sanity.* Lancaster, PA: International Non-Aristotelian Library, Science Press Printing, 1933.

Lampert, Laurence. *Nietzsche's Teaching: An Interpretation of Thus Spoke Zarathustra.* New Haven: Yale University Press, 1986.

Landis, Christine, and Maxine Harris eds. *Sexual Abuse in the Lives of Women Diagnosed with Serious Mental Illness.* Amsterdam, the Netherlands: Harwood Academic Publishers, 1997.

Lavrin, Janko. *Nietzsche: A Biographical Introduction.* New York: Scribner, 1971.

Levi, Oscar, ed. and Anthony Ludovici, trans. *Selected Letters of Friedrich Nietzsche.* London: Heinemann, 1921.

Levi, Oscar, ed. and different trans. *The Complete Works of Friedrich Nietzsche.* 18 vols. Edinburgh and London: T.N. Foulis, 1909-1913. https://archive.org/search.php?query=nietzsche%20epub

Mann, Thomas. *A Sketch of My Life.* Translated by H. T. Lowe-Porter. New York: Alfred A. Knopf, 1960.

Middleton, Christopher, trans. *Selected Letters of Friedrich Nietzsche.* Chicago: University of Chicago Press, 1969.

Miller, Alice. *For Your Own Good: Hidden Cruelty in Child-Rearing and the Roots of Violence.* 3rd ed. New York: Farrar, Straus and Giroux, 1990.

Miller, Jim. *Examined Lives: From Socrates to Nietzsche.* New York: Farrar, Straus and Giroux, 2011.

Nehamas, Alexander. *Nietzsche, Life as Literature.* Cambridge, Mass.: Harvard University Press, 1985.

Nietzsche, Friedrich. *Ecce Homo: And the Birth of Tragedy.* Translated by Clifton Fadiman. New York: Modern Library, 1927.

___________*Daybreak: Thoughts on the Prejudices of Morality.* Translated by R. J. Hollingdale. Cambridge, New York: Cambridge University Press, 1982.

___________*Human, All Too Human.* Translated by R. J. Hollingdale. Two vols. In one. Cambridge, New York: Cambridge University Press, 1986.

___________Untimely Meditations. Translated by R. J. Hollingdale. Cambridge; New York: Cambridge University Press, 1983.

___________*The Will to Power.* Edited and translated by Walter Kaufmann. New York: Vintage, 1968

Parkes, Graham. *Composing the Soul: Reaches of Nietzsche's Psychology.* Chicago: University of Chicago Press, 1994.

Pearson, Ansell, and Duncan Large, Eds. *The Nietzsche Reader.* Oxford: John Wiley & Sons, 2005.

Safranski, Ruediger. *Nietzsche: A Philosophical Biography.* Translated by Shelley Frisch. New York: W.W. Norton, 2002.

Sanderson, Christiane. *Counseling Adult Survivors of Sexual Abuse.* Third Edition. London and Philadelphia: Jessica Kingsly Publishers, 2006.

Schopenhauer, Arthur. *The World as Will and Representation.* Translated by E. F. J. Payne. New York: Dover Publications, 1966.

Solomon, Robert C., and Kathleen Marie Higgins. *What Nietzsche Really Said.* New York: Schocken Books, 2000.

Solomon, Robert C., *Living With Nietzsche: What the Great "Immoralist" Has to Teach Us.* Oxford: Oxford University Press, 2003.

Szasz, Thomas. *The Myth of Mental Illness: Foundations of a Theory of Personal Conduct.* New York: Harper & Row, 1974.

Tedeschi, Richard G., Crystal L. Park, and Lawrence G. Calhoun. *Posttraumatic Growth: Positive Changes in the Aftermath of Crisis.* New York: Psychology Press, 2008.

Thiele, Leslie Paul, *Friedrich Nietzsche and the Politics of the Soul: A Study of Heroic Individualism.* Princeton, N.J.: Princeton University Press, 1990.

Tick, Edward. *War and the Soul: Healing Our Nation's Veterans from Post-Traumatic Stress Disorder.* Wheaton, IL: Quest Books, 2005.

Verrecchia, Anacleto. "Nietzsche's Breakdown in Turin." In *Nietzsche in Italy*, edited by Thomas Harrison, 105-112. Stanford, CA: ANMA Libri, 1988.

Wernik, Uri. *Chance Action and Therapy the Playful Way of Changing.* Hauppauge, N.Y.: Nova Science Publishers, 2011.

___________ Nietzschean Psychology and Psychotherapy: The new doctors of the soul. Lanham, Maryland: Lexington Books, 2016.

Whitaker, Robert. Anatomy of an Epidemic: Magic Bullets, Psychiatric Drugs, and the Astonishing Rise of Mental Illness in America. New York: Crown Publishers, 2010.

Young, Julian. *Friedrich Nietzsche: A Philosophical Biography.* Cambridge: Cambridge University Press, 2010.

ABOUT THE AUTHOR

Uri Wernik, Psy.D is a senior clinical and medical psychologist, and certified sex therapist. He is in private practice and his work experience includes heading a unit for autistic adolescents in a psychiatric hospital, working with staff and students in an Academy of Art and Design, and facilitating groups for bereaved parents.

Dr. Wernik is a graduate of the Hebrew University of Jerusalem and the University of Illinois at Urbana-Champaign. He is a founding member and former chairman of The Israeli Association for Sex Therapy, and a member of the board of directors of Transtherapy.org. He is the author of *Nietzschean Psychology and Psychotherapy: The new doctors of the soul* (Lexington Books: Lanham, Maryland, 2016), *Chance Action Therapy: The playful way of changing* (New York, Nova Science Publishers, 2010), and eight books in Hebrew, among them *I Qoheleth* [Ecclesiastes]*: Psychologist, Philosopher, Poet* (Jerusalem: Carmel, 1998). He also published articles on psychotherapy, sexuality, psychology of religion, and creativity. Additional information can be found on his website http://www.therapy.co.il

INDEX

G

H

I

J

K

L

M

N

O

P

www.ingramcontent.com/pod-product-compliance
Lightning Source LLC
LaVergne TN
LVHW010721210926
848485LV00007B/1405/J